STATISTICAL REINFORCEMENT LEARNING

Modern Machine Learning Approaches

Chapman & Hall/CRC
Machine Learning & Pattern Recognition Series

SERIES EDITORS

Ralf Herbrich
Amazon Development Center
Berlin, Germany

Thore Graepel
Microsoft Research Ltd.
Cambridge, UK

AIMS AND SCOPE

This series reflects the latest advances and applications in machine learning and pattern recognition through the publication of a broad range of reference works, textbooks, and handbooks. The inclusion of concrete examples, applications, and methods is highly encouraged. The scope of the series includes, but is not limited to, titles in the areas of machine learning, pattern recognition, computational intelligence, robotics, computational/statistical learning theory, natural language processing, computer vision, game AI, game theory, neural networks, computational neuroscience, and other relevant topics, such as machine learning applied to bioinformatics or cognitive science, which might be proposed by potential contributors.

PUBLISHED TITLES

BAYESIAN PROGRAMMING
Pierre Bessière, Emmanuel Mazer, Juan-Manuel Ahuactzin, and Kamel Mekhnacha

UTILITY-BASED LEARNING FROM DATA
Craig Friedman and Sven Sandow

HANDBOOK OF NATURAL LANGUAGE PROCESSING, SECOND EDITION
Nitin Indurkhya and Fred J. Damerau

COST-SENSITIVE MACHINE LEARNING
Balaji Krishnapuram, Shipeng Yu, and Bharat Rao

COMPUTATIONAL TRUST MODELS AND MACHINE LEARNING
Xin Liu, Anwitaman Datta, and Ee-Peng Lim

MULTILINEAR SUBSPACE LEARNING: DIMENSIONALITY REDUCTION OF MULTIDIMENSIONAL DATA
Haiping Lu, Konstantinos N. Plataniotis, and Anastasios N. Venetsanopoulos

MACHINE LEARNING: An Algorithmic Perspective, Second Edition
Stephen Marsland

SPARSE MODELING: THEORY, ALGORITHMS, AND APPLICATIONS
Irina Rish and Genady Ya. Grabarnik

A FIRST COURSE IN MACHINE LEARNING
Simon Rogers and Mark Girolami

STATISTICAL REINFORCEMENT LEARNING: MODERN MACHINE LEARNING APPROACHES
Masashi Sugiyama

MULTI-LABEL DIMENSIONALITY REDUCTION
Liang Sun, Shuiwang Ji, and Jieping Ye

REGULARIZATION, OPTIMIZATION, KERNELS, AND SUPPORT VECTOR MACHINES
Johan A. K. Suykens, Marco Signoretto, and Andreas Argyriou

ENSEMBLE METHODS: FOUNDATIONS AND ALGORITHMS
Zhi-Hua Zhou

Chapman & Hall/CRC
Machine Learning & Pattern Recognition Series

STATISTICAL REINFORCEMENT LEARNING

Modern Machine Learning Approaches

Masashi Sugiyama
University of Tokyo
Tokyo, Japan

CRC Press
Taylor & Francis Group
Boca Raton London New York

CRC Press is an imprint of the
Taylor & Francis Group, an **informa** business
A CHAPMAN & HALL BOOK

CRC Press
Taylor & Francis Group
6000 Broken Sound Parkway NW, Suite 300
Boca Raton, FL 33487-2742

First issued in paperback 2020

Version Date: 20150128

ISBN 13: 978-0-367-57586-1 (pbk)
ISBN 13: 978-1-4398-5689-5 (hbk)

Visit the Taylor & Francis Web site at
http://www.taylorandfrancis.com

and the CRC Press Web site at
http://www.crcpress.com

Contents

Foreword

How can agents learn from experience without an omniscient teacher explicitly telling them what to do? Reinforcement learning is the area within machine learning that investigates how an agent can learn an optimal behavior by correlating generic reward signals with its past actions. The discipline draws upon and connects key ideas from behavioral psychology, economics, control theory, operations research, and other disparate fields to model the learning process. In reinforcement learning, the environment is typically modeled as a Markov decision process that provides immediate reward and state information to the agent. However, the agent does not have access to the transition structure of the environment and needs to learn how to choose appropriate actions to maximize its overall reward over time.

This book by Prof. Masashi Sugiyama covers the range of reinforcement learning algorithms from a fresh, modern perspective. With a focus on the statistical properties of estimating parameters for reinforcement learning, the book relates a number of different approaches across the gamut of learning scenarios. The algorithms are divided into model-free approaches that do not explicitly model the dynamics of the environment, and model-based approaches that construct descriptive process models for the environment. Within each of these categories, there are policy iteration algorithms which estimate value functions, and policy search algorithms which directly manipulate policy parameters.

For each of these different reinforcement learning scenarios, the book meticulously lays out the associated optimization problems. A careful analysis is given for each of these cases, with an emphasis on understanding the statistical properties of the resulting estimators and learned parameters. Each chapter contains illustrative examples of applications of these algorithms, with quantitative comparisons between the different techniques. These examples are drawn from a variety of practical problems, including robot motion control and Asian brush painting.

In summary, the book provides a thought provoking statistical treatment of reinforcement learning algorithms, reflecting the author's work and sustained research in this area. It is a contemporary and welcome addition to the rapidly growing machine learning literature. Both beginner students and experienced researchers will find it to be an important source for understanding the latest reinforcement learning techniques.

Daniel D. Lee
GRASP Laboratory
School of Engineering and Applied Science
University of Pennsylvania, Philadelphia, PA, USA

Preface

In the coming *big data* era, *statistics* and *machine learning* are becoming indispensable tools for data mining. Depending on the type of data analysis, machine learning methods are categorized into three groups:

- **Supervised learning:** Given input-output paired data, the objective of supervised learning is to analyze the input-output relation behind the data. Typical tasks of supervised learning include *regression* (predicting the real value), *classification* (predicting the category), and *ranking* (predicting the order). Supervised learning is the most common data analysis and has been extensively studied in the statistics community for long time. A recent trend of supervised learning research in the machine learning community is to utilize side information in addition to the input-output paired data to further improve the prediction accuracy. For example, *semi-supervised learning* utilizes additional input-only data, *transfer learning* borrows data from other similar learning tasks, and *multi-task learning* solves multiple related learning tasks simultaneously.

- **Unsupervised learning:** Given input-only data, the objective of unsupervised learning is to find something useful in the data. Due to this ambiguous definition, unsupervised learning research tends to be more ad hoc than supervised learning. Nevertheless, unsupervised learning is regarded as one of the most important tools in data mining because of its automatic and inexpensive nature. Typical tasks of unsupervised learning include *clustering* (grouping the data based on their similarity), *density estimation* (estimating the probability distribution behind the data), *anomaly detection* (removing outliers from the data), *data visualization* (reducing the dimensionality of the data to 1–3 dimensions), and *blind source separation* (extracting the original source signals from their mixtures). Also, unsupervised learning methods are sometimes used as data pre-processing tools in supervised learning.

- **Reinforcement learning:** Supervised learning is a sound approach, but collecting input-output paired data is often too expensive. Unsupervised learning is inexpensive to perform, but it tends to be ad hoc. Reinforcement learning is placed between supervised learning and unsupervised learning — no explicit supervision (output data) is provided, but we still want to learn the input-output relation behind the data. Instead of output data, reinforcement learning utilizes *rewards*, which evaluate the validity of predicted outputs. Giving implicit supervision such as rewards is usually much easier and less costly than giving explicit supervision, and therefore reinforcement learning can be a vital approach in modern data analysis. Various supervised and unsupervised learning techniques are also utilized in the framework of reinforcement learning.

This book is devoted to introducing fundamental concepts and practical algorithms of statistical reinforcement learning from the modern machine learning viewpoint. Various illustrative examples, mainly in robotics, are also provided to help understand the intuition and usefulness of reinforcement learning techniques. Target readers are graduate-level students in computer science and applied statistics as well as researchers and engineers in related fields. Basic knowledge of probability and statistics, linear algebra, and elementary calculus is assumed.

Machine learning is a rapidly developing area of science, and the author hopes that this book helps the reader grasp various exciting topics in reinforcement learning and stimulate readers' interest in machine learning. Please visit our website at: http://www.ms.k.u-tokyo.ac.jp.

Masashi Sugiyama
University of Tokyo, Japan

Author

Masashi Sugiyama was born in Osaka, Japan, in 1974. He received Bachelor, Master, and Doctor of Engineering degrees in Computer Science from All Tokyo Institute of Technology, Japan in 1997, 1999, and 2001, respectively. In 2001, he was appointed Assistant Professor in the same institute, and he was promoted to Associate Professor in 2003. He moved to the University of Tokyo as Professor in 2014.

He received an Alexander von Humboldt Foundation Research Fellowship and researched at Fraunhofer Institute, Berlin, Germany, from 2003 to 2004. In 2006, he received a European Commission Program Erasmus Mundus Scholarship and researched at the University of Edinburgh, Scotland. He received the Faculty Award from IBM in 2007 for his contribution to machine learning under non-stationarity, the Nagao Special Researcher Award from the Information Processing Society of Japan in 2011 and the Young Scientists' Prize from the Commendation for Science and Technology by the Minister of Education, Culture, Sports, Science and Technology for his contribution to the density-ratio paradigm of machine learning.

His research interests include theories and algorithms of machine learning and data mining, and a wide range of applications such as signal processing, image processing, and robot control. He published *Density Ratio Estimation in Machine Learning* (Cambridge University Press, 2012) and *Machine Learning in Non-Stationary Environments: Introduction to Covariate Shift Adaptation* (MIT Press, 2012).

The author thanks his collaborators, Hirotaka Hachiya, Sethu Vijayakumar, Jan Peters, Jun Morimoto, Zhao Tingting, Ning Xie, Voot Tangkaratt, Tetsuro Morimura, and Norikazu Sugimoto, for exciting and creative discussions. He acknowledges support from MEXT KAKENHI 17700142, 18300057, 20680007, 23120004, 23300069, 25700022, and 26280054, the Okawa Foundation, EU Erasmus Mundus Fellowship, AOARD, SCAT, the JST PRESTO program, and the FIRST program.

Part I

Introduction

Chapter 1

Introduction to Reinforcement Learning

Reinforcement learning is aimed at controlling a computer agent so that a target task is achieved in an unknown environment.

In this chapter, we first give an informal overview of reinforcement learning in Section 1.1. Then we provide a more formal formulation of reinforcement learning in Section 1.2. Finally, the book is summarized in Section 1.3.

1.1 Reinforcement Learning

A schematic of reinforcement learning is given in Figure 1.1. In an unknown environment (e.g., in a maze), a computer agent (e.g., a robot) takes an action (e.g., to walk) based on its own control policy. Then its state is updated (e.g., by moving forward) and evaluation of that action is given as a "reward" (e.g., praise, neutral, or scolding). Through such interaction with the environment, the agent is trained to achieve a certain task (e.g., getting out of the maze) without explicit guidance. A crucial advantage of reinforcement learning is its non-greedy nature. That is, the agent is trained not to improve performance in a short term (e.g., greedily approaching an exit of the maze), but to optimize the long-term achievement (e.g., successfully getting out of the maze).

A reinforcement learning problem contains various technical components such as states, actions, transitions, rewards, policies, and values. Before going into mathematical details (which will be provided in Section 1.2), we intuitively explain these concepts through illustrative reinforcement learning problems here.

Let us consider a *maze problem* (Figure 1.2), where a robot agent is located in a maze and we want to guide him to the goal without explicit supervision about which direction to go. *States* are positions in the maze which the robot agent can visit. In the example illustrated in Figure 1.3, there are 21 states in the maze. *Actions* are possible directions along which the robot agent can move. In the example illustrated in Figure 1.4, there are 4 actions which correspond to movement toward the north, south, east, and west directions. States

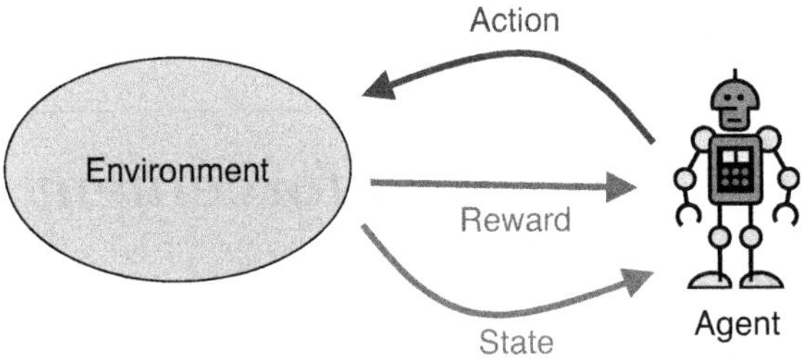

FIGURE 1.1: Reinforcement learning.

and actions are fundamental elements that define a reinforcement learning problem.

Transitions specify how states are connected to each other through actions (Figure 1.5). Thus, knowing the transitions intuitively means knowing the map of the maze. *Rewards* specify the incomes/costs that the robot agent receives when making a transition from one state to another by a certain action. In the case of the maze example, the robot agent receives a positive reward when it reaches the goal. More specifically, a positive reward is provided when making a transition from state 12 to state 17 by action "east" or from state 18 to state 17 by action "north" (Figure 1.6). Thus, knowing the rewards intuitively means knowing the location of the goal state. To emphasize the fact that a reward is given to the robot agent right after taking an action and making a transition to the next state, it is also referred to as an *immediate reward*.

Under the above setup, the goal of reinforcement learning to find the *policy* for controlling the robot agent that allows it to receive the maximum amount of rewards in the long run. Here, a policy specifies an action the robot agent takes at each state (Figure 1.7). Through a policy, a series of states and actions that the robot agent takes from a start state to an end state is specified. Such a series is called a *trajectory* (see Figure 1.7 again). The sum of immediate rewards along a trajectory is called the *return*. In practice, rewards that can be obtained in the distant future are often discounted because receiving rewards earlier is regarded as more preferable. In the maze task, such a discounting strategy urges the robot agent to reach the goal as quickly as possible.

To find the optimal policy efficiently, it is useful to view the return as a function of the initial state. This is called the (state-)*value*. The values can be efficiently obtained via *dynamic programming*, which is a general method for solving a complex optimization problem by breaking it down into simpler subproblems recursively. With the hope that many subproblems are actually the same, dynamic programming solves such overlapped subproblems only once and reuses the solutions to reduce the computation costs.

In the maze problem, the value of a state can be computed from the values of neighboring states. For example, let us compute the value of state 7 (see

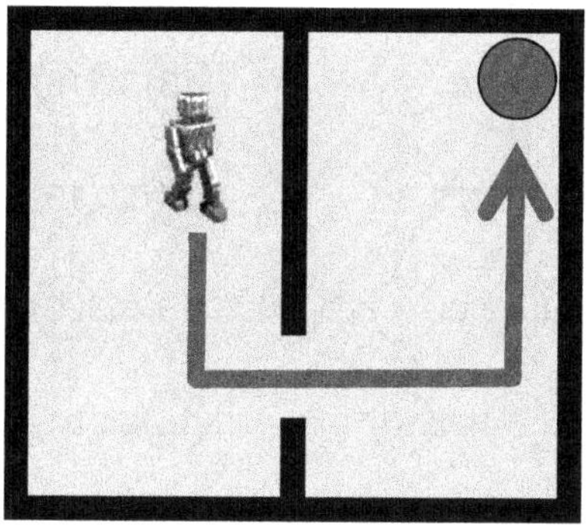

FIGURE 1.2: A maze problem. We want to guide the robot agent to the goal.

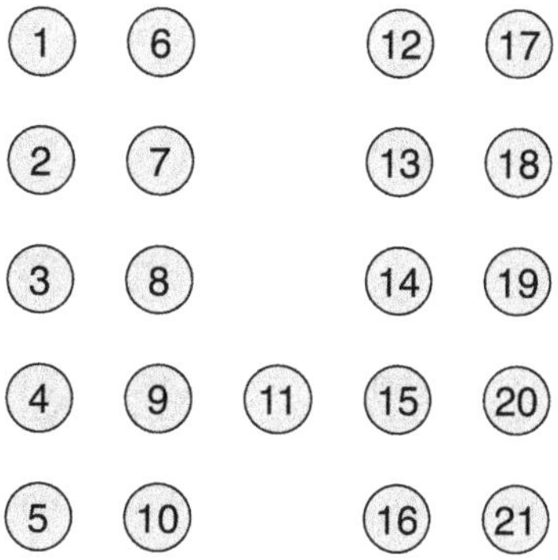

FIGURE 1.3: States are visitable positions in the maze.

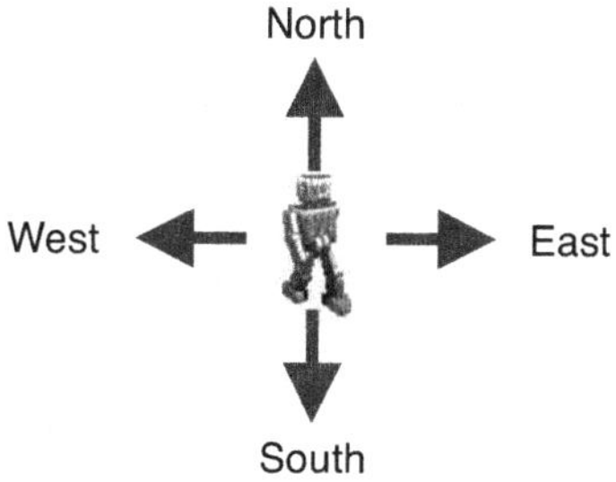

FIGURE 1.4: Actions are possible movements of the robot agent.

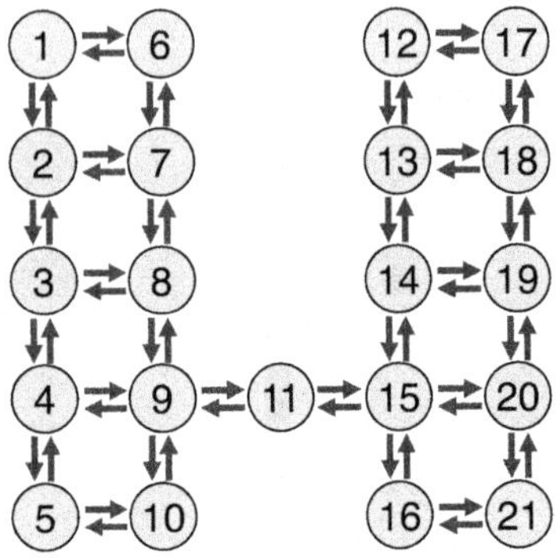

FIGURE 1.5: Transitions specify connections between states via actions. Thus, knowing the transitions means knowing the map of the maze.

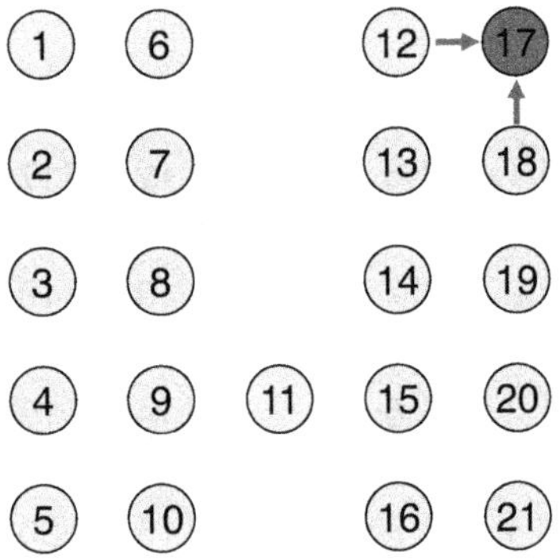

FIGURE 1.6: A positive reward is given when the robot agent reaches the goal. Thus, the reward specifies the goal location.

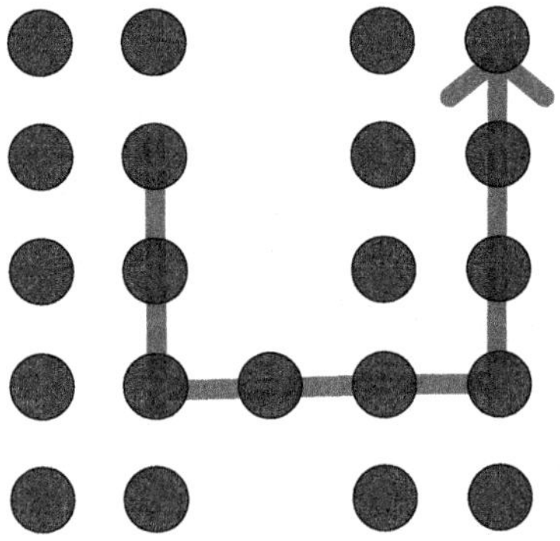

FIGURE 1.7: A policy specifies an action the robot agent takes at each state. Thus, a policy also specifies a trajectory, which is a series of states and actions that the robot agent takes from a start state to an end state.

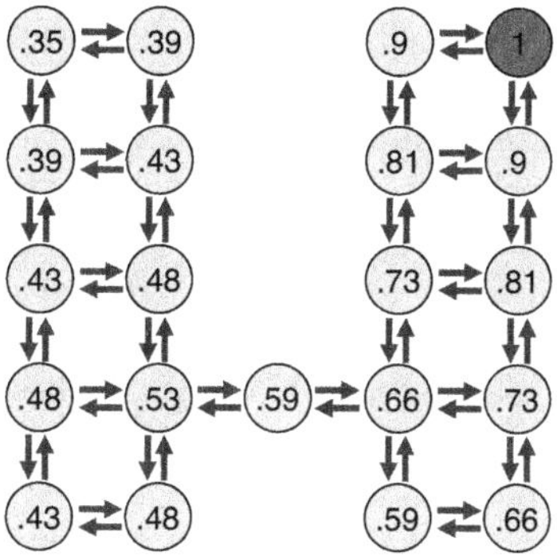

FIGURE 1.8: Values of each state when reward +1 is given at the goal state and the reward is discounted at the rate of 0.9 according to the number of steps.

Figure 1.5 again). From state 7, the robot agent can reach state 2, state 6, and state 8 by a single step. If the robot agent knows the values of these neighboring states, the best action the robot agent should take is to visit the neighboring state with the largest value, because this allows the robot agent to earn the largest amount of rewards in the long run. However, the values of neighboring states are unknown in practice and thus they should also be computed.

Now, we need to solve 3 subproblems of computing the values of state 2, state 6, and state 8. Then, in the same way, these subproblems are further decomposed as follows:

- The problem of computing the value of state 2 is decomposed into 3 subproblems of computing the values of state 1, state 3, and state 7.
- The problem of computing the value of state 6 is decomposed into 2 subproblems of computing the values of state 1 and state 7.
- The problem of computing the value of state 8 is decomposed into 3 subproblems of computing the values of state 3, state 7, and state 9.

Thus, by removing overlaps, the original problem of computing the value of state 7 has been decomposed into 6 unique subproblems: computing the values of state 1, state 2, state 3, state 6, state 8, and state 9.

If we further continue this problem decomposition, we encounter the problem of computing the values of state 17, where the robot agent can receive reward +1. Then the values of state 12 and state 18 can be explicitly computed. Indeed, if a discounting factor (a multiplicative penalty for delayed rewards) is 0.9, the values of state 12 and state 18 are $(0.9)^1 = 0.9$. Then we can further know that the values of state 13 and state 19 are $(0.9)^2 = 0.81$. By repeating this procedure, we can compute the values of all states (as illustrated in Figure 1.8). Based on these values, we can know the optimal action the robot agent should take, i.e., an action that leads the robot agent to the neighboring state with the largest value.

Note that, in real-world reinforcement learning tasks, transitions are often not deterministic but stochastic, because of some external disturbance; in the case of the above maze example, the floor may be slippery and thus the robot agent cannot move as perfectly as it desires. Also, stochastic policies in which mapping from a state to an action is not deterministic are often employed in many reinforcement learning formulations. In these cases, the formulation becomes slightly more complicated, but essentially the same idea can still be used for solving the problem.

To further highlight the notable advantage of reinforcement learning that not the immediate rewards but the long-term accumulation of rewards is maximized, let us consider a *mountain-car problem* (Figure 1.9). There are two mountains and a car is located in a valley between the mountains. The goal is to guide the car to the top of the right-hand hill. However, the engine of the car is not powerful enough to directly run up the right-hand hill and reach the goal. The optimal policy in this problem is to first climb the left-hand hill and then go down the slope to the right with full acceleration to get to the goal (Figure 1.10).

Suppose we define the immediate reward such that moving the car to the right gives a positive reward $+1$ and moving the car to the left gives a negative reward -1. Then, a greedy solution that maximizes the immediate reward moves the car to the right, which does not allow the car to get to the goal due to lack of engine power. On the other hand, reinforcement learning seeks a solution that maximizes the return, i.e., the discounted sum of immediate rewards that the agent can collect over the entire trajectory. This means that the reinforcement learning solution will first move the car to the left even though negative rewards are given for a while, to receive more positive rewards in the future. Thus, the notion of "prior investment" can be naturally incorporated in the reinforcement learning framework.

1.2 Mathematical Formulation

In this section, the reinforcement learning problem is mathematically formulated as the problem of controlling a computer agent under a Markov decision process.

We consider the problem of controlling a computer agent under a discrete-time *Markov decision process* (MDP). That is, at each discrete time-step t, the agent observes a state $\boldsymbol{s}_t \in \mathcal{S}$, selects an action $a_t \in \mathcal{A}$, makes a transition $\boldsymbol{s}_{t+1} \in \mathcal{S}$, and receives an immediate reward,

$$r_t = r(\boldsymbol{s}_t, a_t, \boldsymbol{s}_{t+1}) \in \mathbb{R}.$$

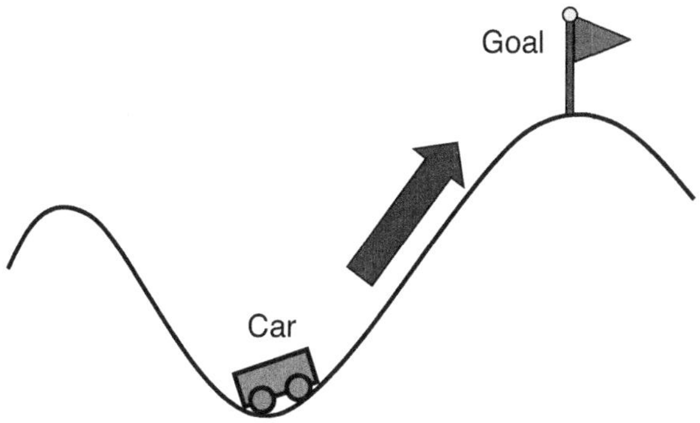

FIGURE 1.9: A mountain-car problem. We want to guide the car to the goal. However, the engine of the car is not powerful enough to directly run up the right-hand hill.

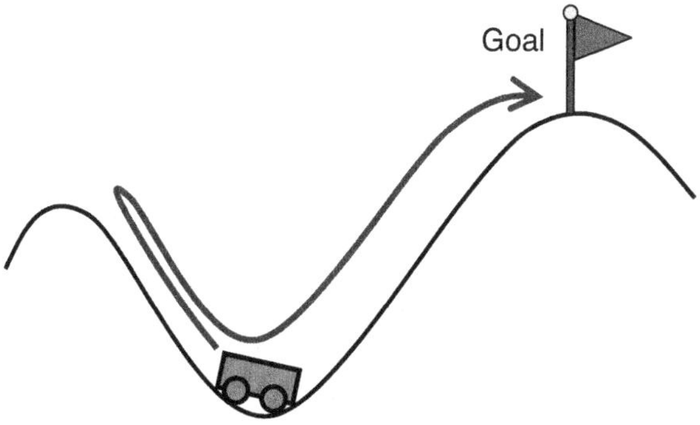

FIGURE 1.10: The optimal policy to reach the goal is to first climb the left-hand hill and then head for the right-hand hill with full acceleration.

$\mathcal{S}$ and $\mathcal{A}$ are called the *state space* and the *action space*, respectively. $r(\boldsymbol{s}, a, \boldsymbol{s}')$ is called the *immediate reward function*.

The initial position of the agent, $\boldsymbol{s}_1$, is drawn from the initial probability distribution. If the state space $\mathcal{S}$ is discrete, the initial probability distribution is specified by the *probability mass function* $P(\boldsymbol{s})$ such that

$$0 \leq P(\boldsymbol{s}) \leq 1, \ \forall \boldsymbol{s} \in \mathcal{S},$$
$$\sum_{\boldsymbol{s} \in \mathcal{S}} P(\boldsymbol{s}) = 1.$$

If the state space $\mathcal{S}$ is continuous, the initial probability distribution is specified by the *probability density function* $p(\boldsymbol{s})$ such that

$$p(\boldsymbol{s}) \geq 0, \ \forall \boldsymbol{s} \in \mathcal{S},$$

$$\int_{s \in \mathcal{S}} p(s)\mathrm{d}s = 1.$$

Because the probability mass function $P(s)$ can be expressed as a probability density function $p(s)$ by using the *Dirac delta function*[1] $\delta(s)$ as

$$p(s) = \sum_{s' \in \mathcal{S}} \delta(s' - s)P(s'),$$

we focus only on the continuous state space below.

The dynamics of the environment, which represent the transition probability from state s to state s' when action a is taken, are characterized by the *transition probability distribution* with conditional probability density $p(s'|s,a)$:

$$p(s'|s,a) \geq 0, \ \forall s, s' \in \mathcal{S}, \ \forall a \in \mathcal{A},$$

$$\int_{s' \in \mathcal{S}} p(s'|s,a)\mathrm{d}s' = 1, \ \forall s \in \mathcal{S}, \ \forall a \in \mathcal{A}.$$

The agent's decision is determined by a *policy* π. When we consider a *deterministic* policy where the action to take at each state is uniquely determined, we regard the policy as a function of states:

$$\pi(s) \in \mathcal{A}, \ \forall s \in \mathcal{S}.$$

Action a can be either discrete or continuous. On the other hand, when developing more sophisticated reinforcement learning algorithms, it is often more convenient to consider a *stochastic* policy, where an action to take at a state is probabilistically determined. Mathematically, a stochastic policy is a conditional probability density of taking action a at state s:

$$\pi(a|s) \geq 0, \ \forall s \in \mathcal{S}, \ \forall a \in \mathcal{A},$$

$$\int_{a \in \mathcal{A}} \pi(a|s)\mathrm{d}a = 1, \ \forall s \in \mathcal{S}.$$

By introducing stochasticity in action selection, we can more actively *explore* the entire state space. Note that when action a is discrete, the stochastic policy is expressed using Dirac's delta function, as in the case of the state densities.

A sequence of states and actions obtained by the procedure described in Figure 1.11 is called a *trajectory*.

---

[1]The Dirac delta function $\delta(\cdot)$ allows us to obtain the value of a function f at a point τ via the *convolution* with f:

$$\int_{-\infty}^{\infty} f(s)\delta(s - \tau)\mathrm{d}s = f(\tau).$$

Dirac's delta function $\delta(\cdot)$ can be expressed as the Gaussian density with standard deviation $\sigma \to 0$:

$$\delta(a) = \lim_{\sigma \to 0} \frac{1}{\sqrt{2\pi\sigma^2}} \exp\left(-\frac{a^2}{2\sigma^2}\right).$$

1. The initial state $\boldsymbol{s}_1$ is chosen following the initial probability $p(\boldsymbol{s})$.
2. For $t = 1, \ldots, T$,
   (a) The action a_t is chosen following the policy $\pi(a_t|\boldsymbol{s}_t)$.
   (b) The next state $\boldsymbol{s}_{t+1}$ is determined according to the transition probability $p(\boldsymbol{s}_{t+1}|\boldsymbol{s}_t, a_t)$.

FIGURE 1.11: Generation of a trajectory sample.

When the number of steps, T, is finite or infinite, the situation is called the *finite horizon* or *infinite horizon*, respectively. Below, we focus on the finite-horizon case because the trajectory length is always finite in practice. We denote a trajectory by h (which stands for a "*history*"):

$$h = [\boldsymbol{s}_1, a_1, \ldots, \boldsymbol{s}_T, a_T, \boldsymbol{s}_{T+1}].$$

The discounted sum of immediate rewards along the trajectory h is called the *return*:

$$R(h) = \sum_{t=1}^{T} \gamma^{t-1} r(\boldsymbol{s}_t, a_t, \boldsymbol{s}_{t+1}),$$

where $\gamma \in [0, 1)$ is called the *discount factor* for future rewards.

The goal of reinforcement learning is to learn the optimal policy π^* that maximizes the *expected return*:

$$\pi^* = \underset{\pi}{\operatorname{argmax}}\, \mathbb{E}_{p^\pi(h)} \Big[R(h) \Big],$$

where $\mathbb{E}_{p^\pi(h)}$ denotes the expectation over trajectory h drawn from $p^\pi(h)$, and $p^\pi(h)$ denotes the probability density of observing trajectory h under policy π:

$$p^\pi(h) = p(\boldsymbol{s}_1) \prod_{t=1}^{T} p(\boldsymbol{s}_{t+1}|\boldsymbol{s}_t, a_t) \pi(a_t|\boldsymbol{s}_t).$$

"argmax" gives the maximizer of a function (Figure 1.12).

For policy learning, various methods have been developed so far. These methods can be classified into *model-based reinforcement learning* and *model-free reinforcement learning*. The term "model" indicates a model of the transition probability $p(\boldsymbol{s}'|\boldsymbol{s}, a)$. In the model-based reinforcement learning approach, the transition probability is learned in advance and the learned transition model is explicitly used for policy learning. On the other hand, in the model-free reinforcement learning approach, policies are learned without explicitly estimating the transition probability. If strong prior knowledge of the

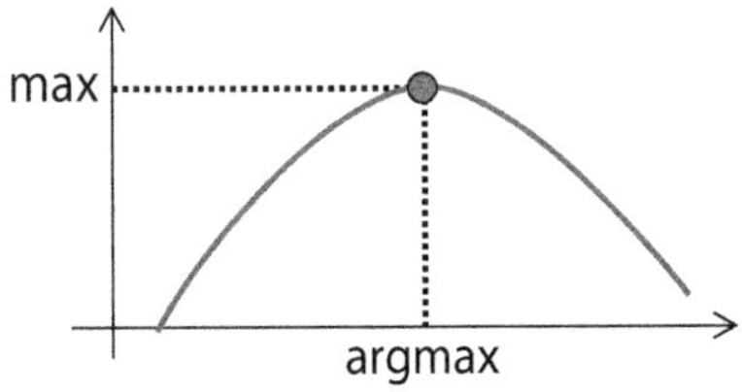

FIGURE 1.12: "argmax" gives the maximizer of a function, while "max" gives the maximum value of a function.

transition model is available, the model-based approach would be more favorable. On the other hand, learning the transition model without prior knowledge itself is a hard statistical estimation problem. Thus, if good prior knowledge of the transition model is not available, the model-free approach would be more promising.

1.3 Structure of the Book

In this section, we explain the structure of this book, which covers major reinforcement learning approaches.

1.3.1 Model-Free Policy Iteration

Policy iteration is a popular and well-studied approach to reinforcement learning. The key idea of policy iteration is to determine policies based on the *value function*.

Let us first introduce the *state-action value function* $Q^\pi(\boldsymbol{s}, a) \in \mathbb{R}$ for policy π, which is defined as the expected return the agent will receive when taking action a at state $\boldsymbol{s}$ and following policy π thereafter:

$$Q^\pi(\boldsymbol{s}, a) = \mathbb{E}_{p^\pi(h)}\left[R(h)\middle|\boldsymbol{s}_1 = \boldsymbol{s}, a_1 = a\right],$$

where "$|\boldsymbol{s}_1 = \boldsymbol{s}, a_1 = a$" means that the initial state $\boldsymbol{s}_1$ and the first action a_1 are fixed at $\boldsymbol{s}_1 = \boldsymbol{s}$ and $a_1 = a$, respectively. That is, the right-hand side of the above equation denotes the conditional expectation of $R(h)$ given $\boldsymbol{s}_1 = \boldsymbol{s}$ and $a_1 = a$.

Let $Q^*(\boldsymbol{s}, a)$ be the optimal state-action value at state $\boldsymbol{s}$ for action a defined as

$$Q^*(\boldsymbol{s}, a) = \max_\pi Q^\pi(\boldsymbol{s}, a).$$

Based on the optimal state-action value function, the optimal action the agent should take at state $\boldsymbol{s}$ is deterministically given as the maximizer of $Q^*(\boldsymbol{s}, a)$

1. Initialize policy $\pi(a|\boldsymbol{s})$.
2. Repeat the following two steps until the policy $\pi(a|\boldsymbol{s})$ converges.
   (a) Policy evaluation: Compute the state-action value function $Q^{\pi}(\boldsymbol{s}, a)$ for the current policy $\pi(a|\boldsymbol{s})$.
   (b) Policy improvement: Update the policy as

$$\pi(a|\boldsymbol{s}) \longleftarrow \delta\left(a - \operatorname*{argmax}_{a'} Q^{\pi}(\boldsymbol{s}, a')\right).$$

FIGURE 1.13: Algorithm of policy iteration.

with respect to a. Thus, the optimal policy $\pi^*(a|\boldsymbol{s})$ is given by

$$\pi^*(a|\boldsymbol{s}) = \delta\left(a - \operatorname*{argmax}_{a'} Q^*(\boldsymbol{s}, a')\right),$$

where $\delta(\cdot)$ denotes Dirac's delta function.

Because the optimal state-action value Q^* is unknown in practice, the policy iteration algorithm alternately evaluates the value Q^{π} for the current policy π and updates the policy π based on the current value Q^{π} (Figure 1.13).

The performance of the above policy iteration algorithm depends on the quality of policy evaluation; i.e., how to learn the state-action value function from data is the key issue. Value function approximation corresponds to a *regression* problem in statistics and machine learning. Thus, various statistical machine learning techniques can be utilized for better value function approximation. Part II of this book addresses this issue, including least-squares estimation and model selection (Chapter 2), basis function design (Chapter 3), efficient sample reuse (Chapter 4), active learning (Chapter 5), and robust learning (Chapter 6).

1.3.2 Model-Free Policy Search

One of the potential weaknesses of policy iteration is that policies are learned via value functions. Thus, improving the quality of value function approximation does not necessarily contribute to improving the quality of resulting policies. Furthermore, a small change in value functions can cause a big difference in policies, which is problematic in, e.g., robot control because such instability can damage the robot's physical system. Another weakness of policy iteration is that policy improvement, i.e., finding the maximizer of $Q^{\pi}(\boldsymbol{s}, a)$ with respect to a, is computationally expensive or difficult when the action space $\mathcal{A}$ is continuous.

Policy search, which directly learns policy functions without estimating value functions, can overcome the above limitations. The basic idea of policy search is to find the policy that maximizes the expected return:

$$\pi^* = \underset{\pi}{\operatorname{argmax}}\, \mathbb{E}_{p^\pi(h)}\Big[R(h)\Big].$$

In policy search, how to find a good policy function in a vast function space is the key issue to be addressed. Part III of this book focuses on policy search and introduces gradient-based methods and the expectation-maximization method in Chapter 7 and Chapter 8, respectively. However, a potential weakness of these direct policy search methods is their instability due to the stochasticity of policies. To overcome the instability problem, an alternative approach called *policy-prior search*, which learns the policy-prior distribution for deterministic policies, is introduced in Chapter 9. Efficient sample reuse in policy-prior search is also discussed there.

1.3.3 Model-Based Reinforcement Learning

In the above model-free approaches, policies are learned without explicitly modeling the unknown environment (i.e., the transition probability of the agent in the environment, $p(\boldsymbol{s}'|\boldsymbol{s}, a)$). On the other hand, the model-based approach explicitly learns the environment in advance and uses the learned environment model for policy learning.

No additional sampling cost is necessary to generate artificial samples from the learned environment model. Thus, the model-based approach is particularly useful when data collection is expensive (e.g., robot control). However, accurately estimating the transition model from a limited amount of trajectory data in multi-dimensional continuous state and action spaces is highly challenging. Part IV of this book focuses on model-based reinforcement learning. In Chapter 10, a non-parametric transition model estimator that possesses the optimal convergence rate with high computational efficiency is introduced. However, even with the optimal convergence rate, estimating the transition model in high-dimensional state and action spaces is still challenging. In Chapter 11, a *dimensionality reduction* method that can be efficiently embedded into the transition model estimation procedure is introduced and its usefulness is demonstrated through experiments.

Part II

Model-Free Policy Iteration

In Part II, we introduce a reinforcement learning approach based on value functions called *policy iteration.*

The key issue in the policy iteration framework is how to accurately approximate the value function from a small number of data samples. In Chapter 2, a fundamental framework of value function approximation based on least squares is explained. In this least-squares formulation, how to design good basis functions is critical for better value function approximation. A practical basis design method based on *manifold-based smoothing* (Chapelle et al., 2006) is explained in Chapter 3.

In real-world reinforcement learning tasks, gathering data is often costly. In Chapter 4, we describe a method for efficiently reusing previously corrected samples in the framework of *covariate shift adaptation* (Sugiyama & Kawanabe, 2012). In Chapter 5, we apply a statistical *active learning* technique (Sugiyama & Kawanabe, 2012) to optimizing data collection strategies for reducing the sampling cost.

Finally, in Chapter 6, an outlier-robust extension of the least-squares method based on *robust regression* (Huber, 1981) is introduced. Such a robust method is highly useful in handling noisy real-world data.

Chapter 2

Policy Iteration with Value Function Approximation

In this chapter, we introduce the framework of least-squares policy iteration. In Section 2.1, we first explain the framework of policy iteration, which iteratively executes the policy evaluation and policy improvement steps for finding better policies. Then, in Section 2.2, we show how value function approximation in the policy evaluation step can be formulated as a regression problem and introduce a least-squares algorithm called *least-squares policy iteration* (Lagoudakis & Parr, 2003). Finally, this chapter is concluded in Section 2.3.

2.1 Value Functions

A traditional way to learn the optimal policy is based on *value function*. In this section, we introduce two types of value functions, the *state value function* and the *state-action value function*, and explain how they can be used for finding better policies.

2.1.1 State Value Functions

The *state value function* $V^\pi(\boldsymbol{s}) \in \mathbb{R}$ for policy π measures the "value" of state $\boldsymbol{s}$, which is defined as the expected return the agent will receive when following policy π from state $\boldsymbol{s}$:

$$V^\pi(\boldsymbol{s}) = \mathbb{E}_{p^\pi(h)}\Big[R(h)\Big|\boldsymbol{s}_1 = \boldsymbol{s}\Big],$$

where "$|\boldsymbol{s}_1 = \boldsymbol{s}$" means that the initial state $\boldsymbol{s}_1$ is fixed at $\boldsymbol{s}_1 = \boldsymbol{s}$. That is, the right-hand side of the above equation denotes the conditional expectation of return $R(h)$ given $\boldsymbol{s}_1 = \boldsymbol{s}$.

By recursion, $V^\pi(\boldsymbol{s})$ can be expressed as

$$V^\pi(\boldsymbol{s}) = \mathbb{E}_{p(\boldsymbol{s}'|\boldsymbol{s},a)\pi(a|\boldsymbol{s})}\Big[r(\boldsymbol{s}, a, \boldsymbol{s}') + \gamma V^\pi(\boldsymbol{s}')\Big],$$

where $\mathbb{E}_{p(\boldsymbol{s}'|\boldsymbol{s},a)\pi(a|\boldsymbol{s})}$ denotes the conditional expectation over a and $\boldsymbol{s}'$ drawn from $p(s'|s,a)\pi(a|s)$ given s. This recursive expression is called the *Bellman equation for state values*. $V^{\pi}(s)$ may be obtained by repeating the following update from some initial estimate:

$$V^{\pi}(s) \longleftarrow \mathbb{E}_{p(s'|s,a)\pi(a|s)}\left[r(s,a,s') + \gamma V^{\pi}(s')\right].$$

The optimal state value at state s, $V^*(s)$, is defined as the maximizer of state value $V^{\pi}(s)$ with respect to policy π:

$$V^*(s) = \max_{\pi} V^{\pi}(s).$$

Based on the optimal state value $V^*(s)$, the optimal policy π^*, which is deterministic, can be obtained as

$$\pi^*(a|s) = \delta\left(a - a^*(s)\right),$$

where $\delta(\cdot)$ denotes Dirac's delta function and

$$a^*(s) = \underset{a \in \mathcal{A}}{\operatorname{argmax}} \left\{\mathbb{E}_{p(s'|s,a)}\left[r(s,a,s') + \gamma V^*(s')\right]\right\}.$$

$\mathbb{E}_{p(s'|s,a)}$ denotes the conditional expectation over s' drawn from $p(s'|s,a)$ given s and a. This algorithm, first computing the optimal value function and then obtaining the optimal policy based on the optimal value function, is called *value iteration*.

A possible variation is to iteratively perform policy evaluation and improvement as

$$\text{Policy evaluation:} \quad V^{\pi}(s) \longleftarrow \mathbb{E}_{p(s'|s,a)\pi(a|s)}\left[r(s,a,s') + \gamma V^{\pi}(s')\right].$$

$$\text{Policy improvement:} \quad \pi^*(a|s) \longleftarrow \delta\left(a - a^{\pi}(s)\right),$$

where

$$a^{\pi}(s) = \underset{a \in \mathcal{A}}{\operatorname{argmax}} \left\{\mathbb{E}_{p(s'|s,a)}\left[r(s,a,s') + \gamma V^{\pi}(s')\right]\right\}.$$

These two steps may be iterated either for all states at once or in a state-by-state manner. This iterative algorithm is called the *policy iteration* (based on state value functions).

2.1.2 State-Action Value Functions

In the above policy improvement step, the action to take is optimized based on the state value function $V^{\pi}(s)$. A more direct way to handle this action optimization is to consider the *state-action value function* $Q^{\pi}(s,a)$ for policy π:

$$Q^{\pi}(s,a) = \mathbb{E}_{p^{\pi}(h)}\left[R(h)\middle| s_1 = s, a_1 = a\right],$$

where "$|s_1 = s, a_1 = a$" means that the initial state s_1 and the first action a_1 are fixed at $s_1 = s$ and $a_1 = a$, respectively. That is, the right-hand side of the above equation denotes the conditional expectation of return $R(h)$ given $s_1 = s$ and $a_1 = a$.

Let $r(s,a)$ be the expected immediate reward when action a is taken at state s:

$$r(s,a) = \mathbb{E}_{p(s'|s,a)}[r(s,a,s')].$$

Then, in the same way as $V^\pi(s)$, $Q^\pi(s,a)$ can be expressed by recursion as

$$Q^\pi(s,a) = r(s,a) + \gamma \mathbb{E}_{\pi(a'|s')p(s'|s,a)}\left[Q^\pi(s',a')\right], \tag{2.1}$$

where $\mathbb{E}_{\pi(a'|s')p(s'|s,a)}$ denotes the conditional expectation over s' and a' drawn from $\pi(a'|s')p(s'|s,a)$ given s and a. This recursive expression is called the *Bellman equation for state-action values.*

Based on the Bellman equation, the optimal policy may be obtained by iterating the following two steps:

$$\text{Policy evaluation:} \quad Q^\pi(s,a) \longleftarrow r(s,a) + \gamma \mathbb{E}_{\pi(a'|s')p(s'|s,a)}\left[Q^\pi(s',a')\right].$$

$$\text{Policy improvement:} \quad \pi(a|s) \longleftarrow \delta\left(a - \operatorname*{argmax}_{a' \in \mathcal{A}} Q^\pi(s,a')\right).$$

In practice, it is sometimes preferable to use an explorative policy. For example, *Gibbs policy improvement* is given by

$$\pi(a|s) \longleftarrow \frac{\exp(Q^\pi(s,a)/\tau)}{\int_{\mathcal{A}} \exp(Q^\pi(s,a')/\tau)\mathrm{d}a'},$$

where $\tau > 0$ determines the degree of exploration. When the action space $\mathcal{A}$ is discrete, *ϵ-greedy policy improvement* is also used:

$$\pi(a|s) \longleftarrow \begin{cases} 1 - \epsilon + \epsilon/|\mathcal{A}| & \text{if } a = \operatorname*{argmax}_{a' \in \mathcal{A}} Q^\pi(s,a'), \\ \epsilon/|\mathcal{A}| & \text{otherwise,} \end{cases}$$

where $\epsilon \in (0, 1]$ determines the randomness of the new policy.

The above policy improvement step based on $Q^\pi(s,a)$ is essentially the same as the one based on $V^\pi(s)$ explained in Section 2.1.1. However, the policy improvement step based on $Q^\pi(s,a)$ does not contain the expectation operator and thus policy improvement can be more directly carried out. For this reason, we focus on the above formulation, called *policy iteration* based on state-action value functions.

2.2 Least-Squares Policy Iteration

As explained in the previous section, the optimal policy function may be learned via state-action value function $Q^\pi(\boldsymbol{s}, a)$. However, learning the state-action value function from data is a challenging task for continuous state $\boldsymbol{s}$ and action a.

Learning the state-action value function from data can actually be regarded as a *regression* problem in statistics and machine learning. In this section, we explain how the least-squares regression technique can be employed in value function approximation, which is called *least-squares policy iteration* (Lagoudakis & Parr, 2003).

2.2.1 Immediate-Reward Regression

Let us approximate the state-action value function $Q^\pi(\boldsymbol{s}, a)$ by the following *linear-in-parameter model*:

$$\sum_{b=1}^{B} \theta_b \phi_b(\boldsymbol{s}, a),$$

where $\{\phi_b(\boldsymbol{s}, a)\}_{b=1}^{B}$ are basis functions, B denotes the number of basis functions, and $\{\theta_b\}_{b=1}^{B}$ are parameters. Specific designs of basis functions will be discussed in Chapter 3. Below, we use the following vector representation for compactly expressing the parameters and basis functions:

$$\boldsymbol{\theta}^\top \boldsymbol{\phi}(\boldsymbol{s}, a),$$

where $^\top$ denotes the transpose and

$$\boldsymbol{\theta} = (\theta_1, \ldots, \theta_B)^\top \in \mathbb{R}^B,$$

$$\boldsymbol{\phi}(\boldsymbol{s}, a) = \left(\phi_1(\boldsymbol{s}, a), \ldots, \phi_B(\boldsymbol{s}, a)\right)^\top \in \mathbb{R}^B.$$

From the Bellman equation for state-action values (2.1), we can express the expected immediate reward $r(\boldsymbol{s}, a)$ as

$$r(\boldsymbol{s}, a) = Q^\pi(\boldsymbol{s}, a) - \gamma \mathbb{E}_{\pi(a'|\boldsymbol{s}')p(\boldsymbol{s}'|\boldsymbol{s},a)}\left[Q^\pi(\boldsymbol{s}', a')\right].$$

By substituting the value function model $\boldsymbol{\theta}^\top \boldsymbol{\phi}(\boldsymbol{s}, a)$ in the above equation, the expected immediate reward $r(\boldsymbol{s}, a)$ may be approximated as

$$r(\boldsymbol{s}, a) \approx \boldsymbol{\theta}^\top \boldsymbol{\phi}(\boldsymbol{s}, a) - \gamma \mathbb{E}_{\pi(a'|\boldsymbol{s}')p(\boldsymbol{s}'|\boldsymbol{s},a)}\left[\boldsymbol{\theta}^\top \boldsymbol{\phi}(\boldsymbol{s}', a')\right].$$

Now let us define a new basis function vector $\boldsymbol{\psi}(\boldsymbol{s}, a)$:

$$\boldsymbol{\psi}(\boldsymbol{s}, a) = \boldsymbol{\phi}(\boldsymbol{s}, a) - \gamma \mathbb{E}_{\pi(a'|\boldsymbol{s}')p(\boldsymbol{s}'|\boldsymbol{s},a)}\left[\boldsymbol{\phi}(\boldsymbol{s}', a')\right].$$

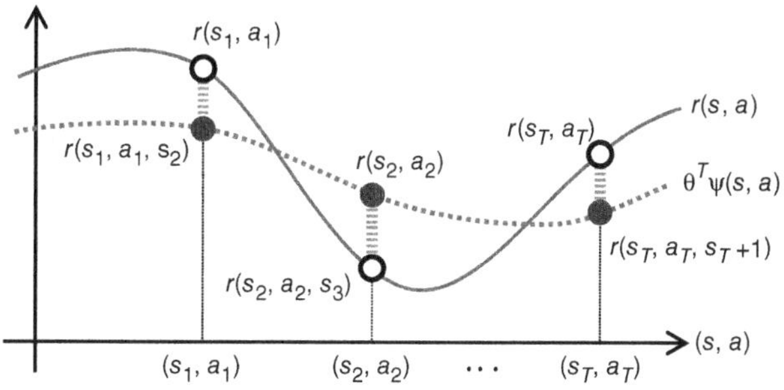

FIGURE 2.1: Linear approximation of state-action value function $Q^{\pi}(\boldsymbol{s}, a)$ as linear regression of expected immediate reward $r(\boldsymbol{s}, a)$.

Then the expected immediate reward $r(\boldsymbol{s}, a)$ may be approximated as

$$r(\boldsymbol{s}, a) \approx \boldsymbol{\theta}^{\top} \boldsymbol{\psi}(\boldsymbol{s}, a).$$

As explained above, the linear approximation problem of the state-action value function $Q^{\pi}(\boldsymbol{s}, a)$ can be reformulated as the linear regression problem of the expected immediate reward $r(\boldsymbol{s}, a)$ (see Figure 2.1). The key trick was to push the recursive nature of the state-action value function $Q^{\pi}(\boldsymbol{s}, a)$ into the composite basis function $\boldsymbol{\psi}(\boldsymbol{s}, a)$.

2.2.2 Algorithm

Now, we explain how the parameters $\boldsymbol{\theta}$ are learned in the least-squares framework. That is, the model $\boldsymbol{\theta}^{\top} \boldsymbol{\psi}(\boldsymbol{s}, a)$ is fitted to the expected immediate reward $r(\boldsymbol{s}, a)$ under the squared loss:

$$\min_{\boldsymbol{\theta}} \left\{ \mathbb{E}_{p^{\pi}(h)} \left[\frac{1}{T} \sum_{t=1}^{T} \left(\boldsymbol{\theta}^{\top} \boldsymbol{\psi}(\boldsymbol{s}_t, a_t) - r(\boldsymbol{s}_t, a_t) \right)^2 \right] \right\},$$

where h denotes the history sample following the current policy π:

$$h = [\boldsymbol{s}_1, a_1, \ldots, \boldsymbol{s}_T, a_T, \boldsymbol{s}_{T+1}].$$

For history samples $\mathcal{H} = \{h_1, \ldots, h_N\}$, where

$$h_n = [\boldsymbol{s}_{1,n}, a_{1,n}, \ldots, \boldsymbol{s}_{T,n}, a_{T,n}, \boldsymbol{s}_{T+1,n}],$$

an empirical version of the above least-squares problem is given as

$$\min_{\boldsymbol{\theta}} \left\{ \frac{1}{N} \sum_{n=1}^{N} \left[\frac{1}{T} \sum_{t=1}^{T} \left(\boldsymbol{\theta}^{\top} \widehat{\boldsymbol{\psi}}(\boldsymbol{s}_{t,n}, a_{t,n}; \mathcal{H}) - r(\boldsymbol{s}_{t,n}, a_{t,n}, \boldsymbol{s}_{t+1,n}) \right)^2 \right] \right\}.$$

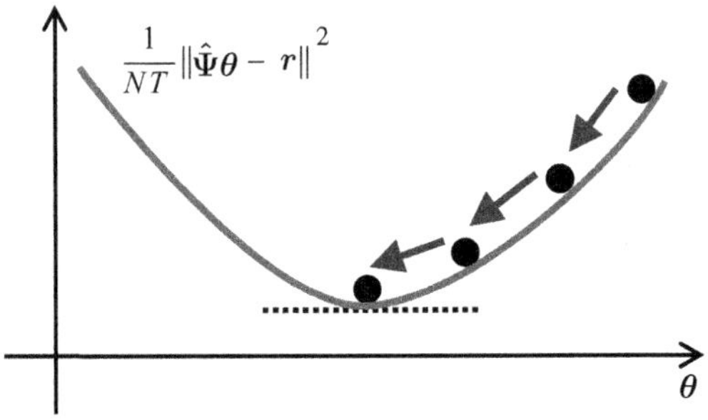

FIGURE 2.2: Gradient descent.

Here, $\widehat{\psi}(s, a; \mathcal{H})$ is an empirical estimator of $\psi(s, a)$ given by

$$\widehat{\psi}(s, a; \mathcal{H}) = \phi(s, a) - \frac{1}{|\mathcal{H}_{(s,a)}|} \sum_{s' \in \mathcal{H}_{(s,a)}} \mathbb{E}_{\pi(a'|s')}\Big[\gamma\phi(s', a')\Big],$$

where $\mathcal{H}_{(s,a)}$ denotes a subset of $\mathcal{H}$ that consists of all transition samples from state s by action a, $|\mathcal{H}_{(s,a)}|$ denotes the number of elements in the set $\mathcal{H}_{(s,a)}$, and $\sum_{s' \in \mathcal{H}_{s,a)}}$ denotes the summation over all destination states s' in the set $\mathcal{H}_{(s,a)}$.

Let $\widehat{\Psi}$ be the $NT \times B$ matrix and r be the NT-dimensional vector defined as

$$\widehat{\Psi}_{N(t-1)+n,b} = \widehat{\psi}_b(s_{t,n}, a_{t,n}),$$
$$r_{N(t-1)+n} = r(s_{t,n}, a_{t,n}, s_{t+1,n}).$$

$\widehat{\Psi}$ is sometimes called the *design matrix*. Then the above least-squares problem can be compactly expressed as

$$\min_{\theta} \left\{ \frac{1}{NT} \|\widehat{\Psi}\theta - r\|^2 \right\},$$

where $\|\cdot\|$ denotes the ℓ_2-norm. Because this is a quadratic function with respect to θ, its global minimizer $\widehat{\theta}$ can be analytically obtained by setting its derivative to zero as

$$\widehat{\theta} = (\widehat{\Psi}^\top \widehat{\Psi})^{-1} \widehat{\Psi}^\top r. \tag{2.2}$$

If B is too large and computing the inverse of $\widehat{\Psi}^\top \widehat{\Psi}$ is intractable, we may use a *gradient descent* method. That is, starting from some initial estimate θ, the solution is updated until convergence, as follows (see Figure 2.2):

$$\theta \longleftarrow \theta - \varepsilon(\widehat{\Psi}^\top \widehat{\Psi}\theta - \widehat{\Psi}^\top r),$$

where $\widehat{\boldsymbol{\Psi}}^\top \widehat{\boldsymbol{\Psi}}\boldsymbol{\theta} - \widehat{\boldsymbol{\Psi}}^\top \boldsymbol{r}$ corresponds to the gradient of the objective function $\|\widehat{\boldsymbol{\Psi}}\boldsymbol{\theta} - \boldsymbol{r}\|^2$ and ε is a small positive constant representing the step size of gradient descent.

A notable variation of the above least-squares method is to compute the solution by

$$\widetilde{\boldsymbol{\theta}} = (\boldsymbol{\Phi}^\top \widehat{\boldsymbol{\Psi}})^{-1} \boldsymbol{\Phi}^\top \boldsymbol{r},$$

where $\boldsymbol{\Phi}$ is the $NT \times B$ matrix defined as

$$\Phi_{N(t-1)+n,b} = \phi(\boldsymbol{s}_{t,n}, a_{t,n}).$$

This variation is called the *least-squares fixed-point approximation* (Lagoudakis & Parr, 2003) and is shown to handle the estimation error included in the basis function $\widehat{\psi}$ in a sound way (Bradtke & Barto, 1996). However, for simplicity, we focus on Eq. (2.2) below.

2.2.3 Regularization

Regression techniques in machine learning are generally formulated as minimization of a goodness-of-fit term and a regularization term. In the above least-squares framework, the goodness-of-fit of our model is measured by the squared loss. In the following chapters, we discuss how other loss functions can be utilized in the policy iteration framework, e.g., sample reuse in Chapter 4 and outlier-robust learning in Chapter 6. Here we focus on the regularization term and introduce practically useful regularization techniques.

The *ℓ_2-regularizer* is the most standard regularizer in statistics and machine learning; it is also called the *ridge regression* (Hoerl & Kennard, 1970):

$$\min_{\boldsymbol{\theta}} \left\{ \frac{1}{NT} \|\widehat{\boldsymbol{\Psi}}\boldsymbol{\theta} - \boldsymbol{r}\|^2 + \lambda \|\boldsymbol{\theta}\|^2 \right\},$$

where $\lambda \geq 0$ is the regularization parameter. The role of the ℓ_2-regularizer $\|\boldsymbol{\theta}\|^2$ is to penalize the growth of the parameter vector $\boldsymbol{\theta}$ to avoid overfitting to noisy samples. A practical advantage of the use of the ℓ_2-regularizer is that the minimizer $\widehat{\boldsymbol{\theta}}$ can still be obtained analytically:

$$\widehat{\boldsymbol{\theta}} = (\widehat{\boldsymbol{\Psi}}^\top \widehat{\boldsymbol{\Psi}} + \lambda \boldsymbol{I}_B)^{-1} \widehat{\boldsymbol{\Psi}}^\top \boldsymbol{r},$$

where $\boldsymbol{I}_B$ denotes the $B \times B$ identity matrix. Because of the addition of $\lambda \boldsymbol{I}_B$, the matrix to be inverted above has a better numerical condition and thus the solution tends to be more stable than the solution obtained by plain least squares without regularization.

Note that the same solution as the above ℓ_2-penalized least-squares problem can be obtained by solving the following ℓ_2-constrained least-squares problem:

$$\min_{\boldsymbol{\theta}} \frac{1}{NT} \|\widehat{\boldsymbol{\Psi}}\boldsymbol{\theta} - \boldsymbol{r}\|^2$$

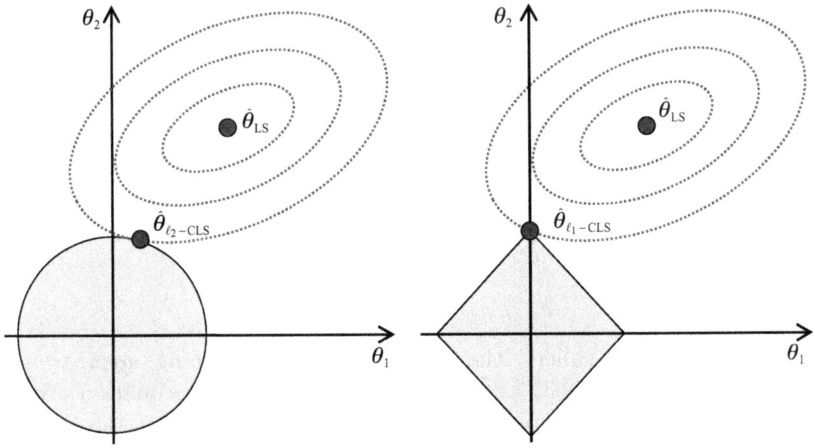

(a) ℓ_2-constraint (b) ℓ_1-constraint

FIGURE 2.3: Feasible regions (i.e., regions where the constraint is satisfied). The least-squares (LS) solution is the bottom of the elliptical hyperboloid, whereas the solution of constrained least-squares (CLS) is located at the point where the hyperboloid touches the feasible region.

$$\text{subject to } \|\boldsymbol{\theta}\|^2 \leq C,$$

where C is determined from λ. Note that the larger the value of λ is (i.e., the stronger the effect of regularization is), the smaller the value of C is (i.e., the smaller the feasible region is). The feasible region (i.e., the region where the constraint $\|\boldsymbol{\theta}\|^2 \leq C$ is satisfied) is illustrated in Figure 2.3(a).

Another popular choice of regularization in statistics and machine learning is the *ℓ_1-regularizer*, which is also called the *least absolute shrinkage and selection operator* (LASSO) (Tibshirani, 1996):

$$\min_{\boldsymbol{\theta}} \left\{ \frac{1}{NT} \|\widehat{\boldsymbol{\Psi}}\boldsymbol{\theta} - \boldsymbol{r}\|^2 + \lambda \|\boldsymbol{\theta}\|_1 \right\},$$

where $\|\cdot\|_1$ denotes the ℓ_1-norm defined as the absolute sum of elements:

$$\|\boldsymbol{\theta}\|_1 = \sum_{b=1}^{B} |\theta_b|.$$

In the same way as the ℓ_2-regularization case, the same solution as the above ℓ_1-penalized least-squares problem can be obtained by solving the following constrained least-squares problem:

$$\min_{\boldsymbol{\theta}} \frac{1}{NT} \|\widehat{\boldsymbol{\Psi}}\boldsymbol{\theta} - \boldsymbol{r}\|^2$$
$$\text{subject to } \|\boldsymbol{\theta}\|_1 \leq C,$$

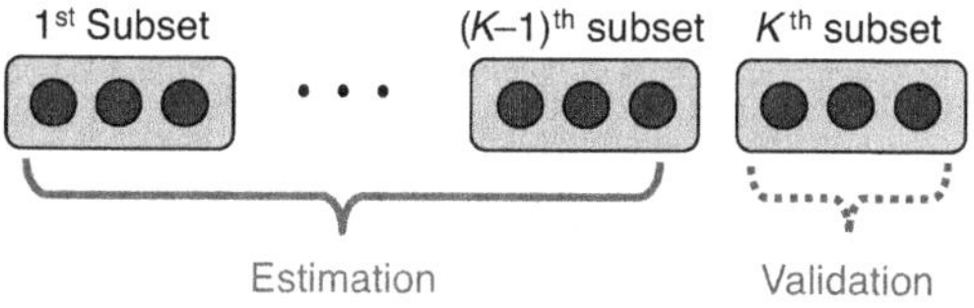

FIGURE 2.4: Cross validation.

where C is determined from λ. The feasible region is illustrated in Figure 2.3(b).

A notable property of ℓ_1-regularization is that the solution tends to be *sparse*, i.e., many of the elements $\{\theta_b\}_{b=1}^{B}$ become exactly zero. The reason why the solution becomes sparse can be intuitively understood from Figure 2.3(b): the solution tends to be on one of the corners of the feasible region, where the solution is sparse. On the other hand, in the ℓ_2-constraint case (see Figure 2.3(a) again), the solution is similar to the ℓ_1-constraint case, but it is not generally on an axis and thus the solution is not sparse. Such a sparse solution has various computational advantages. For example, the solution for large-scale problems can be computed efficiently, because all parameters do not have to be explicitly handled; see, e.g., Tomioka et al., 2011. Furthermore, the solutions for all different regularization parameters can be computed efficiently (Efron et al., 2004), and the output of the learned model can be computed efficiently.

2.2.4 Model Selection

In regression, tuning parameters are often included in the algorithm, such as basis parameters and the regularization parameter. Such tuning parameters can be objectively and systematically optimized based on *cross-validation* (Wahba, 1990) as follows (see Figure 2.4).

First, the training dataset $\mathcal{H}$ is divided into K disjoint subsets of approximately the same size, $\{\mathcal{H}_k\}_{k=1}^{K}$. Then the regression solution $\widehat{\boldsymbol{\theta}}_k$ is obtained using $\mathcal{H}\backslash\mathcal{H}_k$ (i.e., all samples without $\mathcal{H}_k$), and its squared error for the hold-out samples $\mathcal{H}_k$ is computed. This procedure is repeated for $k = 1, \ldots, K$, and the model (such as the basis parameter and the regularization parameter) that minimizes the average error is chosen as the most suitable one.

One may think that the ordinary squared error is directly used for model selection, instead of its cross-validation estimator. However, the ordinary squared error is heavily biased (or in other words, *over-fitted*) since the same training samples are used twice for learning parameters and estimating the generalization error (i.e., the out-of-sample prediction error). On the other hand, the cross-validation estimator of squared error is almost unbiased, where "almost" comes from the fact that the number of training samples is reduced due to data splitting in the cross-validation procedure.

In general, cross-validation is computationally expensive because the squared error needs to be estimated many times. For example, when performing 5-fold cross-validation for 10 model candidates, the learning procedure has to be repeated $5 \times 10 = 50$ times. However, this is often acceptable in practice because sensible model selection gives an accurate solution even with a small number of samples. Thus, in total, the computation time may not grow that much. Furthermore, cross-validation is suitable for parallel computing since error estimation for different models and different folds are independent of each other. For instance, when performing 5-fold cross-validation for 10 model candidates, the use of 50 computing units allows us to compute everything at once.

2.3 Remarks

Reinforcement learning via regression of state-action value functions is a highly powerful and flexible approach, because we can utilize various regression techniques developed in statistics and machine learning such as least-squares, regularization, and cross-validation.

In the following chapters, we introduce more sophisticated regression techniques such as manifold-based smoothing (Chapelle et al., 2006) in Chapter 3, covariate shift adaptation (Sugiyama & Kawanabe, 2012) in Chapter 4, active learning (Sugiyama & Kawanabe, 2012) in Chapter 5, and robust regression (Huber, 1981) in Chapter 6.

Chapter 3

Basis Design for Value Function Approximation

Least-squares policy iteration explained in Chapter 2 works well, given appropriate basis functions for value function approximation. Because of its smoothness, the Gaussian kernel is a popular and useful choice as a basis function. However, it does not allow for discontinuity, which is conceivable in many reinforcement learning tasks. In this chapter, we introduce an alternative basis function based on *geodesic Gaussian kernels* (GGKs), which exploit the non-linear manifold structure induced by the Markov decision processes (MDPs). The details of GGK are explained in Section 3.1, and its relation to other basis function designs is discussed in Section 3.2. Then, experimental performance is numerically evaluated in Section 3.3, and this chapter is concluded in Section 3.4.

3.1 Gaussian Kernels on Graphs

In least-squares policy iteration, the choice of basis functions $\{\phi_b(\boldsymbol{s}, a)\}_{b=1}^{B}$ is an open design issue (see Chapter 2). Traditionally, Gaussian kernels have been a popular choice (Lagoudakis & Parr, 2003; Engel et al., 2005), but they cannot approximate discontinuous functions well. To cope with this problem, more sophisticated methods of constructing suitable basis functions have been proposed which effectively make use of the *graph* structure induced by MDPs (Mahadevan, 2005). In this section, we introduce an alternative way of constructing basis functions by incorporating the graph structure of the state space.

3.1.1 MDP-Induced Graph

Let $\mathcal{G}$ be a graph induced by an MDP, where states $\mathcal{S}$ are nodes of the graph and the transitions with non-zero transition probabilities from one node to another are edges. The edges may have weights determined, e.g., based on the transition probabilities or the distance between nodes. The graph structure corresponding to an example grid world shown in Figure 3.1(a) is illustrated

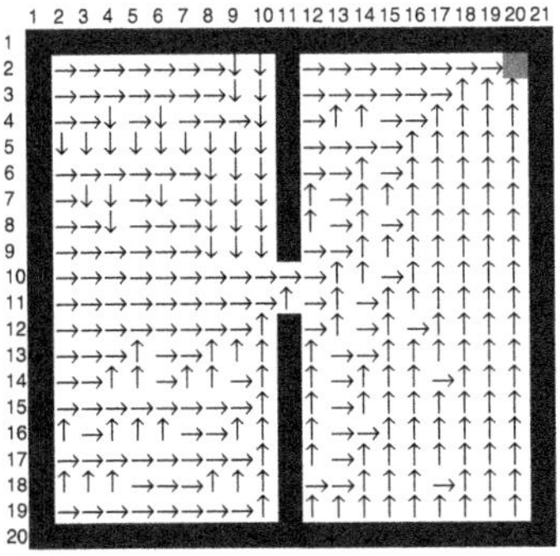

(a) Black areas are walls over which the agent cannot move, while the goal is represented in gray. Arrows on the grids represent one of the optimal policies.

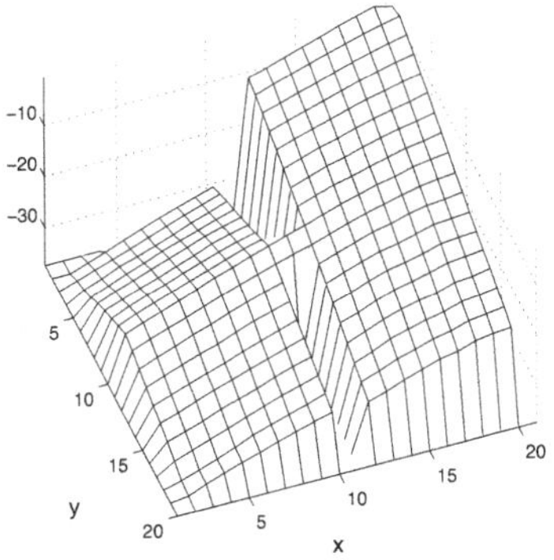

(b) Optimal state value function (in log-scale).

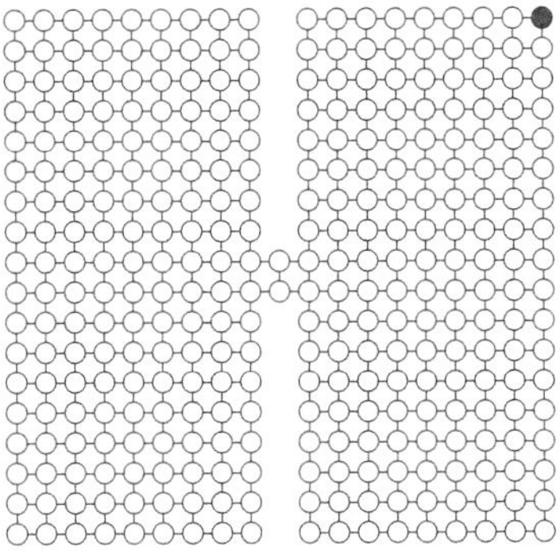

(c) Graph induced by the MDP and a random policy.

FIGURE 3.1: An illustrative example of a reinforcement learning task of guiding an agent to a goal in the grid world.

in Figure 3.1(c). In practice, such graph structure (including the connection weights) is estimated from samples of a finite length. We assume that the graph $\mathcal{G}$ is connected. Typically, the graph is *sparse* in reinforcement learning tasks, i.e.,

$$\ell \ll n(n-1)/2,$$

where ℓ is the number of edges and n is the number of nodes.

3.1.2 Ordinary Gaussian Kernels

Ordinary Gaussian kernels (OGKs) on the Euclidean space are defined as

$$K(\boldsymbol{s}, \boldsymbol{s}') = \exp\left(-\frac{\mathrm{ED}(\boldsymbol{s}, \boldsymbol{s}')^2}{2\sigma^2}\right),$$

where $\mathrm{ED}(\boldsymbol{s}, \boldsymbol{s}')$ are the Euclidean distance between states $\boldsymbol{s}$ and $\boldsymbol{s}'$; for example,

$$\mathrm{ED}(\boldsymbol{s}, \boldsymbol{s}') = \|\boldsymbol{x} - \boldsymbol{x}'\|,$$

when the Cartesian positions of $\boldsymbol{s}$ and $\boldsymbol{s}'$ in the state space are given by $\boldsymbol{x}$ and $\boldsymbol{x}'$, respectively. σ^2 is the variance parameter of the Gaussian kernel.

The above Gaussian function is defined on the state space $\mathcal{S}$, where $\boldsymbol{s}'$ is treated as a center of the kernel. In order to employ the Gaussian kernel in least-squares policy iteration, it needs to be extended over the state-action space $\mathcal{S} \times \mathcal{A}$. This is usually carried out by simply "copying" the Gaussian function over the action space (Lagoudakis & Parr, 2003; Mahadevan, 2005). More precisely, let the total number k of basis functions be mp, where m is the number of possible actions and p is the number of Gaussian centers. For the i-th action $a^{(i)}$ $(\in \mathcal{A})$ $(i = 1, 2, \ldots, m)$ and for the j-th Gaussian center $\boldsymbol{c}^{(j)}$ $(\in \mathcal{S})$ $(j = 1, 2, \ldots, p)$, the $(i + (j-1)m)$-th basis function is defined as

$$\phi_{i+(j-1)m}(\boldsymbol{s}, a) = I(a = a^{(i)})K(\boldsymbol{s}, \boldsymbol{c}^{(j)}), \tag{3.1}$$

where $I(\cdot)$ is the indicator function:

$$I(a = a^{(i)}) = \begin{cases} 1 & \text{if } a = a^{(i)}, \\ 0 & \text{otherwise.} \end{cases}$$

3.1.3 Geodesic Gaussian Kernels

On graphs, a natural definition of the distance would be the *shortest path*. The Gaussian kernel based on the shortest path is given by

$$K(\boldsymbol{s}, \boldsymbol{s}') = \exp\left(-\frac{\mathrm{SP}(\boldsymbol{s}, \boldsymbol{s}')^2}{2\sigma^2}\right), \tag{3.2}$$

where $\mathrm{SP}(\boldsymbol{s}, \boldsymbol{s}')$ denotes the shortest path from state $\boldsymbol{s}$ to state $\boldsymbol{s}'$. The shortest path on a graph can be interpreted as a discrete approximation to the *geodesic distance* on a non-linear manifold (Chung, 1997). For this reason, we call Eq. (3.2) a *geodesic Gaussian kernel* (GGK) (Sugiyama et al., 2008).

Shortest paths on graphs can be efficiently computed using the *Dijkstra algorithm* (Dijkstra, 1959). With its naive implementation, computational complexity for computing the shortest paths from a single node to all other nodes is $O(n^2)$, where n is the number of nodes. If the *Fibonacci heap* is employed, computational complexity can be reduced to $O(n \log n + \ell)$ (Fredman & Tarjan, 1987), where ℓ is the number of edges. Since the graph in value function approximation problems is typically sparse (i.e., $\ell \ll n^2$), using the Fibonacci heap provides significant computational gains. Furthermore, there exist various approximation algorithms which are computationally very efficient (see Goldberg & Harrelson, 2005 and references therein).

Analogously to OGKs, we need to extend GGKs to the state-action space to use them in least-squares policy iteration. A naive way is to just employ Eq. (3.1), but this can cause a shift in the Gaussian centers since the state usually changes when some action is taken. To incorporate this transition, the basis functions are defined as the expectation of Gaussian functions after transition:

$$\phi_{i+(j-1)m}(\boldsymbol{s}, a) = I(a = a^{(i)}) \sum_{\boldsymbol{s}' \in \mathcal{S}} \mathcal{P}(\boldsymbol{s}'|\boldsymbol{s}, a) K(\boldsymbol{s}', \boldsymbol{c}^{(j)}). \tag{3.3}$$

This shifting scheme is shown to work very well when the transition is predominantly deterministic (Sugiyama et al., 2008).

3.1.4 Extension to Continuous State Spaces

So far, we focused on discrete state spaces. However, the concept of GGKs can be naturally extended to continuous state spaces, which is explained here. First, the continuous state space is discretized, which gives a graph as a discrete approximation to the non-linear *manifold* structure of the continuous state space. Based on the graph, GGKs can be constructed in the same way as the discrete case. Finally, the discrete GGKs are interpolated, e.g., using a linear method to give continuous GGKs.

Although this procedure discretizes the continuous state space, it must be noted that the discretization is only for the purpose of obtaining the graph as a discrete approximation of the continuous non-linear manifold; the resulting basis functions themselves are continuously interpolated and hence the state space is still treated as continuous, as opposed to conventional discretization procedures.

3.2 Illustration

In this section, the characteristics of GGKs are discussed in comparison to existing basis functions.

3.2.1 Setup

Let us consider a toy reinforcement learning task of guiding an agent to a goal in a deterministic grid world (see Figure 3.1(a)). The agent can take 4 actions: up, down, left, and right. Note that actions which make the agent collide with the wall are disallowed. A positive immediate reward +1 is given if the agent reaches a goal state; otherwise it receives no immediate reward. The discount factor is set at $\gamma = 0.9$.

In this task, a state $\boldsymbol{s}$ corresponds to a two-dimensional Cartesian grid position $\boldsymbol{x}$ of the agent. For illustration purposes, let us display the state value function,

$$V^{\pi}(\boldsymbol{s}) : \mathcal{S} \rightarrow \mathbb{R},$$

which is the expected long-term discounted sum of rewards the agent receives when the agent takes actions following policy π from state $\boldsymbol{s}$. From the definition, it can be confirmed that $V^{\pi}(\boldsymbol{s})$ is expressed in terms of $Q^{\pi}(\boldsymbol{s}, a)$ as

$$V^{\pi}(\boldsymbol{s}) = Q^{\pi}(\boldsymbol{s}, \pi(\boldsymbol{s})).$$

The optimal state value function $V^{*}(\boldsymbol{s})$ (in log-scale) is illustrated in Figure 3.1(b). An MDP-induced graph structure estimated from 20 series of random walk samples[1] of length 500 is illustrated in Figure 3.1(c). Here, the edge weights in the graph are set at 1 (which is equivalent to the Euclidean distance between two nodes).

3.2.2 Geodesic Gaussian Kernels

An example of GGKs for this graph is depicted in Figure 3.2(a), where the variance of the kernel is set at a large value ($\sigma^2 = 30$) for illustration purposes. The graph shows that GGKs have a nice smooth surface *along* the maze, but not *across* the partition between two rooms. Since GGKs have "centers," they are extremely useful for adaptively choosing a subset of bases, e.g., using a uniform allocation strategy, sample-dependent allocation strategy, or maze-dependent allocation strategy of the centers. This is a practical advantage over some non-ordered basis functions. Moreover, since GGKs are local by nature, the ill effects of local noise are constrained locally, which is another useful property in practice.

The approximated value functions obtained by 40 GGKs[2] are depicted in Figure 3.3(a), where one GGK center is put at the goal state and the remaining 9 centers are chosen randomly. For GGKs, kernel functions are extended over the action space using the shifting scheme (see Eq. (3.3)) since the transition is

---

[1]More precisely, in each random walk, an initial state is chosen randomly. Then, an action is chosen randomly and transition is made; this is repeated 500 times. This entire procedure is independently repeated 20 times to generate the training set.

[2]Note that the total number k of basis functions is 160 since each GGK is copied over the action space as per Eq. (3.3).

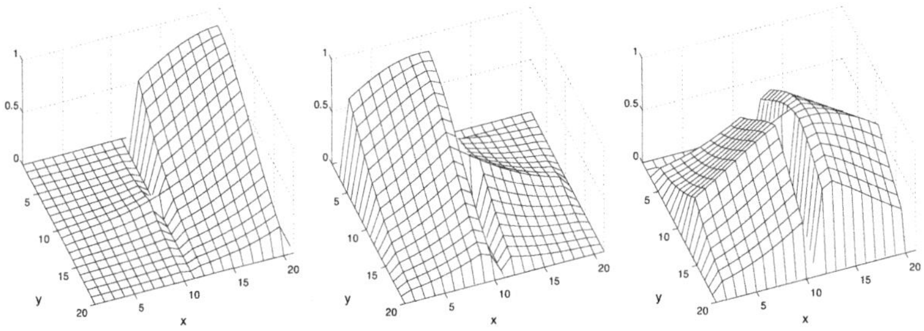

(a) Geodesic Gaussian kernels

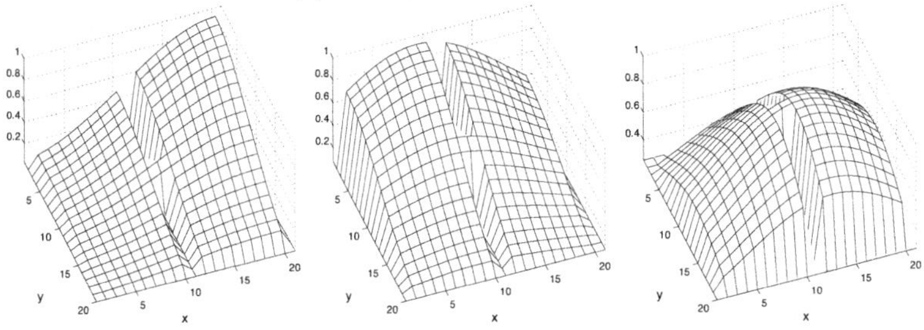

(b) Ordinary Gaussian kernels

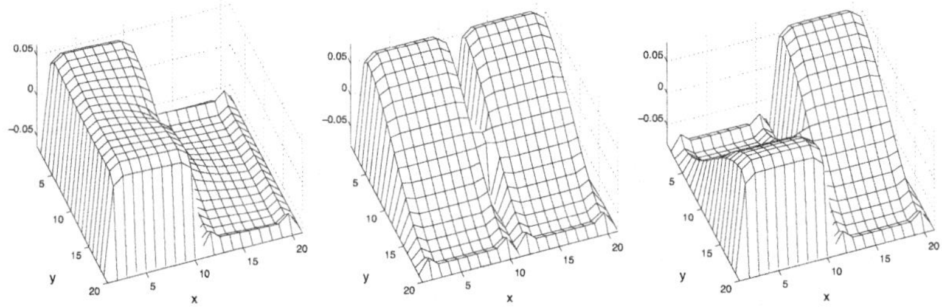

(c) Graph-Laplacian eigenbases

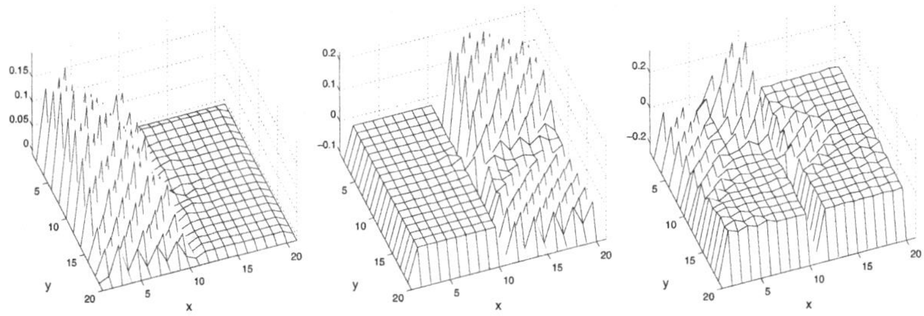

(d) Diffusion wavelets

FIGURE 3.2: Examples of basis functions.

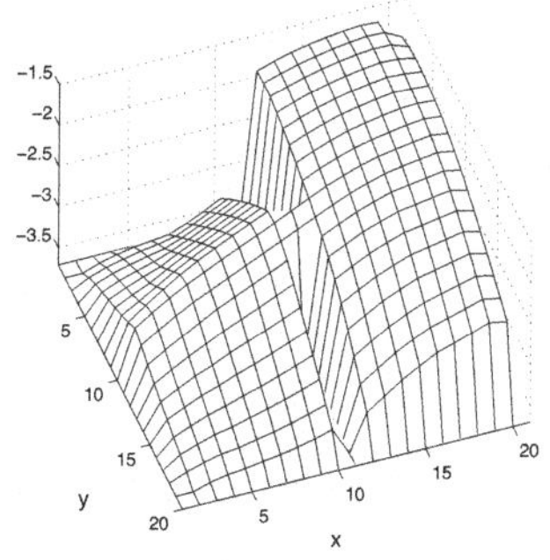

(a) Geodesic Gaussian kernels (MSE = 1.03×10^{-2})

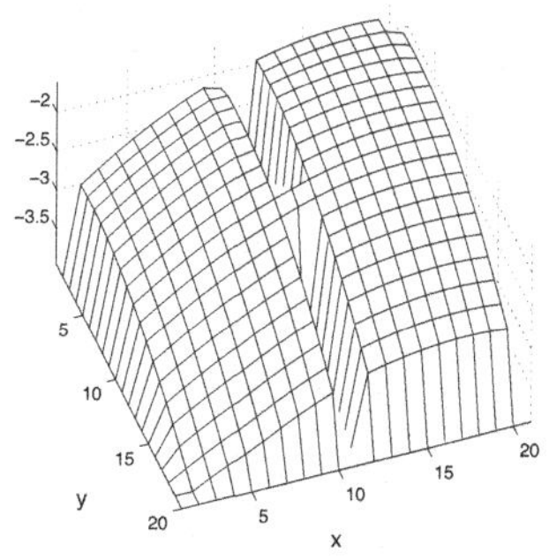

(b) Ordinary Gaussian kernels (MSE = 1.19×10^{-2})

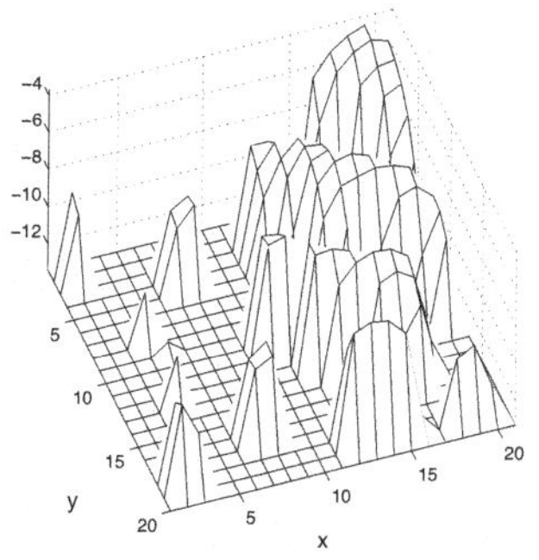

(c) Graph-Laplacian eigenbases (MSE = 4.73×10^{-4})

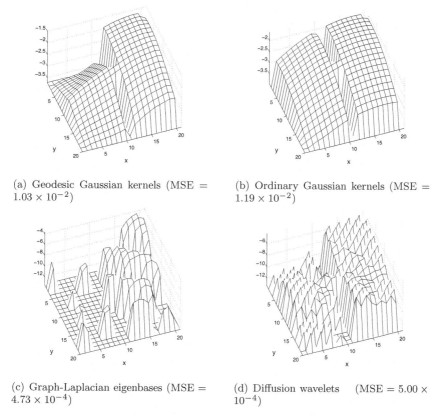

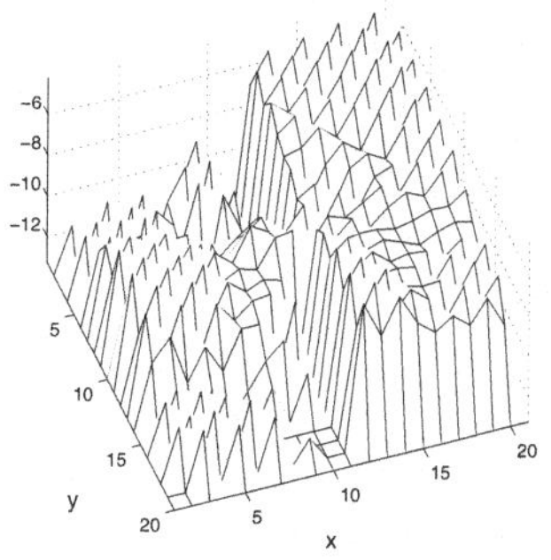

(d) Diffusion wavelets (MSE = 5.00×10^{-4})

FIGURE 3.3: Approximated value functions in log-scale. The errors are computed with respect to the optimal value function illustrated in Figure 3.1(b).

deterministic (see Section 3.1.3). The proposed GGK-based method produces a nice smooth function along the maze while the discontinuity around the partition between two rooms is sharply maintained (cf. Figure 3.1(b)). As a result, for this particular case, GGKs give the optimal policy (see Figure 3.4(a)).

As discussed in Section 3.1.3, the sparsity of the state transition matrix allows efficient and fast computations of shortest paths on the graph. Therefore, least-squares policy iteration with GGK-based bases is still computationally attractive.

3.2.3 Ordinary Gaussian Kernels

OGKs share some of the preferable properties of GGKs described above. However, as illustrated in Figure 3.2(b), the tail of OGKs extends beyond the partition between two rooms. Therefore, OGKs tend to undesirably smooth out the discontinuity of the value function around the barrier wall (see

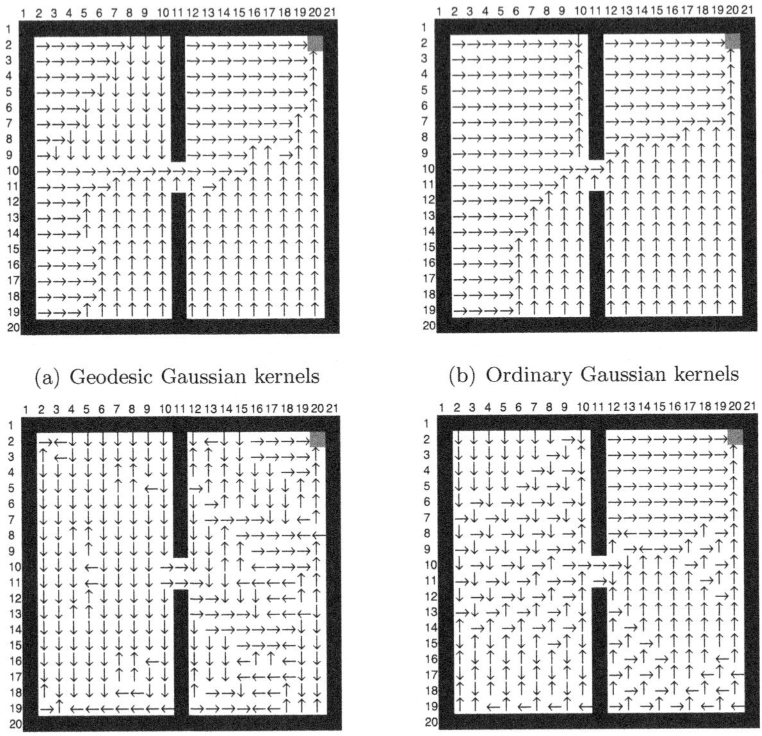

(a) Geodesic Gaussian kernels

(b) Ordinary Gaussian kernels

(c) Graph-Laplacian eigenbases

(d) Diffusion wavelets

FIGURE 3.4: Obtained policies.

Figure 3.3(b)). This causes an error in the policy around the partition (see $x = 10$, $y = 2, 3, \ldots, 9$ of Figure 3.4(b)).

3.2.4 Graph-Laplacian Eigenbases

Mahadevan (2005) proposed employing the *smoothest* vectors on graphs as bases in value function approximation. According to the spectral graph theory (Chung, 1997), such smooth bases are given by the minor eigenvectors of the *graph-Laplacian* matrix, which are called *graph-Laplacian eigenbases* (GLEs). GLEs may be regarded as a natural extension of Fourier bases to graphs.

Examples of GLEs are illustrated in Figure 3.2(c), showing that they have Fourier-like structure on the graph. It should be noted that GLEs are rather global in nature, implying that noise in a local region can potentially degrade the global quality of approximation. An advantage of GLEs is that they have a natural ordering of the basis functions according to the smoothness. This is practically very helpful in choosing a subset of basis functions. Figure 3.3(c) depicts the approximated value function in log-scale, where the top

40 smoothest GLEs out of 326 GLEs are used (note that the actual number of bases is 160 because of the duplication over the action space). It shows that GLEs globally give a very good approximation, although the small local fluctuation is significantly emphasized since the graph is in log-scale. Indeed, the mean squared error (MSE) between the approximated and optimal value functions described in the captions of Figure 3.3 shows that GLEs give a much smaller MSE than GGKs and OGKs. However, the obtained value function contains systematic local fluctuation and this results in an inappropriate policy (see Figure 3.4(c)).

MDP-induced graphs are typically sparse. In such cases, the resultant graph-Laplacian matrix is also sparse and GLEs can be obtained just by solving a sparse eigenvalue problem, which is computationally efficient. However, finding minor eigenvectors could be numerically unstable.

3.2.5 Diffusion Wavelets

Coifman and Maggioni (2006) proposed *diffusion wavelets* (DWs), which are a natural extension of wavelets to the graph. The construction is based on a symmetrized random walk on a graph. It is diffused on the graph up to a desired level, resulting in a multi-resolution structure. A detailed algorithm for constructing DWs and mathematical properties are described in Coifman and Maggioni (2006).

When constructing DWs, the maximum nest level of wavelets and tolerance used in the construction algorithm needs to be specified by users. The maximum nest level is set at 10 and the tolerance is set at 10^{-10}, which are suggested by the authors. Examples of DWs are illustrated in Figure 3.2(d), showing a nice multi-resolution structure on the graph. DWs are over-complete bases, so one has to appropriately choose a subset of bases for better approximation. Figure 3.3(d) depicts the approximated value function obtained by DWs, where we chose the most global 40 DWs from 1626 over-complete DWs (note that the actual number of bases is 160 because of the duplication over the action space). The choice of the subset bases could possibly be enhanced using multiple heuristics. However, the current choice is reasonable since Figure 3.3(d) shows that DWs give a much smaller MSE than Gaussian kernels. Nevertheless, similar to GLEs, the obtained value function contains a lot of small fluctuations (see Figure 3.3(d)) and this results in an erroneous policy (see Figure 3.4(d)).

Thanks to the multi-resolution structure, computation of diffusion wavelets can be carried out recursively. However, due to the over-completeness, it is still rather demanding in computation time. Furthermore, appropriately determining the tuning parameters as well as choosing an appropriate basis subset is not straightforward in practice.

3.3 Numerical Examples

As discussed in the previous section, GGKs bring a number of preferable properties for making value function approximation effective. In this section, the behavior of GGKs is illustrated numerically.

3.3.1 Robot-Arm Control

Here, a simulator of a two-joint robot arm (moving in a plane), illustrated in Figure 3.5(a), is employed. The task is to lead the end-effector ("hand") of the arm to an object while avoiding the obstacles. Possible actions are to increase or decrease the angle of each joint ("shoulder" and "elbow") by 5 degrees in the plane, simulating coarse stepper-motor joints. Thus, the state space $\mathcal{S}$ is the 2-dimensional discrete space consisting of two joint-angles, as illustrated in Figure 3.5(b). The black area in the middle corresponds to the obstacle in the joint-angle state space. The action space $\mathcal{A}$ involves 4 actions: increase or decrease one of the joint angles. A positive immediate reward $+1$ is given when the robot's end-effector touches the object; otherwise the robot receives no immediate reward. Note that actions which make the arm collide with obstacles are disallowed. The discount factor is set at $\gamma = 0.9$. In this environment, the robot can change the joint angle exactly by 5 degrees, and therefore the environment is deterministic. However, because of the obstacles, it is difficult to explicitly compute an inverse kinematic model. Furthermore, the obstacles introduce discontinuity in value functions. Therefore, this robot-arm control task is an interesting test bed for investigating the behavior of GGKs.

Training samples from 50 series of 1000 random arm movements are collected, where the start state is chosen randomly in each trial. The graph induced by the above MDP consists of 1605 nodes and uniform weights are assigned to the edges. Since there are 16 goal states in this environment (see Figure 3.5(b)), the first 16 Gaussian centers are put at the goals and the remaining centers are chosen randomly in the state space. For GGKs, kernel functions are extended over the action space using the shifting scheme (see Eq. (3.3)) since the transition is deterministic in this experiment.

Figure 3.6 illustrates the value functions approximated using GGKs and OGKs. The graphs show that GGKs give a nice smooth surface with obstacle-induced discontinuity sharply preserved, while OGKs tend to smooth out the discontinuity. This makes a significant difference in avoiding the obstacle. From "A" to "B" in Figure 3.5(b), the GGK-based value function results in a trajectory that avoids the obstacle (see Figure 3.6(a)). On the other hand, the OGK-based value function yields a trajectory that tries to move the arm *through* the obstacle by following the gradient upward (see Figure 3.6(b)), causing the arm to get stuck behind the obstacle.

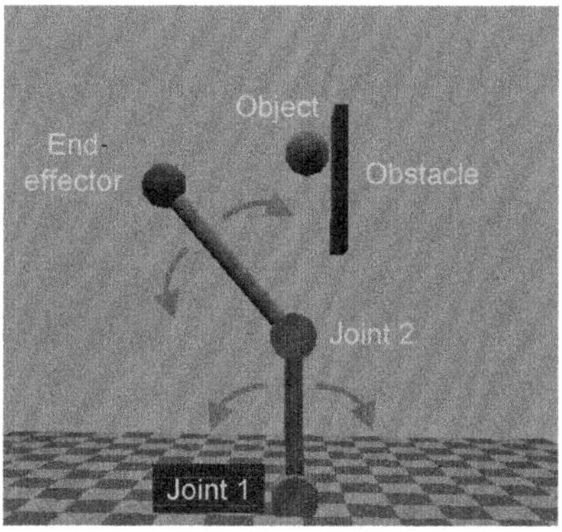

(a) A schematic

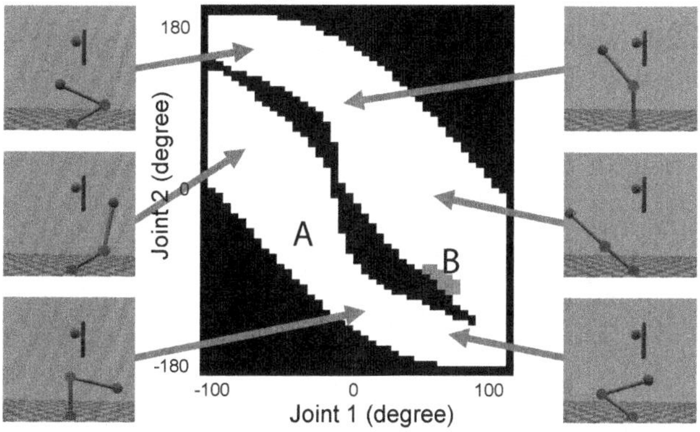

(b) State space

FIGURE 3.5: A two-joint robot arm. In this experiment, GGKs are put at all the goal states and the remaining kernels are distributed uniformly over the maze; the shifting scheme is used in GGKs.

Figure 3.7 summarizes the performance of GGKs and OGKs measured by the percentage of successful trials (i.e., the end-effector reaches the object) over 30 independent runs. More precisely, in each run, 50,000 training samples are collected using a different random seed, a policy is then computed by the GGK- or OGK-based least-squares policy iteration, and finally the obtained policy is tested. This graph shows that GGKs remarkably outperform OGKs since the arm can successfully avoid the obstacle. The performance of OGKs does not go beyond 0.6 even when the number of kernels is increased. This is caused by the tail effect of OGKs. As a result, the OGK-based policy cannot lead the end-effector to the object if it starts from the bottom left half of the state space.

When the number of kernels is increased, the performance of both GGKs and OGKs gets worse at around $k = 20$. This is caused by the kernel alloca-

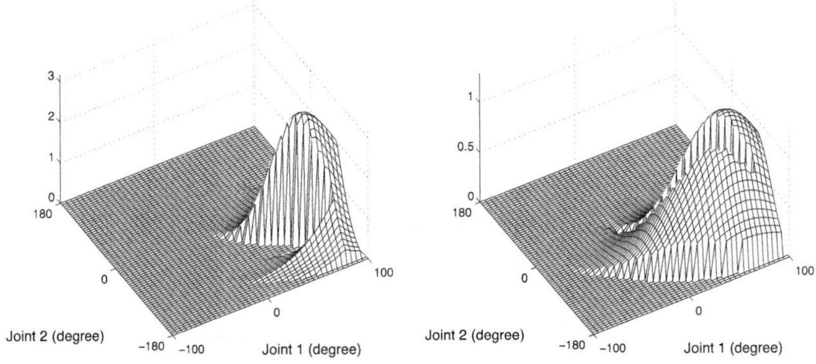

(a) Geodesic Gaussian kernels (b) Ordinary Gaussian kernels

FIGURE 3.6: Approximated value functions with 10 kernels (the actual number of bases is 40 because of the duplication over the action space).

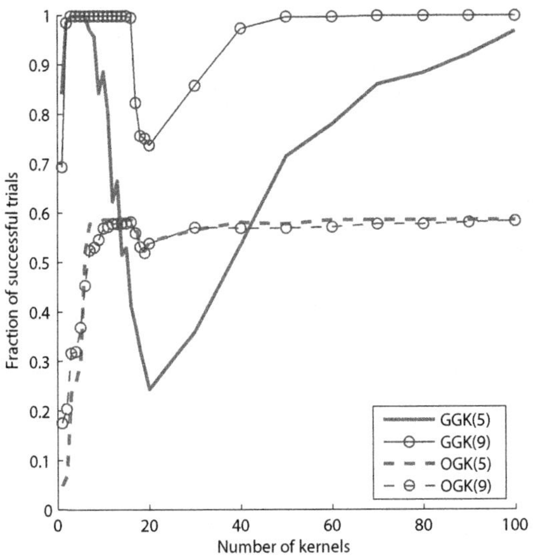

FIGURE 3.7: Fraction of successful trials.

tion strategy: the first 16 kernels are put at the goal states and the remaining kernel centers are chosen randomly. When k is less than or equal to 16, the approximated value function tends to have a unimodal profile since all kernels are put at the goal states. However, when k is larger than 16, this unimodality is broken and the surface of the approximated value function has slight fluctuations, causing an error in policies and degrading performance at around

$k = 20$. This performance degradation tends to recover as the number of kernels is further increased.

Motion examples of the robot arm trained with GGK and OGK are illustrated in Figure 3.8 and Figure 3.9, respectively.

Overall, the above result shows that when GGKs are combined with the above-mentioned kernel-center allocation strategy, almost perfect policies can be obtained with a small number of kernels. Therefore, the GGK method is computationally highly advantageous.

3.3.2 Robot-Agent Navigation

The above simple robot-arm control simulation shows that GGKs are promising. Here, GGKs are applied to a more challenging task of mobile-robot navigation, which involves a high-dimensional and very large state space.

A *Khepera robot*, illustrated in Figure 3.10(a), is employed for the navigation task. The Khepera robot is equipped with 8 infrared sensors ("s1" to "s8" in the figure), each of which gives a measure of the distance from the surrounding obstacles. Each sensor produces a scalar value between 0 and 1023: the sensor obtains the maximum value 1023 if an obstacle is just in front of the sensor and the value decreases as the obstacle gets farther until it reaches the minimum value 0. Therefore, the state space $\mathcal{S}$ is 8-dimensional. The Khepera robot has two wheels and takes the following defined actions: forward, left rotation, right rotation, and backward (i.e., the action space $\mathcal{A}$ contains actions). The speed of the left and right wheels for each action is described in Figure 3.10(a) in the bracket (the unit is pulse per 10 milliseconds). Note that the sensor values and the wheel speed are highly stochastic due to the cross talk, sensor noise, slip, etc. Furthermore, perceptual aliasing occurs due to the limited range and resolution of sensors. Therefore, the state transition is also highly stochastic. The discount factor is set at $\gamma = 0.9$.

The goal of the navigation task is to make the Khepera robot explore the environment as much as possible. To this end, a positive reward $+1$ is given when the Khepera robot moves forward and a negative reward -2 is given when the Khepera robot collides with an obstacle. No reward is given to the left rotation, right rotation, and backward actions. This reward design encourages the Khepera robot to go forward without hitting obstacles, through which extensive exploration in the environment could be achieved.

Training samples are collected from 200 series of 100 random movements in a fixed environment with several obstacles (see Figure 3.11(a)). Then, a graph is constructed from the gathered samples by discretizing the continuous state space using a *self-organizing map* (SOM) (Kohonen, 1995). A SOM consists of neurons located on a regular grid. Each neuron corresponds to a cluster and neurons are connected to adjacent ones by neighborhood relation. The SOM is similar to the *k-means clustering algorithm*, but it is different in that the topological structure of the entire map is taken into account. Thanks to this, the entire space tends to be covered by the SOM. The number of nodes

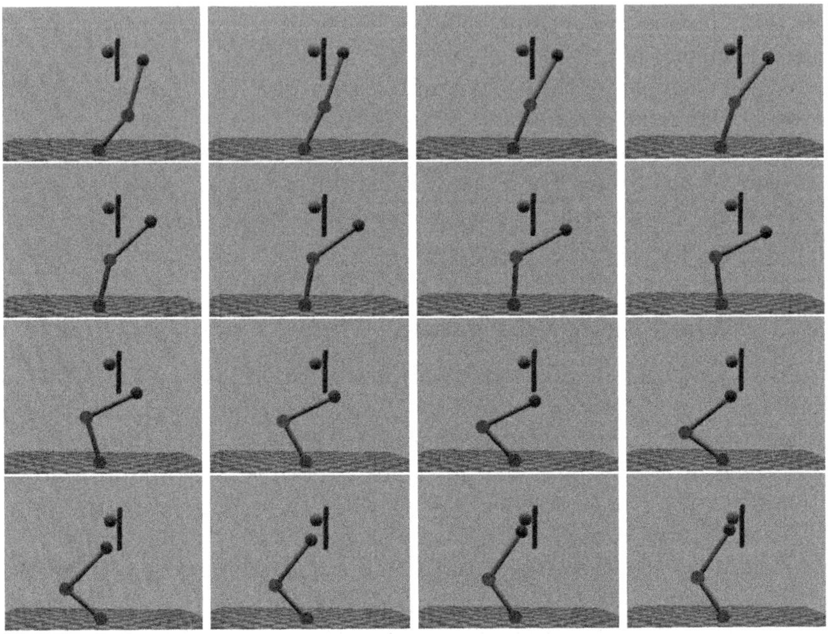

FIGURE 3.8: A motion example of the robot arm trained with GGK (from left to right and top to bottom).

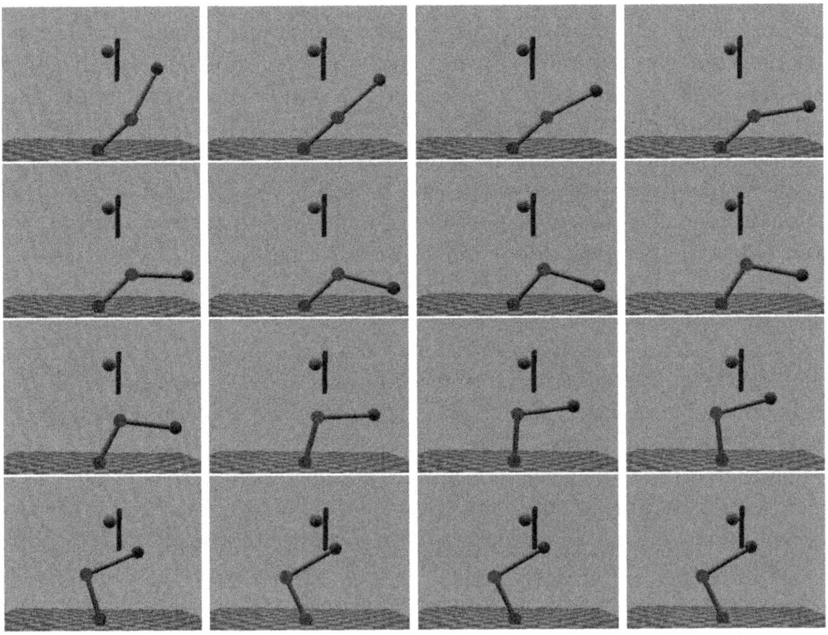

FIGURE 3.9: A motion example of the robot arm trained with OGK (from left to right and top to bottom).

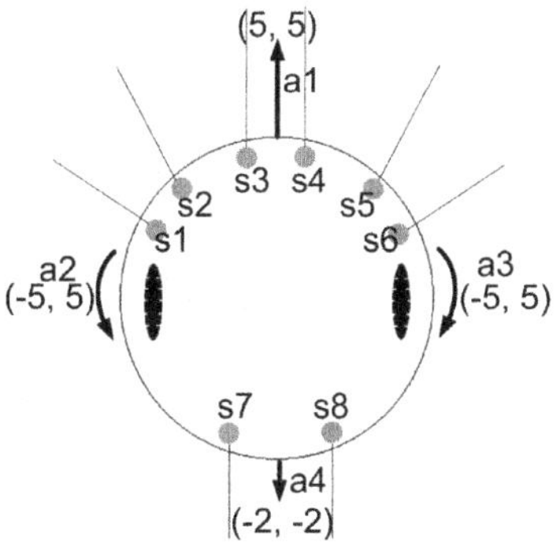

(a) A schematic

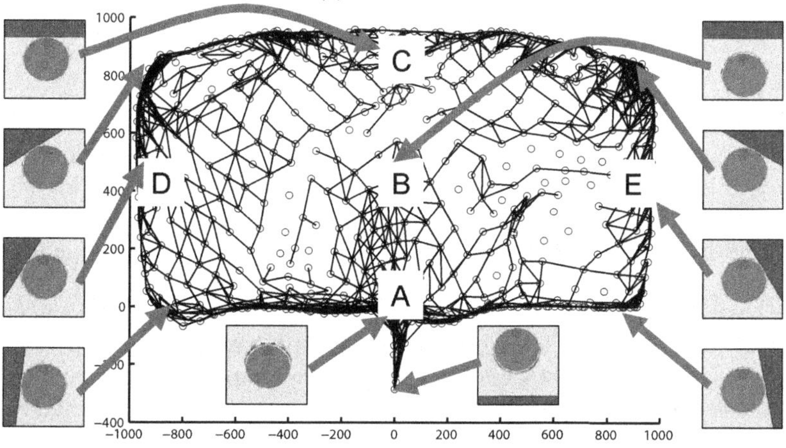

(b) State space projected onto a 2-dimensional subspace for visualization

FIGURE 3.10: Khepera robot. In this experiment, GGKs are distributed uniformly over the maze without the shifting scheme.

(states) in the graph is set at 696 (equivalent to the SOM map size of 24×29). This value is computed by the standard rule-of-thumb formula $5\sqrt{n}$ (Vesanto et al., 2000), where n is the number of samples. The connectivity of the graph is determined by state transitions occurring in the samples. More specifically, if there is a state transition from one node to another in the samples, an edge is established between these two nodes and the edge weight is set according to the Euclidean distance between them.

Figure 3.10(b) illustrates an example of the obtained graph structure. For visualization purposes, the 8-dimensional state space is projected onto a 2-dimensional subspace spanned by

$$\begin{array}{l}(-1 \quad -1 \quad 0 \quad 0 \quad 1 \quad 1 \quad 0 \quad 0),\\(0 \quad 0 \quad 1 \quad 1 \quad 0 \quad 0 \quad -1 \quad -1).\end{array}$$

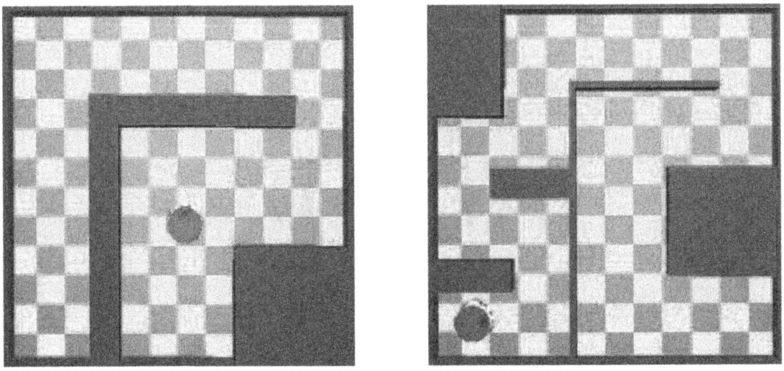

(a) Training (b) Test

FIGURE 3.11: Simulation environment.

Note that this projection is performed *only* for the purpose of visualization. All the computations are carried out using the entire 8-dimensional data. The i-th element in the above bases corresponds to the output of the i-th sensor (see Figure 3.10(a)). The projection onto this subspace roughly means that the horizontal axis corresponds to the distance to the left and right obstacles, while the vertical axis corresponds to the distance to the front and back obstacles. For clear visibility, the edges whose weight is less than 250 are plotted. Representative local poses of the Khepera robot with respect to the obstacles are illustrated in Figure 3.10(b). This graph has a notable feature: the nodes around the region "B" in the figure are directly connected to the nodes at "A," but are very sparsely connected to the nodes at "C," "D," and "E." This implies that the geodesic distance from "B" to "C," "B" to "D," or "B" to "E" is typically larger than the Euclidean distance.

Since the transition from one state to another is highly stochastic in the current experiment, the GGK function is simply duplicated over the action space (see Eq. (3.1)). For obtaining continuous GGKs, GGK functions need to be interpolated (see Section 3.1.4). A simple linear interpolation method may be employed in general, but the current experiment has unique characteristics: at least one of the sensor values is always zero since the Khepera robot is never completely surrounded by obstacles. Therefore, samples are always on the surface of the 8-dimensional hypercube-shaped state space. On the other hand, the node centers determined by the SOM are not generally on the surface. This means that any sample is not included in the convex hull of its nearest nodes and the function value needs to be *extrapolated*. Here, the Euclidean distance between the sample and its nearest node is simply added when computing kernel values. More precisely, for a state $\boldsymbol{s}$ that is not generally located on a node center, the GGK-based basis function is defined as

$$\phi_{i+(j-1)m}(\boldsymbol{s}, a) = I(a = a^{(i)}) \exp\left(-\frac{(\mathrm{ED}(\boldsymbol{s}, \tilde{\boldsymbol{s}}) + \mathrm{SP}(\tilde{\boldsymbol{s}}, \boldsymbol{c}^{(j)}))^2}{2\sigma^2}\right),$$

where $\tilde{s}$ is the node closest to s in the Euclidean distance.

Figure 3.12 illustrates an example of actions selected at each node by the GGK-based and OGK-based policies. One hundred kernels are used and the width is set at 1000. The symbols $\uparrow$, $\downarrow$, $\subset$, and $\supset$ in the figure indicate forward, backward, left rotation, and right rotation actions. This shows that there is a clear difference in the obtained policies at the state "C." The backward action is most likely to be taken by the OGK-based policy, while the left rotation and right rotation are most likely to be taken by the GGK-based policy. This causes a significant difference in the performance. To explain this, suppose that the Khepera robot is at the state "C," i.e., it faces a wall. The GGK-based policy guides the Khepera robot from "C" to "A" via "D" or "E" by taking the left and right rotation actions and it can avoid the obstacle successfully. On the other hand, the OGK-based policy tries to plan a path from "C" to "A" via "B" by activating the backward action. As a result, the forward action is taken at "B." For this reason, the Khepera robot returns to "C" again and ends up moving back and forth between "C" and "B."

For the performance evaluation, a more complicated environment than the one used for gathering training samples (see Figure 3.11) is used. This means that how well the obtained policies can be *generalized* to an unknown environment is evaluated here. In this test environment, the Khepera robot runs from a fixed starting position (see Figure 3.11(b)) and takes 150 steps following the obtained policy, with the sum of rewards (+1 for the forward action) computed. If the Khepera robot collides with an obstacle before 150 steps, the evaluation is stopped. The mean test performance over 30 independent runs is depicted in Figure 3.13 as a function of the number of kernels. More precisely, in each run, a graph is constructed based on the training samples taken from the training environment and the specified number of kernels is put randomly on the graph. Then, a policy is learned by the GGK- or OGK-based least-squares policy iteration using the training samples. Note that the actual number of bases is four times more because of the extension of basis functions over the action space. The test performance is measured 5 times for each policy and the average is output. Figure 3.13 shows that GGKs significantly outperform OGKs, demonstrating that GGKs are promising even in the challenging setting with a high-dimensional large state space.

Figure 3.14 depicts the computation time of each method as a function of the number of kernels. This shows that the computation time monotonically increases as the number of kernels increases and the GGK-based and OGK-based methods have comparable computation time. However, given that the GGK-based method works much better than the OGK-based method with a smaller number of kernels (see Figure 3.13), the GGK-based method could be regarded as a computationally efficient alternative to the standard OGK-based method.

Finally, the trained Khepera robot is applied to map building. Starting from an initial position (indicated by a square in Figure 3.15), the Khepera

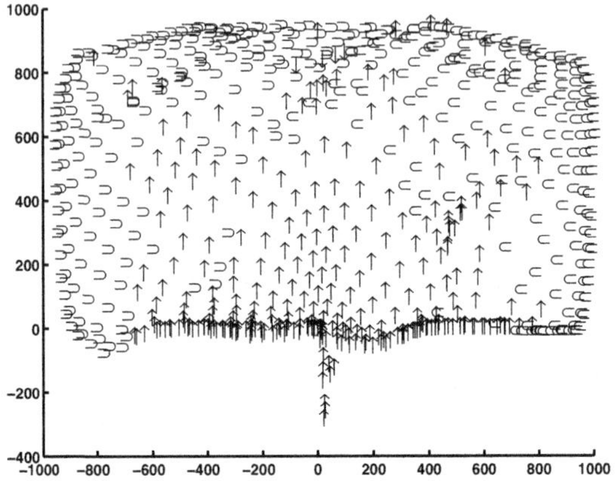

(a) Geodesic Gaussian kernels

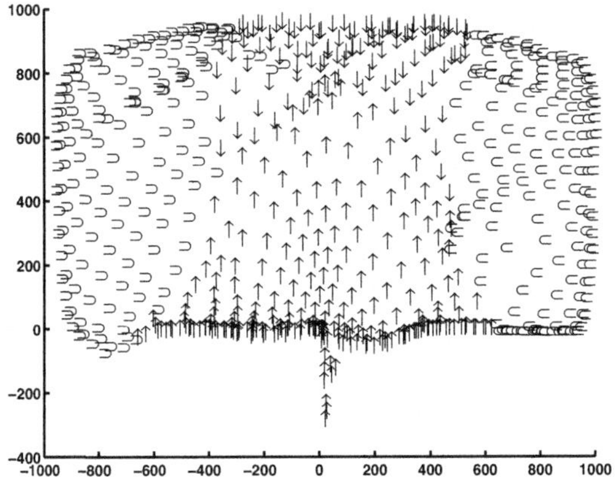

(b) Ordinary Gaussian kernels

FIGURE 3.12: Examples of obtained policies. The symbols $\uparrow$, $\downarrow$, $\subset$, and $\supset$ indicate forward, backward, left rotation, and right rotation actions.

robot takes an action 2000 times following the learned policy. Eighty kernels with Gaussian width $\sigma = 1000$ are used for value function approximation. The results of GGKs and OGKs are depicted in Figure 3.15. The graphs show that the GGK result gives a broader profile of the environment, while the OGK result only reveals a local area around the initial position.

Motion examples of the Khepera robot trained with GGK and OGK are illustrated in Figure 3.16 and Figure 3.17, respectively.

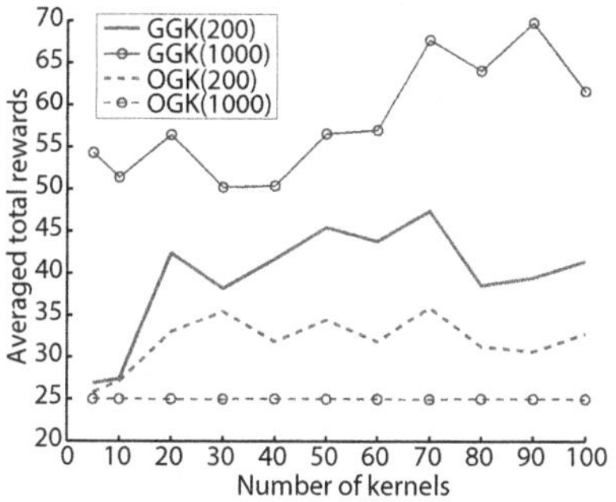

FIGURE 3.13: Average amount of exploration.

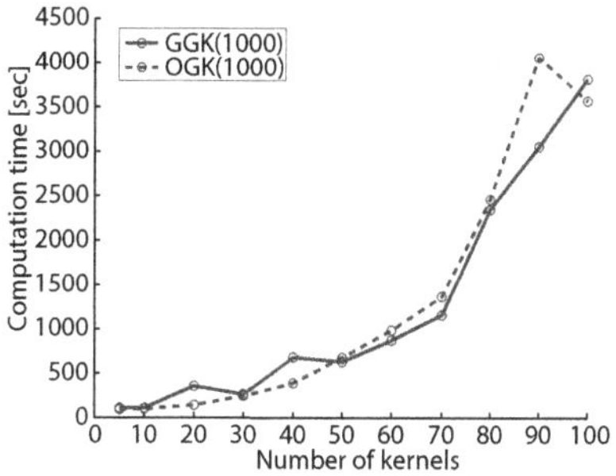

FIGURE 3.14: Computation time.

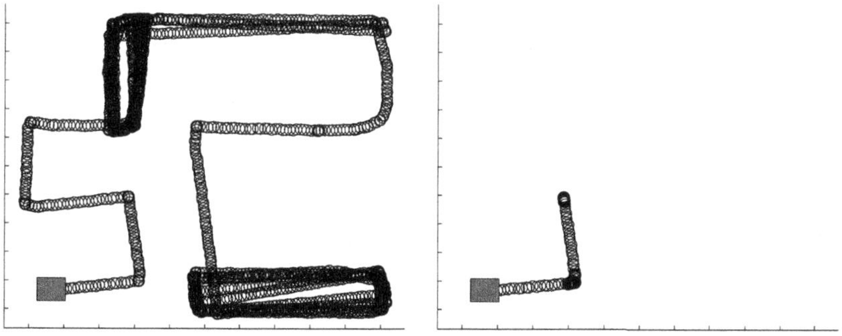

(a) Geodesic Gaussian kernels (b) Ordinary Gaussian kernels

FIGURE 3.15: Results of map building (cf. Figure 3.11(b)).

3.4 Remarks

The performance of least-squares policy iteration depends heavily on the choice of basis functions for value function approximation. In this chapter, the geodesic Gaussian kernel (GGK) was introduced and shown to possess several preferable properties such as smoothness along the graph and easy computability. It was also demonstrated that the policies obtained by GGKs are not as sensitive to the choice of the Gaussian kernel width, which is a useful property in practice. Also, the heuristics of putting Gaussian centers on goal states was shown to work well.

However, when the transition is highly stochastic (i.e., the transition probability has a wide support), the graph constructed based on the transition samples could be noisy. When an erroneous transition results in a short-cut

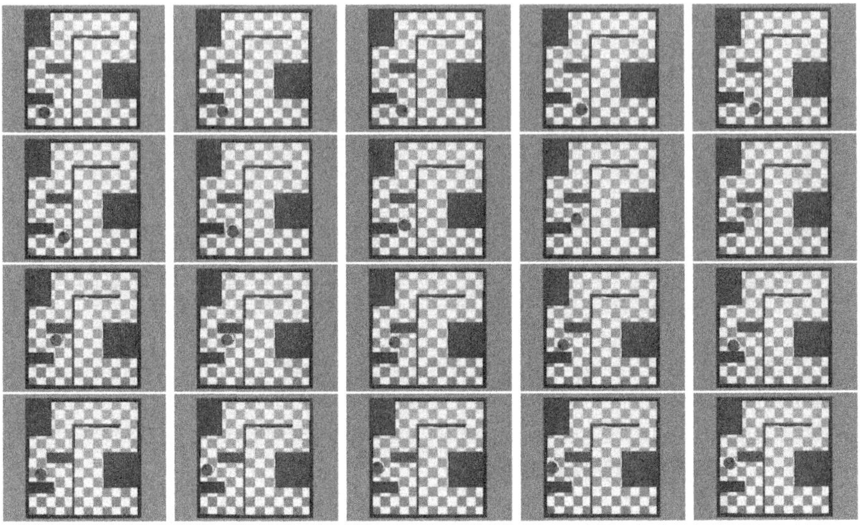

FIGURE 3.16: A motion example of the Khepera robot trained with GGK (from left to right and top to bottom).

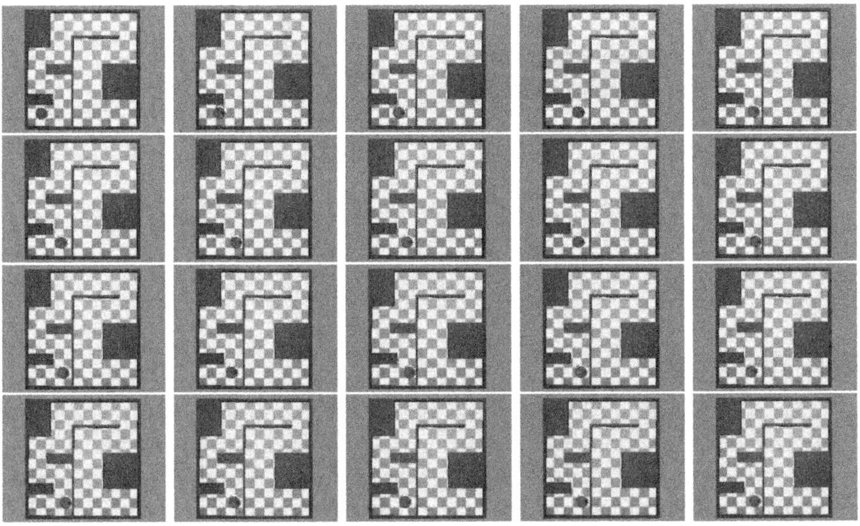

FIGURE 3.17: A motion example of the Khepera robot trained with OGK (from left to right and top to bottom).

over obstacles, the graph-based approach may not work well since the topology of the state space changes significantly.

Chapter 4

Sample Reuse in Policy Iteration

Off-policy reinforcement learning is aimed at efficiently using data samples gathered from a policy that is different from the currently optimized policy. A common approach is to use *importance sampling* techniques for compensating for the bias caused by the difference between the data-sampling policy and the target policy. In this chapter, we explain how importance sampling can be utilized to efficiently reuse previously collected data samples in policy iteration. After formulating the problem of off-policy value function approximation in Section 4.1, representative off-policy value function approximation techniques including adaptive importance sampling are reviewed in Section 4.2. Then, in Section 4.3, how the adaptivity of importance sampling can be optimally controlled is explained. In Section 4.4, off-policy value function approximation techniques are integrated in the framework of least-squares policy iteration for efficient sample reuse. Experimental results are shown in Section 4.5, and finally this chapter is concluded in Section 4.6.

4.1 Formulation

As explained in Section 2.2, least-squares policy iteration models the state-action value function $Q^\pi(\boldsymbol{s}, a)$ by a linear architecture,

$$\boldsymbol{\theta}^\top \boldsymbol{\phi}(\boldsymbol{s}, a),$$

and learns the parameter $\boldsymbol{\theta}$ so that the *generalization error* G is minimized:

$$G(\boldsymbol{\theta}) = \mathbb{E}_{p^\pi(h)}\left[\frac{1}{T}\sum_{t=1}^{T}\Big(\boldsymbol{\theta}^\top \boldsymbol{\psi}(\boldsymbol{s}_t, a_t) - r(\boldsymbol{s}_t, a_t)\Big)^2\right]. \tag{4.1}$$

Here, $\mathbb{E}_{p^\pi(h)}$ denotes the expectation over history

$$h = [\boldsymbol{s}_1, a_1, \ldots, \boldsymbol{s}_T, a_T, \boldsymbol{s}_{T+1}]$$

following the target policy π and

$$\boldsymbol{\psi}(\boldsymbol{s}, a) = \boldsymbol{\phi}(\boldsymbol{s}, a) - \gamma \mathbb{E}_{\pi(a'|\boldsymbol{s}')p(\boldsymbol{s}'|\boldsymbol{s},a)}\Big[\boldsymbol{\phi}(\boldsymbol{s}', a')\Big].$$

When history samples following the target policy π are available, the situation is called *on-policy* reinforcement learning. In this case, just replacing the expectation contained in the generalization error G by sample averages gives a statistically consistent estimator (i.e., the estimated parameter converges to the optimal value as the number of samples goes to infinity).

Here, we consider the situation called *off-policy* reinforcement learning, where the *sampling policy* $\widetilde{\pi}$ for collecting data samples is generally different from the target policy π. Let us denote the history samples following $\widetilde{\pi}$ by

$$\mathcal{H}^{\widetilde{\pi}} = \{h_1^{\widetilde{\pi}}, \ldots, h_N^{\widetilde{\pi}}\},$$

where each episodic sample $h_n^{\widetilde{\pi}}$ is given as

$$h_n^{\widetilde{\pi}} = [\boldsymbol{s}_{1,n}^{\widetilde{\pi}}, a_{1,n}^{\widetilde{\pi}}, \ldots, \boldsymbol{s}_{T,n}^{\widetilde{\pi}}, a_{T,n}^{\widetilde{\pi}}, \boldsymbol{s}_{T+1,n}^{\widetilde{\pi}}].$$

Under the off-policy setup, naive learning by minimizing the sample-approximated generalization error $\widehat{G}_{\mathrm{NIW}}$ leads to an inconsistent estimator:

$$\widehat{G}_{\mathrm{NIW}}(\boldsymbol{\theta}) = \frac{1}{NT}\sum_{n=1}^{N}\sum_{t=1}^{T}\left(\boldsymbol{\theta}^\top \widehat{\boldsymbol{\psi}}(\boldsymbol{s}_{t,n}^{\widetilde{\pi}}, a_{t,n}^{\widetilde{\pi}}; \mathcal{H}^{\widetilde{\pi}}) - r(\boldsymbol{s}_{t,n}^{\widetilde{\pi}}, a_{t,n}^{\widetilde{\pi}}, \boldsymbol{s}_{t+1,n}^{\widetilde{\pi}})\right)^2,$$

where

$$\widehat{\boldsymbol{\psi}}(\boldsymbol{s}, a; \mathcal{H}) = \boldsymbol{\phi}(\boldsymbol{s}, a) - \frac{1}{|\mathcal{H}_{(\boldsymbol{s},a)}|}\sum_{\boldsymbol{s}' \in \mathcal{H}_{(\boldsymbol{s},a)}} \mathbb{E}_{\widetilde{\pi}(a'|\boldsymbol{s}')}\left[\gamma \boldsymbol{\phi}(\boldsymbol{s}', a')\right].$$

$\mathcal{H}_{(\boldsymbol{s},a)}$ denotes a subset of $\mathcal{H}$ that consists of all transition samples from state $\boldsymbol{s}$ by action a, $|\mathcal{H}_{(\boldsymbol{s},a)}|$ denotes the number of elements in the set $\mathcal{H}_{(\boldsymbol{s},a)}$, and $\sum_{\boldsymbol{s}' \in \mathcal{H}_{\boldsymbol{s},a)}}$ denotes the summation over all destination states $\boldsymbol{s}'$ in the set $\mathcal{H}_{(\boldsymbol{s},a)}$. NIW stands for "No Importance Weight," which will be explained later.

This inconsistency problem can be avoided by gathering new samples following the target policy π, i.e., when the current policy is updated, new samples are gathered following the updated policy and the new samples are used for policy evaluation. However, when the data sampling cost is high, this is too expensive. It would be more cost efficient if previously gathered samples could be reused effectively.

4.2 Off-Policy Value Function Approximation

Importance sampling is a general technique for dealing with the off-policy situation. Suppose we have i.i.d. (*independent and identically distributed*) samples $\{x_n\}_{n=1}^N$ from a strictly positive probability density function $\widetilde{p}(x)$. Using these samples, we would like to compute the expectation of a function $g(x)$ over another probability density function $p(x)$. A consistent approximation of the expectation is given by the *importance-weighted* average as

$$\frac{1}{N}\sum_{n=1}^{N} g(x_n)\frac{p(x_n)}{\widetilde{p}(x_n)} \overset{N\to\infty}{\longrightarrow} \mathbb{E}_{\widetilde{p}(x)}\left[g(x)\frac{p(x)}{\widetilde{p}(x)}\right]$$
$$= \int g(x)\frac{p(x)}{\widetilde{p}(x)}\widetilde{p}(x)dx = \int g(x)p(x)dx = \mathbb{E}_{p(x)}\left[g(x)\right].$$

However, applying the importance sampling technique in off-policy reinforcement learning is not straightforward since our training samples of state $\boldsymbol{s}$ and action a are not i.i.d. due to the sequential nature of Markov decision processes (MDPs). In this section, representative importance-weighting techniques for MDPs are reviewed.

4.2.1 Episodic Importance Weighting

Based on the independence between episodes,

$$p(h,h') = p(h)p(h') = p(\boldsymbol{s}_1,a_1,\ldots,\boldsymbol{s}_T,a_T,\boldsymbol{s}_{T+1})p(\boldsymbol{s}'_1,a'_1,\ldots,\boldsymbol{s}'_T,a'_T,\boldsymbol{s}'_{T+1}),$$

the generalization error G can be rewritten as

$$G(\boldsymbol{\theta}) = \mathbb{E}_{p^{\widetilde{\pi}}(h)}\left[\frac{1}{T}\sum_{t=1}^{T}\left(\boldsymbol{\theta}^\top\boldsymbol{\psi}(\boldsymbol{s}_t,a_t) - r(\boldsymbol{s}_t,a_t)\right)^2 w_T\right],$$

where w_T is the *episodic importance weight* (EIW):

$$w_T = \frac{p^{\pi}(h)}{p^{\widetilde{\pi}}(h)}.$$

$p^{\pi}(h)$ and $p^{\widetilde{\pi}}(h)$ are the probability densities of observing episodic data h under policy π and $\widetilde{\pi}$:

$$p^{\pi}(h) = p(\boldsymbol{s}_1)\prod_{t=1}^{T}\pi(a_t|\boldsymbol{s}_t)p(\boldsymbol{s}_{t+1}|\boldsymbol{s}_t,a_t),$$
$$p^{\widetilde{\pi}}(h) = p(\boldsymbol{s}_1)\prod_{t=1}^{T}\widetilde{\pi}(a_t|\boldsymbol{s}_t)p(\boldsymbol{s}_{t+1}|\boldsymbol{s}_t,a_t).$$

Note that the importance weights can be computed without explicitly knowing $p(\boldsymbol{s}_1)$ and $p(\boldsymbol{s}_{t+1}|\boldsymbol{s}_t,a_t)$, since they are canceled out:

$$w_T = \frac{\prod_{t=1}^{T}\pi(a_t|\boldsymbol{s}_t)}{\prod_{t=1}^{T}\widetilde{\pi}(a_t|\boldsymbol{s}_t)}.$$

Using the training data $\mathcal{H}^{\widetilde{\pi}}$, we can construct a consistent estimator of G as

$$\widehat{G}_{\mathrm{EIW}}(\boldsymbol{\theta}) = \frac{1}{NT}\sum_{n=1}^{N}\sum_{t=1}^{T}\left(\boldsymbol{\theta}^\top \widehat{\boldsymbol{\psi}}(\boldsymbol{s}_{t,n}^{\widetilde{\pi}}, a_{t,n}^{\widetilde{\pi}}; \mathcal{H}^{\widetilde{\pi}}) - r(\boldsymbol{s}_{t,n}^{\widetilde{\pi}}, a_{t,n}^{\widetilde{\pi}}, \boldsymbol{s}_{t+1,n}^{\widetilde{\pi}})\right)^2 \widehat{w}_{T,n}, \tag{4.2}$$

where

$$\widehat{w}_{T,n} = \frac{\prod_{t=1}^{T}\pi(a_{t,n}^{\widetilde{\pi}}|\boldsymbol{s}_{t,n}^{\widetilde{\pi}})}{\prod_{t=1}^{T}\widetilde{\pi}(a_{t,n}^{\widetilde{\pi}}|\boldsymbol{s}_{t,n}^{\widetilde{\pi}})}.$$

4.2.2 Per-Decision Importance Weighting

A crucial observation in EIW is that the error at the t-th step does not depend on the samples after the t-th step (Precup et al., 2000). Thus, the generalization error G can be rewritten as

$$G(\boldsymbol{\theta}) = \mathbb{E}_{p^{\widetilde{\pi}}(h)}\left[\frac{1}{T}\sum_{t=1}^{T}\left(\boldsymbol{\theta}^\top \boldsymbol{\psi}(\boldsymbol{s}_t, a_t) - r(\boldsymbol{s}_t, a_t)\right)^2 w_t\right],$$

where w_t is the *per-decision importance weight* (PIW):

$$w_t = \frac{p(\boldsymbol{s}_1)\prod_{t'=1}^{t}\pi(a_{t'}|\boldsymbol{s}_{t'})p(\boldsymbol{s}_{t'+1}|\boldsymbol{s}_{t'}, a_{t'})}{p(\boldsymbol{s}_1)\prod_{t'=1}^{t}\widetilde{\pi}(a_{t'}|\boldsymbol{s}_{t'})p(\boldsymbol{s}_{t'+1}|\boldsymbol{s}_{t'}, a_{t'})} = \frac{\prod_{t'=1}^{t}\pi(a_{t'}|\boldsymbol{s}_{t'})}{\prod_{t'=1}^{t}\widetilde{\pi}(a_{t'}|\boldsymbol{s}_{t'})}.$$

Using the training data $\mathcal{H}^{\widetilde{\pi}}$, we can construct a consistent estimator as follows (cf. Eq. (4.2)):

$$\widehat{G}_{\mathrm{PIW}}(\boldsymbol{\theta}) = \frac{1}{NT}\sum_{n=1}^{N}\sum_{t=1}^{T}\left(\boldsymbol{\theta}^\top \widehat{\boldsymbol{\psi}}(\boldsymbol{s}_{t,n}^{\widetilde{\pi}}, a_{t,n}^{\widetilde{\pi}}; \mathcal{H}^{\widetilde{\pi}}) - r(\boldsymbol{s}_{t,n}^{\widetilde{\pi}}, a_{t,n}^{\widetilde{\pi}}, \boldsymbol{s}_{t+1,n}^{\widetilde{\pi}})\right)^2 \widehat{w}_{t,n},$$

where

$$\widehat{w}_{t,n} = \frac{\prod_{t'=1}^{t}\pi(a_{t',n}^{\widetilde{\pi}}|\boldsymbol{s}_{t',n}^{\widetilde{\pi}})}{\prod_{t'=1}^{t}\widetilde{\pi}(a_{t',n}^{\widetilde{\pi}}|\boldsymbol{s}_{t',n}^{\widetilde{\pi}})}.$$

$\widehat{w}_{t,n}$ *only* contains the relevant terms up to the t-th step, while $\widehat{w}_{T,n}$ includes all the terms until the end of the episode.

4.2.3 Adaptive Per-Decision Importance Weighting

The PIW estimator is guaranteed to be consistent. However, both are not *efficient* in the statistical sense (Shimodaira, 2000), i.e., they do not have the smallest admissible variance. For this reason, the PIW estimator can have large variance in finite sample cases and therefore learning with PIW tends to be unstable in practice.

To improve the stability, it is important to control the trade-off between consistency and efficiency (or similarly bias and variance) based on training data. Here, the *flattening parameter* ν ($\in [0,1]$) is introduced to control the trade-off by slightly "flattening" the importance weights (Shimodaira, 2000; Sugiyama et al., 2007):

$$\widehat{G}_{\mathrm{AIW}}(\boldsymbol{\theta}) = \frac{1}{NT}\sum_{n=1}^{N}\sum_{t=1}^{T}\Big(\boldsymbol{\theta}^\top \widehat{\boldsymbol{\psi}}(\boldsymbol{s}_{t,n}^{\widetilde{\pi}}, a_{t,n}^{\widetilde{\pi}}; \mathcal{H}^{\widetilde{\pi}}) - r(\boldsymbol{s}_{t,n}^{\widetilde{\pi}}, a_{t,n}^{\widetilde{\pi}}, \boldsymbol{s}_{t+1,n}^{\widetilde{\pi}})\Big)^2 (\widehat{w}_{t,n})^{\nu},$$

where AIW stands for the *adaptive per-decision importance weight*. When $\nu = 0$, AIW is reduced to NIW and therefore it has large bias but has relatively small variance. On the other hand, when $\nu = 1$, AIW is reduced to PIW. Thus, it has small bias but has relatively large variance. In practice, an intermediate value of ν will yield the best performance.

Let $\widehat{\boldsymbol{\Psi}}$ be the $NT \times B$ matrix, $\widehat{\boldsymbol{W}}$ be the $NT \times NT$ diagonal matrix, and $\boldsymbol{r}$ be the NT-dimensional vector defined as

$$\begin{aligned}\widehat{\Psi}_{N(t-1)+n,b} &= \widehat{\psi}_b(\boldsymbol{s}_{t,n}, a_{t,n}),\\ \widehat{W}_{N(t-1)+n,N(t-1)+n} &= \widehat{w}_{t,n},\\ r_{N(t-1)+n} &= r(\boldsymbol{s}_{t,n}, a_{t,n}, \boldsymbol{s}_{t+1,n}).\end{aligned}$$

Then, $\widehat{G}_{\mathrm{AIW}}$ can be compactly expressed as

$$\widehat{G}_{\mathrm{AIW}}(\boldsymbol{\theta}) = \frac{1}{NT}(\widehat{\boldsymbol{\Psi}}\boldsymbol{\theta} - \boldsymbol{r})^\top \widehat{\boldsymbol{W}}^{\nu}(\widehat{\boldsymbol{\Psi}}\boldsymbol{\theta} - \boldsymbol{r}).$$

Because this is a convex quadratic function with respect to $\boldsymbol{\theta}$, its global minimizer $\widehat{\boldsymbol{\theta}}_{\mathrm{AIW}}$ can be analytically obtained by setting its derivative to zero as

$$\widehat{\boldsymbol{\theta}}_{\mathrm{AIW}} = (\widehat{\boldsymbol{\Psi}}^\top \widehat{\boldsymbol{W}}^{\nu} \widehat{\boldsymbol{\Psi}})^{-1} \widehat{\boldsymbol{\Psi}}^\top \widehat{\boldsymbol{W}}^{\nu} \boldsymbol{r}.$$

This means that the cost for computing $\widehat{\boldsymbol{\theta}}_{\mathrm{AIW}}$ is essentially the same as $\widehat{\boldsymbol{\theta}}_{\mathrm{NIW}}$, which is given as follows (see Section 2.2.2):

$$\widehat{\boldsymbol{\theta}}_{\mathrm{NIW}} = (\widehat{\boldsymbol{\Psi}}^\top \widehat{\boldsymbol{\Psi}})^{-1} \widehat{\boldsymbol{\Psi}}^\top \boldsymbol{r}.$$

4.2.4 Illustration

Here, the influence of the flattening parameter ν on the estimator $\widehat{\boldsymbol{\theta}}_{\mathrm{AIW}}$ is illustrated using the chain-walk MDP illustrated in Figure 4.1.

The MDP consists of 10 states

$$\mathcal{S} = \{s^{(1)}, \ldots, s^{(10)}\}$$

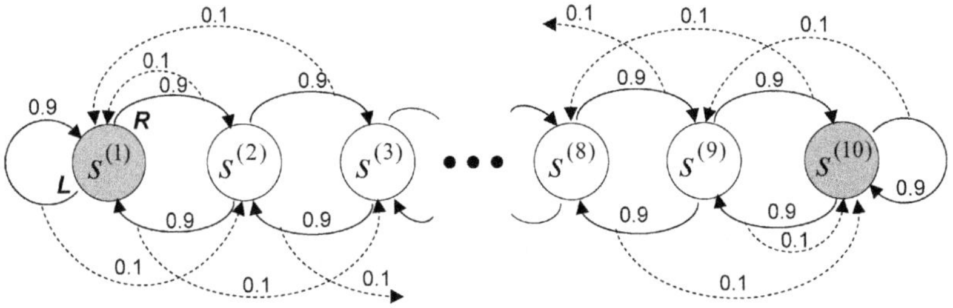

FIGURE 4.1: Ten-state chain-walk MDP.

and two actions

$$\mathcal{A} = \{a^{(1)}, a^{(2)}\} = \{\text{“L,” “R”}\}.$$

The reward +1 is given when visiting $s^{(1)}$ and $s^{(10)}$. The transition probability p is indicated by the numbers attached to the arrows in the figure. For example,

$$p(s^{(2)}|s^{(1)}, a = \text{“R”}) = 0.9 \quad \text{and} \quad p(s^{(1)}|s^{(1)}, a = \text{“R”}) = 0.1$$

mean that the agent can successfully move to the right node with probability 0.9 (indicated by solid arrows in the figure) and the action fails with probability 0.1 (indicated by dashed arrows in the figure). Six Gaussian kernels with standard deviation $\sigma = 10$ are used as basis functions, and kernel centers are located at $s^{(1)}$, $s^{(5)}$, and $s^{(10)}$. More specifically, the basis functions, $\boldsymbol{\phi}(s,a) = (\phi_1(s,a), \ldots, \phi_6(s,a))$ are defined as

$$\phi_{3(i-1)+j}(s,a) = I(a = a^{(i)}) \exp\left(-\frac{(s-c_j)^2}{2\sigma^2}\right),$$

for $i = 1, 2$ and $j = 1, 2, 3$, where

$$c_1 = 1, c_2 = 5, c_3 = 10,$$

and

$$I(x) = \begin{cases} 1 & \text{if } x \text{ is true,} \\ 0 & \text{if } x \text{ is not true.} \end{cases}$$

The experiments are repeated 50 times, where the sampling policy $\widetilde{\pi}(a|s)$ and the current policy $\pi(a|s)$ are chosen randomly in each trial such that $\widetilde{\pi} \neq \pi$. The discount factor is set at $\gamma = 0.9$. The model parameter $\widehat{\boldsymbol{\theta}}_{\mathrm{AIW}}$ is learned from the training samples $\mathcal{H}_{\widetilde{\pi}}$ and its generalization error is computed from the test samples $\mathcal{H}_{\pi}$.

The left column of Figure 4.2 depicts the true generalization error G averaged over 50 trials as a function of the flattening parameter ν for $N = 10$, 30, and 50. Figure 4.2(a) shows that when the number of episodes is large ($N = 50$), the generalization error tends to decrease as the flattening parameter increases. This would be a natural result due to the consistency of $\widehat{\boldsymbol{\theta}}_{\mathrm{AIW}}$

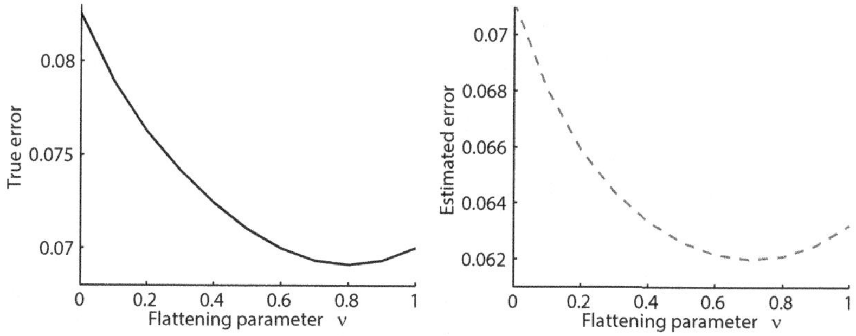

(a) $N = 50$

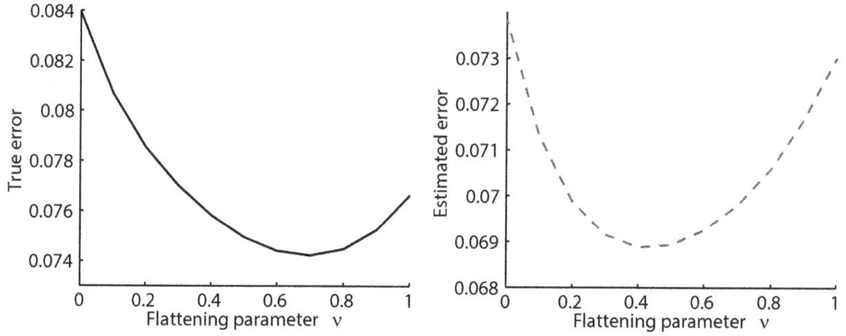

(b) $N = 30$

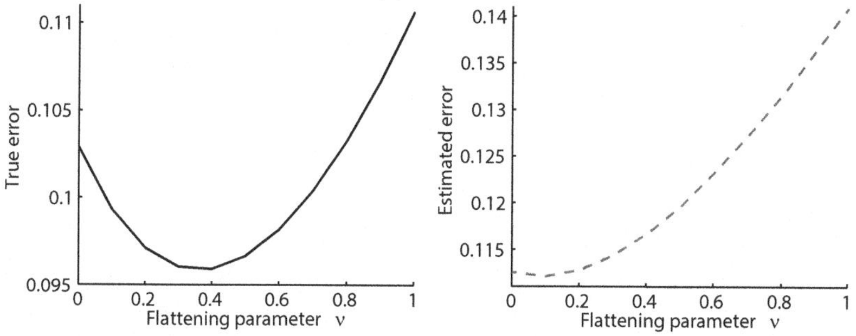

(c) $N = 10$

FIGURE 4.2: Left: True generalization error G averaged over 50 trials as a function of the flattening parameter ν in the 10-state chain-walk problem. The number of steps is fixed at $T = 10$. The trend of G differs depending on the number N of episodic samples. Right: Generalization error estimated by 5-fold importance weighted cross validation (IWCV) ($\widehat{G}_{\mathrm{IWCV}}$) averaged over 50 trials as a function of the flattening parameter ν in the 10-state chain-walk problem. The number of steps is fixed at $T = 10$. IWCV nicely captures the trend of the true generalization error G.

when $\nu = 1$. On the other hand, Figure 4.2(b) shows that when the number of episodes is not large ($N = 30$), $\nu = 1$ performs rather poorly. This implies that the consistent estimator tends to be unstable when the number of episodes is not large enough; $\nu = 0.7$ works the best in this case. Figure 4.2(c) shows the results when the number of episodes is further reduced ($N = 10$). This illustrates that the consistent estimator with $\nu = 1$ is even worse than the ordinary estimator ($\nu = 0$) because the bias is dominated by large variance. In this case, the best ν is even smaller and is achieved at $\nu = 0.4$.

The above results show that AIW can outperform PIW, particularly when only a small number of training samples are available, provided that the flattening parameter ν is chosen appropriately.

4.3 Automatic Selection of Flattening Parameter

In this section, the problem of selecting the flattening parameter in AIW is addressed.

4.3.1 Importance-Weighted Cross-Validation

Generally, the best ν tends to be large (small) when the number of training samples is large (small). However, this general trend is not sufficient to fine-tune the flattening parameter since the best value of ν depends on training samples, policies, the model of value functions, etc. In this section, we discuss how *model selection* is performed to choose the best flattening parameter ν automatically from the training data and policies.

Ideally, the value of ν should be set so that the generalization error G is minimized, but the true G is not accessible in practice. To cope with this problem, we can use cross-validation (see Section 2.2.4) for estimating the generalization error G. However, in the off-policy scenario where the sampling policy $\widetilde{\pi}$ and the target policy π are different, ordinary cross-validation gives a biased estimate of G. In the off-policy scenario, *importance-weighted cross-validation* (IWCV) (Sugiyama et al., 2007) is more useful, where the cross-validation estimate of the generalization error is obtained with importance weighting.

More specifically, let us divide a training dataset $\mathcal{H}^{\widetilde{\pi}}$ containing N episodes into K subsets $\{\mathcal{H}_k^{\widetilde{\pi}}\}_{k=1}^K$ of approximately the same size. For simplicity, we assume that N is divisible by K. Let $\widehat{\boldsymbol{\theta}}_{\mathrm{AIW}}^k$ be the parameter learned from $\mathcal{H} \backslash \mathcal{H}_k$ (i.e., all samples without $\mathcal{H}_k$). Then, the generalization error is estimated with

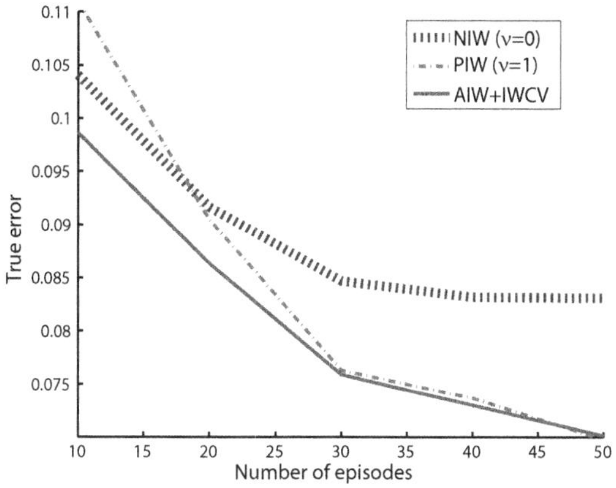

FIGURE 4.3: True generalization error G averaged over 50 trials obtained by NIW ($\nu = 0$), PIW ($\nu = 1$), AIW+IWCV (ν is chosen by IWCV) in the 10-state chain-walk MDP.

importance weighting as

$$\widehat{G}_{\mathrm{IWCV}} = \frac{1}{K}\sum_{k=1}^{K} \widehat{G}^k_{\mathrm{IWCV}},$$

where

$$\widehat{G}^k_{\mathrm{IWCV}} = \frac{K}{NT}\sum_{h\in\mathcal{H}^{\widetilde{\pi}}_k}\sum_{t=1}^{T}\left(\widehat{\boldsymbol{\theta}}^k_{\mathrm{AIW}}{}^\top \widehat{\boldsymbol{\psi}}(\boldsymbol{s}_t, a_t; \mathcal{H}^{\widetilde{\pi}}_k) - r(\boldsymbol{s}_t, a_t, \boldsymbol{s}_{t+1})\right)^2 \widehat{w}_t.$$

The generalization error estimate $\widehat{G}_{\mathrm{IWCV}}$ is computed for all candidate models (in the current setting, a candidate model corresponds to a different value of the flattening parameter ν) and the one that minimizes the estimated generalization error is chosen:

$$\widehat{\nu}_{\mathrm{IWCV}} = \underset{\nu}{\operatorname{argmin}}\, \widehat{G}_{\mathrm{IWCV}}.$$

4.3.2 Illustration

To illustrate how IWCV works, let us use the same numerical examples as Section 4.2.4. The right column of Figure 4.2 depicts the generalization error estimated by 5-fold IWCV averaged over 50 trials as a function of the flattening parameter ν. The graphs show that IWCV nicely captures the trend of the true generalization error for all three cases.

Figure 4.3 describes, as a function of the number N of episodes, the average true generalization error obtained by NIW (AIW with $\nu = 0$), PIW

(AIW with $\nu = 1$), and AIW+IWCV ($\nu \in \{0.0, 0.1, \ldots, 0.9, 1.0\}$ is selected in each trial using 5-fold IWCV). This result shows that the improvement of the performance by NIW saturates when $N \geq 30$, implying that the bias caused by NIW is not negligible. The performance of PIW is worse than NIW when $N \leq 20$, which is caused by the large variance of PIW. On the other hand, AIW+IWCV consistently gives good performance for all N, illustrating the strong adaptation ability of AIW+IWCV.

4.4 Sample-Reuse Policy Iteration

In this section, AIW+IWCV is extended from single-step policy evaluation to full policy iteration. This method is called *sample-reuse policy iteration* (SRPI).

4.4.1 Algorithm

Let us denote the policy at the L-th iteration by π_L. In on-policy policy iteration, new data samples $\mathcal{H}^{\pi_L}$ are collected following the new policy π_L during the policy evaluation step. Thus, previously collected data samples $\{\mathcal{H}^{\pi_1}, \ldots, \mathcal{H}^{\pi_{L-1}}\}$ are not used:

$$\pi_1 \xrightarrow{\text{E}:\{\mathcal{H}^{\pi_1}\}} \widehat{Q}^{\pi_1} \xrightarrow{\text{I}} \pi_2 \xrightarrow{\text{E}:\{\mathcal{H}^{\pi_2}\}} \widehat{Q}^{\pi_2} \xrightarrow{\text{I}} \pi_3 \xrightarrow{\text{E}:\{\mathcal{H}^{\pi_3}\}} \cdots \xrightarrow{\text{I}} \pi_L,$$

where "E : $\{\mathcal{H}\}$" indicates the policy evaluation step using the data sample $\mathcal{H}$ and "I" indicates the policy improvement step. It would be more cost efficient if all previously collected data samples were reused in policy evaluation:

$$\pi_1 \xrightarrow{\text{E}:\{\mathcal{H}^{\pi_1}\}} \widehat{Q}^{\pi_1} \xrightarrow{\text{I}} \pi_2 \xrightarrow{\text{E}:\{\mathcal{H}^{\pi_1},\mathcal{H}^{\pi_2}\}} \widehat{Q}^{\pi_2} \xrightarrow{\text{I}} \pi_3 \xrightarrow{\text{E}:\{\mathcal{H}^{\pi_1},\mathcal{H}^{\pi_2},\mathcal{H}^{\pi_3}\}} \cdots \xrightarrow{\text{I}} \pi_L.$$

Since the previous policies and the current policy are different in general, an *off-policy* scenario needs to be explicitly considered to reuse previously collected data samples. Here, we explain how AIW+IWCV can be used in this situation. For this purpose, the definition of $\widehat{G}_{\text{AIW}}$ is extended so that multiple sampling policies $\pi_1, \ldots, \pi_L$ are taken into account:

$$\widehat{G}^L_{\text{AIW}} = \frac{1}{LNT} \sum_{l=1}^{L} \sum_{n=1}^{N} \sum_{t=1}^{T} \Big(\boldsymbol{\theta}^\top \widehat{\boldsymbol{\psi}}(\boldsymbol{s}^{\pi_l}_{t,n}, a^{\pi_l}_{t,n}; \{\mathcal{H}^{\pi_l}\}^L_{l=1}) - r(\boldsymbol{s}^{\pi_l}_{t,n}, a^{\pi_l}_{t,n}, \boldsymbol{s}^{\pi_l}_{t+1,n}) \Big)^2 \left(\frac{\prod_{t'=1}^{t} \pi_L(a^{\pi_l}_{t',n} | \boldsymbol{s}^{\pi_l}_{t',n})}{\prod_{t'=1}^{t} \pi_l(a^{\pi_l}_{t',n} | \boldsymbol{s}^{\pi_l}_{t',n})} \right)^{\nu_L}, \tag{4.3}$$

where $\widehat{G}^L_{\text{AIW}}$ is the generalization error estimated at the L-th policy evaluation using AIW. The flattening parameter ν_L is chosen based on IWCV before performing policy evaluation.

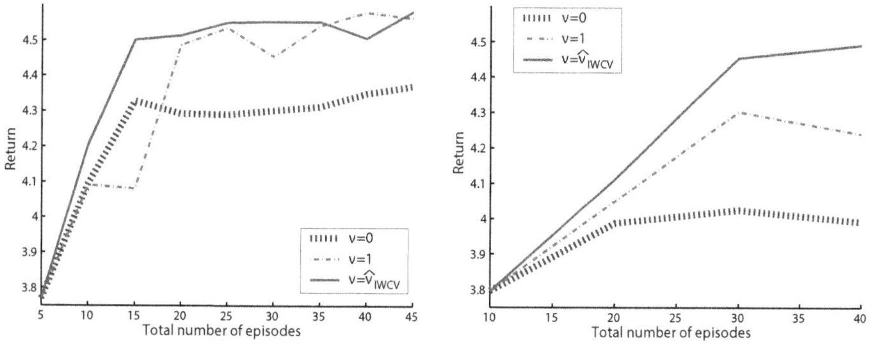

(a) $N = 5$ (b) $N = 10$

FIGURE 4.4: The performance of policies learned in three scenarios: $\nu = 0$, $\nu = 1$, and SRPI (ν is chosen by IWCV) in the 10-state chain-walk problem. The performance is measured by the average return computed from test samples over 30 trials. The agent collects training sample $\mathcal{H}^{\pi_L}$ ($N = 5$ or 10 with $T = 10$) at every iteration and performs policy evaluation using all collected samples $\mathcal{H}^{\pi_1}, \ldots, \mathcal{H}^{\pi_L}$. The total number of episodes means the number of training episodes ($N \times L$) collected by the agent in policy iteration.

4.4.2 Illustration

Here, the behavior of SRPI is illustrated under the same experimental setup as Section 4.3.2. Let us consider three scenarios: ν is fixed at 0, ν is fixed at 1, and ν is chosen by IWCV (i.e., SRPI). The agent collects samples $\mathcal{H}^{\pi_L}$ in each policy iteration following the current policy π_L and computes $\widehat{\boldsymbol{\theta}}^{L}_{\mathrm{AIW}}$ from all collected samples $\mathcal{H}^{\pi_1}, \ldots, \mathcal{H}^{\pi_L}$ using Eq. (4.3). Three Gaussian kernels are used as basis functions, where kernel centers are randomly selected from the state space $\mathcal{S}$ in each trial. The initial policy π_1 is chosen randomly and *Gibbs policy improvement*,

$$\pi(a|\boldsymbol{s}) \longleftarrow \frac{\exp(Q^{\pi}(\boldsymbol{s}, a)/\tau)}{\sum_{a' \in \mathcal{A}} \exp(Q^{\pi}(\boldsymbol{s}, a')/\tau)}, \tag{4.4}$$

is performed with $\tau = 2L$.

Figure 4.4 depicts the average return over 30 trials when $N = 5$ and 10 with a fixed number of steps ($T = 10$). The graphs show that SRPI provides stable and fast learning of policies, while the performance improvement of policies learned with $\nu = 0$ saturates in early iterations. The method with $\nu = 1$ can improve policies well, but its progress tends to be behind SRPI.

Figure 4.5 depicts the average value of the flattening parameter used in SRPI as a function of the total number of episodic samples. The graphs show that the value of the flattening parameter chosen by IWCV tends to rise in the beginning and go down later. At first sight, this does not agree with the general trend of preferring a low-variance estimator in early stages and preferring a

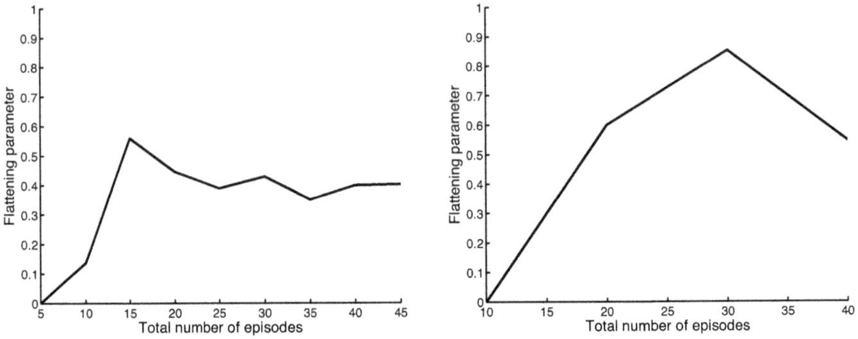

(a) $N = 5$ (b) $N = 10$

FIGURE 4.5: Flattening parameter values used by SRPI averaged over 30 trials as a function of the total number of episodic samples in the 10-state chain-walk problem.

low-bias estimator later. However, this result is still consistent with the general trend: when the return increases rapidly (the total number of episodic samples is up to 15 when $N = 5$ and 30 when $N = 10$ in Figure 4.5), the value of the flattening parameter increases (see Figure 4.4). After that, the return does not increase any more (see Figure 4.4) since the policy iteration has already been converged. Then, it is natural to prefer a small flattening parameter (Figure 4.5) since the sample selection bias becomes mild after convergence.

These results show that SRPI can effectively reuse previously collected samples by appropriately tuning the flattening parameter according to the condition of data samples, policies, etc.

4.5 Numerical Examples

In this section, the performance of SRPI is numerically investigated in more complex tasks.

4.5.1 Inverted Pendulum

First, we consider the task of the *swing-up inverted pendulum* illustrated in Figure 4.6, which consists of a pole hinged at the top of a cart. The goal of the task is to swing the pole up by moving the cart. There are three actions: applying positive force $+50$ ($\mathrm{kg} \cdot \mathrm{m/s^2}$) to the cart to move right, negative force -50 to move left, and zero force to just coast. That is, the action space

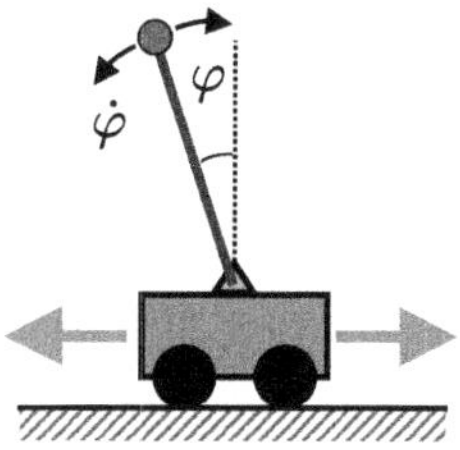

FIGURE 4.6: Illustration of the inverted pendulum task.

$\mathcal{A}$ is discrete and described by

$$\mathcal{A} = \{50, -50, 0\} \ \text{kg} \cdot \text{m/s}^2.$$

Note that the force itself is not strong enough to swing the pole up. Thus the cart needs to be moved back and forth several times to swing the pole up. The state space $\mathcal{S}$ is continuous and consists of the angle φ [rad] ($\in [0, 2\pi]$) and the angular velocity $\dot{\varphi}$ [rad/s] ($\in [-\pi, \pi]$). Thus, a state $\boldsymbol{s}$ is described by two-dimensional vector $\boldsymbol{s} = (\varphi, \dot{\varphi})^\top$. The angle φ and angular velocity $\dot{\varphi}$ are updated as follows:

$$\begin{aligned}
\varphi_{t+1} =& \varphi_t + \dot{\varphi}_{t+1}\Delta t, \\
\dot{\varphi}_{t+1} =& \dot{\varphi}_t + \frac{9.8\sin(\varphi_t) - \alpha w d(\dot{\varphi}_t)^2 \sin(2\varphi_t)/2 + \alpha \cos(\varphi_t) a_t}{4l/3 - \alpha w d \cos^2(\varphi_t)} \Delta t,
\end{aligned}$$

where $\alpha = 1/(W + w)$ and a_t ($\in \mathcal{A}$) is the action chosen at time t. The reward function $r(\boldsymbol{s}, a, \boldsymbol{s}')$ is defined as

$$r(\boldsymbol{s}, a, \boldsymbol{s}') = \cos(\varphi_{\boldsymbol{s}'}),$$

where $\varphi_{\boldsymbol{s}'}$ denotes the angle φ of state $\boldsymbol{s}'$. The problem parameters are set as follows: the mass of the cart W is 8 [kg], the mass of the pole w is 2 [kg], the length of the pole d is 0.5 [m], and the simulation time step Δt is 0.1[s].

Forty-eight Gaussian kernels with standard deviation $\sigma = \pi$ are used as basis functions, and kernel centers are located over the following grid points:

$$\{0, 2/3\pi, 4/3\pi, 2\pi\} \times \{-3\pi, -\pi, \pi, 3\pi\}.$$

That is, the basis functions $\boldsymbol{\phi}(\boldsymbol{s}, a) = \{\phi_1(\boldsymbol{s}, a), \ldots, \phi_{16}(\boldsymbol{s}, a)\}$ are set as

$$\phi_{16(i-1)+j}(\boldsymbol{s}, a) = I(a = a^{(i)})\exp\left(-\frac{\|\boldsymbol{s} - \boldsymbol{c}_j\|^2}{2\sigma^2}\right),$$

for $i = 1, 2, 3$ and $j = 1, \ldots, 16$, where

$$\boldsymbol{c}_1 = (0, -3\pi)^\top, \boldsymbol{c}_2 = (0, -\pi)^\top, \ldots, \boldsymbol{c}_{12} = (2\pi, 3\pi)^\top.$$

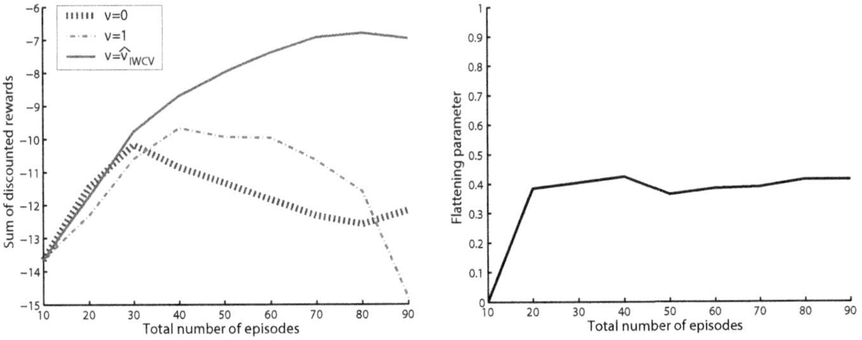

(a) Performance of policy (b) Average flattening parameter

FIGURE 4.7: Results of SRPI in the inverted pendulum task. The agent collects training sample $\mathcal{H}^{\pi_L}$ ($N = 10$ and $T = 100$) in each iteration and policy evaluation is performed using all collected samples $\{\mathcal{H}^{\pi_1}, \ldots, \mathcal{H}^{\pi_L}\}$. (a) The performance of policies learned with $\nu = 0$, $\nu = 1$, and SRPI. The performance is measured by the average return computed from test samples over 20 trials. The total number of episodes means the number of training episodes ($N \times L$) collected by the agent in policy iteration. (b) Average flattening parameter values chosen by IWCV in SRPI over 20 trials.

The initial policy $\pi_1(a|\boldsymbol{s})$ is chosen randomly, and the initial-state probability density $p(\boldsymbol{s})$ is set to be uniform. The agent collects data samples $\mathcal{H}^{\pi_L}$ ($N = 10$ and $T = 100$) at each policy iteration following the current policy π_L. The discounted factor is set at $\gamma = 0.95$ and the policy is updated by Gibbs policy improvement (4.4) with $\tau = L$.

Figure 4.7(a) describes the performance of learned policies. The graph shows that SRPI nicely improves the performance throughout the entire policy iteration. On the other hand, the performance when the flattening parameter is fixed at $\nu = 0$ or $\nu = 1$ is not properly improved after the middle of iterations. The average flattening parameter values depicted in Figure 4.7(b) show that the flattening parameter tends to increase quickly in the beginning and then is kept at medium values. Motion examples of the inverted pendulum by SRPI with ν chosen by IWCV and $\nu = 1$ are illustrated in Figure 4.8 and Figure 4.9, respectively.

These results indicate that the flattening parameter is well adjusted to reuse the previously collected samples effectively for policy evaluation, and thus SRPI can outperform the other methods.

4.5.2 Mountain Car

Next, we consider the *mountain car task* illustrated in Figure 4.10. The task consists of a car and two hills whose landscape is described by $\sin(3x)$.

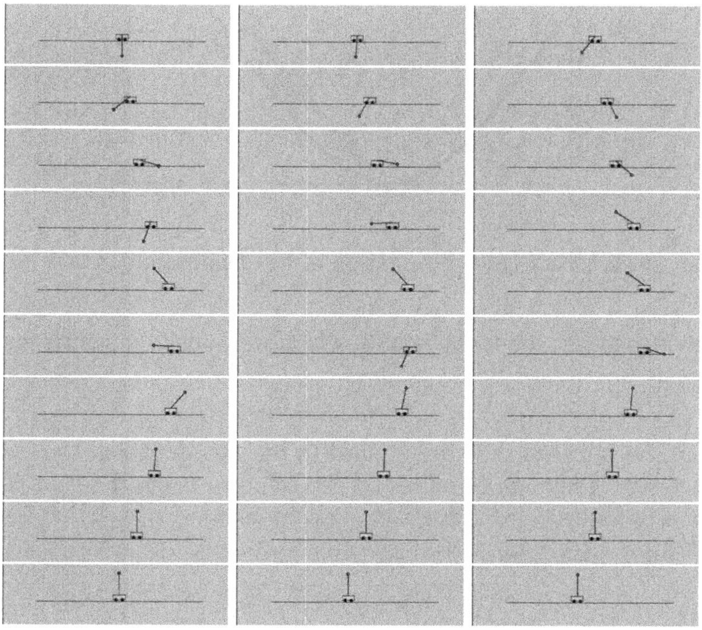

FIGURE 4.8: Motion examples of the inverted pendulum by SRPI with ν chosen by IWCV (from left to right and top to bottom).

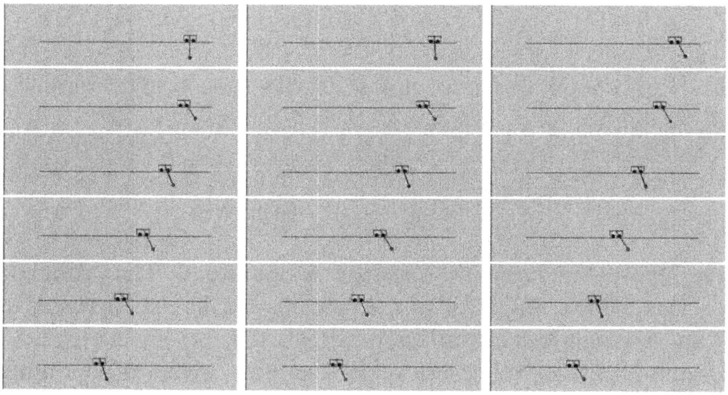

FIGURE 4.9: Motion examples of the inverted pendulum by SRPI with $\nu = 1$ (from left to right and top to bottom).

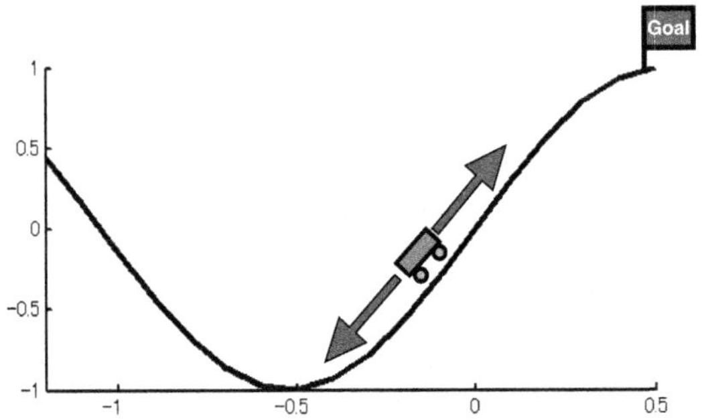

FIGURE 4.10: Illustration of the mountain car task.

The top of the right hill is the goal to which we want to guide the car. There are three actions,

$$\{+0.2, -0.2, 0\},$$

which are the values of the force applied to the car. Note that the force of the car is not strong enough to climb up the slope to reach the goal. The state space $\mathcal{S}$ is described by the horizontal position x $[m]$ ($\in [-1.2, 0.5]$) and the velocity $\dot{x}$ [m/s] ($\in [-1.5, 1.5]$):

$$\boldsymbol{s} = (x, \dot{x})^\top.$$

The position x and velocity $\dot{x}$ are updated by

$$\begin{aligned} x_{t+1} &= x_t + \dot{x}_{t+1}\Delta t, \\ \dot{x}_{t+1} &= \dot{x}_t + \Big(-9.8w\cos(3x_t) + \frac{a_t}{w} - k\dot{x}_t \Big)\Delta t, \end{aligned}$$

where a_t ($\in \mathcal{A}$) is the action chosen at the time t. The reward function $R(\boldsymbol{s}, a, \boldsymbol{s}')$ is defined as

$$R(\boldsymbol{s}, a, \boldsymbol{s}') = \begin{cases} 1 & \text{if } x_{\boldsymbol{s}'} \geq 0.5, \\ -0.01 & \text{otherwise,} \end{cases}$$

where $x_{\boldsymbol{s}'}$ denotes the horizontal position x of state $\boldsymbol{s}'$. The problem parameters are set as follows: the mass of the car w is 0.2 [kg], the friction coefficient k is 0.3, and the simulation time step Δt is 0.1 [s].

The same experimental setup as the swing-up inverted pendulum task in Section 4.5.1 is used, except that the number of Gaussian kernels is 36, the kernel standard deviation is set at $\sigma = 1$, and the kernel centers are allocated over the following grid points:

$$\{-1.2, 0.35, 0.5\} \times \{-1.5, -0.5, 0.5, 1.5\}.$$

Figure 4.11(a) shows the performance of learned policies measured by the

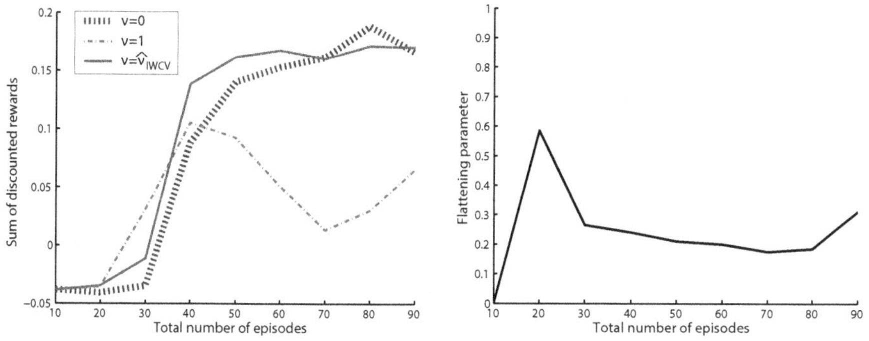

(a) Performance of policy

(b) Average flattening parameter

FIGURE 4.11: Results of sample-reuse policy iteration in the mountain-car task. The agent collects training sample $\mathcal{H}^{\pi_L}$ ($N = 10$ and $T = 100$) at every iteration and policy evaluation is performed using all collected samples $\mathcal{H}^{\pi_1}, \ldots, \mathcal{H}^{\pi_L}$. (a) The performance is measured by the average return computed from test samples over 20 trials. The total number of episodes means the number of training episodes ($N \times L$) collected by the agent in policy iteration. (b) Average flattening parameter values used by SRPI over 20 trials.

average return computed from the test samples. The graph shows similar tendencies to the swing-up inverted pendulum task for SRPI and $\nu = 1$, while the method with $\nu = 0$ performs relatively well this time. This implies that the bias in the previously collected samples does not affect the estimation of the value functions that strongly, because the function approximator is better suited to represent the value function for this problem. The average flattening parameter values (cf. Figure 4.11(b)) show that the flattening parameter decreases soon after the increase in the beginning, and then the smaller values tend to be chosen. This indicates that SRPI tends to use low-variance estimators in this task. Motion examples by SRPI with ν chosen by IWCV are illustrated in Figure 4.12.

These results show that SRPI can perform stable and fast learning by effectively reusing previously collected data.

4.6 Remarks

Instability has been one of the critical limitations of importance-sampling techniques, which often makes off-policy methods impractical. To overcome this weakness, an *adaptive* importance-sampling technique was introduced for controlling the trade-off between consistency and stability in value function

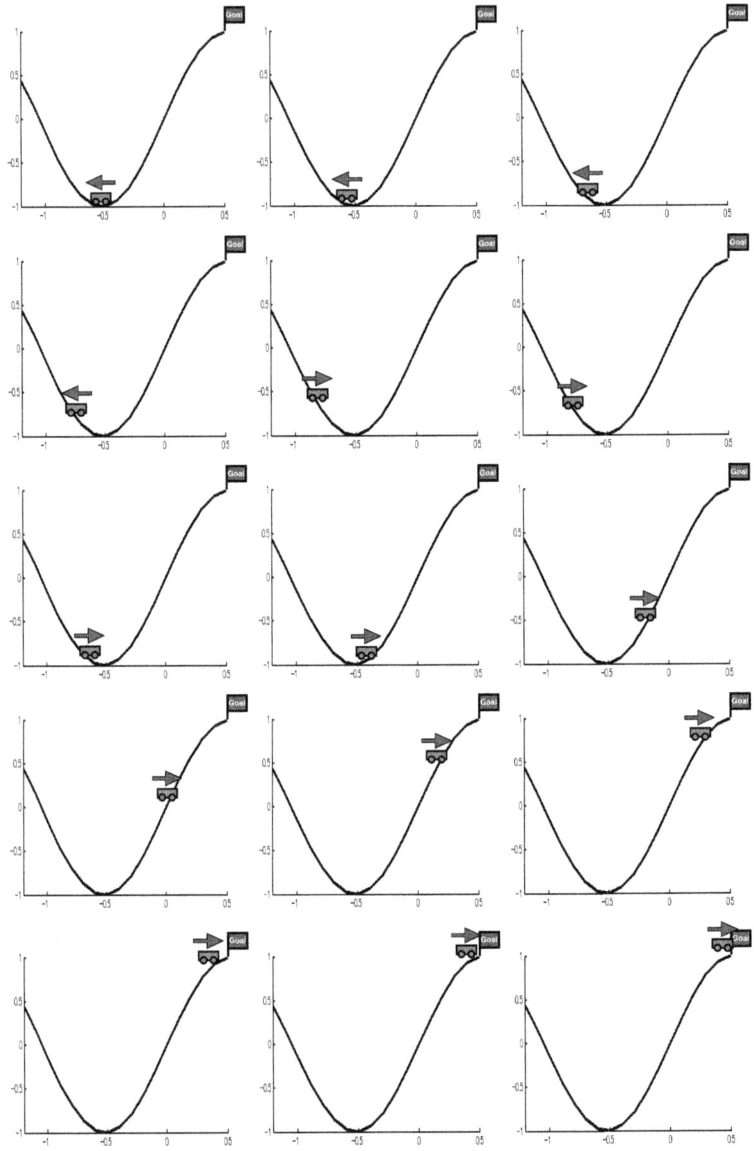

FIGURE 4.12: Motion examples of the mountain car by SRPI with ν chosen by IWCV (from left to right and top to bottom).

approximation. Furthermore, importance-weighted cross-validation was introduced for automatically choosing the trade-off parameter.

The range of application of importance sampling is not limited to policy iteration. We will explain how importance sampling can be utilized for sample reuse in the policy search frameworks in Chapter 8 and Chapter 9.

Chapter 5

Active Learning in Policy Iteration

In Chapter 4, we considered the off-policy situation where a data-collecting policy and the target policy are different. In the framework of *sample-reuse policy iteration*, new samples are always chosen following the target policy. However, a clever choice of sampling policies can actually further improve the performance. The topic of choosing sampling policies is called *active learning* in statistics and machine learning. In this chapter, we address the problem of choosing sampling policies in sample-reuse policy iteration. In Section 5.1, we explain how a statistical active learning method can be employed for optimizing the sampling policy in value function approximation. In Section 5.2, we introduce *active policy iteration*, which incorporates the active learning idea into the framework of sample-reuse policy iteration. The effectiveness of active policy iteration is numerically investigated in Section 5.3, and finally this chapter is concluded in Section 5.4.

5.1 Efficient Exploration with Active Learning

The accuracy of estimated value functions depends on training samples collected following sampling policy $\widetilde{\pi}(a|\boldsymbol{s})$. In this section, we explain how a statistical active learning method (Sugiyama, 2006) can be employed for value function approximation.

5.1.1 Problem Setup

Let us consider a situation where collecting state-action trajectory samples is easy and cheap, but gathering immediate reward samples is hard and expensive. For example, consider a robot-arm control task of hitting a ball with a bat and driving the ball as far away as possible (see Figure 5.6). Let us adopt the carry of the ball as the immediate reward. In this setting, obtaining state-action trajectory samples of the robot arm is easy and relatively cheap since we just need to control the robot arm and record its state-action trajectories over time. However, explicitly computing the carry of the ball from the state-action samples is hard due to friction and elasticity of links, air resistance, air currents, and so on. For this reason, in practice, we may have to put the robot in open space, let the robot really hit the ball, and measure the carry of the ball manually. Thus, gathering immediate reward samples is much more expensive than the state-action trajectory samples. In such a situation, immediate reward samples are too expensive to be used for designing the sampling policy. Only state-action trajectory samples may be used for designing sampling policies.

The goal of active learning in the current setup is to determine the sampling policy so that the expected generalization error is minimized. However, since the generalization error is not accessible in practice, it needs to be estimated from samples for performing active learning. A difficulty of estimating the generalization error in the context of active learning is that its estimation needs to be carried out only from state-action trajectory samples *without* using immediate reward samples. This means that standard generalization error estimation techniques such as cross-validation cannot be employed. Below, we explain how the generalization error can be estimated without the reward samples.

5.1.2 Decomposition of Generalization Error

The information we are allowed to use for estimating the generalization error is a set of roll-out samples *without* immediate rewards:

$$\mathcal{H}^{\widetilde{\pi}} = \{h_1^{\widetilde{\pi}}, \ldots, h_N^{\widetilde{\pi}}\},$$

where each episodic sample $h_n^{\widetilde{\pi}}$ is given as

$$h_n^{\widetilde{\pi}} = [\boldsymbol{s}_{1,n}^{\widetilde{\pi}}, a_{1,n}^{\widetilde{\pi}}, \ldots, \boldsymbol{s}_{T,n}^{\widetilde{\pi}}, a_{T,n}^{\widetilde{\pi}}, \boldsymbol{s}_{T+1,n}^{\widetilde{\pi}}].$$

Let us define the deviation of an observed immediate reward $r_{t,n}^{\widetilde{\pi}}$ from its expectation $r(\boldsymbol{s}_{t,n}^{\widetilde{\pi}}, a_{t,n}^{\widetilde{\pi}})$ as

$$\epsilon_{t,n}^{\widetilde{\pi}} = r_{t,n}^{\widetilde{\pi}} - r(\boldsymbol{s}_{t,n}^{\widetilde{\pi}}, a_{t,n}^{\widetilde{\pi}}).$$

Note that $\epsilon_{t,n}^{\widetilde{\pi}}$ could be regarded as additive noise in the context of least-squares function fitting. By definition, $\epsilon_{t,n}^{\widetilde{\pi}}$ has mean zero and its variance generally depends on $\boldsymbol{s}_{t,n}^{\widetilde{\pi}}$ and $a_{t,n}^{\widetilde{\pi}}$, i.e., *heteroscedastic noise* (Bishop, 2006). However, since estimating the variance of $\epsilon_{t,n}^{\widetilde{\pi}}$ without using reward samples is not generally possible, we ignore the dependence of the variance on $\boldsymbol{s}_{t,n}^{\widetilde{\pi}}$ and $a_{t,n}^{\widetilde{\pi}}$. Let us denote the *input-independent* common variance by σ^2.

We would like to estimate the generalization error,

$$G(\widehat{\boldsymbol{\theta}}) = \mathbb{E}_{p^{\widetilde{\pi}}(h)}\left[\frac{1}{T}\sum_{t=1}^{T}\left(\widehat{\boldsymbol{\theta}}^{\top}\widehat{\boldsymbol{\psi}}(\boldsymbol{s}_t, a_t; \mathcal{H}^{\widetilde{\pi}}) - r(\boldsymbol{s}_t, a_t)\right)^2\right],$$

from $\mathcal{H}^{\widetilde{\pi}}$. Its expectation over "noise" can be decomposed as follows (Sugiyama, 2006):

$$\mathbb{E}_{\epsilon^{\widetilde{\pi}}}\left[G(\widehat{\boldsymbol{\theta}})\right] = \text{Bias} + \text{Variance} + \text{ModelError},$$

where $\mathbb{E}_{\epsilon^{\widetilde{\pi}}}$ denotes the expectation over "noise" $\{\epsilon_{t,n}^{\widetilde{\pi}}\}_{t=1,n=1}^{T,N}$. "Bias," "Variance," and "ModelError" are the *bias* term, the *variance* term, and the *model error* term defined by

$$\text{Bias} = \mathbb{E}_{p^{\widetilde{\pi}}(h)}\left[\frac{1}{T}\sum_{t=1}^{T}\left\{(\mathbb{E}_{\epsilon^{\widetilde{\pi}}}\left[\widehat{\boldsymbol{\theta}}\right] - \boldsymbol{\theta}^*)^\top \widehat{\boldsymbol{\psi}}(\boldsymbol{s}_t, a_t; \mathcal{H}^{\widetilde{\pi}})\right\}^2\right],$$

$$\text{Variance} = \mathbb{E}_{p^{\widetilde{\pi}}(h)}\left[\frac{1}{T}\sum_{t=1}^{T}\left\{(\widehat{\boldsymbol{\theta}} - \mathbb{E}_{\epsilon^{\widetilde{\pi}}}\left[\widehat{\boldsymbol{\theta}}\right])^\top \widehat{\boldsymbol{\psi}}(\boldsymbol{s}_t, a_t; \mathcal{H}^{\widetilde{\pi}})\right\}^2\right],$$

$$\text{ModelError} = \mathbb{E}_{p^{\widetilde{\pi}}(h)}\left[\frac{1}{T}\sum_{t=1}^{T}(\boldsymbol{\theta}^{*\top} \widehat{\boldsymbol{\psi}}(\boldsymbol{s}_t, a_t; \mathcal{H}^{\widetilde{\pi}}) - r(\boldsymbol{s}_t, a_t))^2\right].$$

$\boldsymbol{\theta}^*$ denotes the optimal parameter in the model:

$$\boldsymbol{\theta}^* = \underset{\boldsymbol{\theta}}{\operatorname{argmin}}\, \mathbb{E}_{p^{\widetilde{\pi}}(h)}\left[\frac{1}{T}\sum_{t=1}^{T}(\boldsymbol{\theta}^\top \boldsymbol{\psi}(\boldsymbol{s}_t, a_t) - r(\boldsymbol{s}_t, a_t))^2\right].$$

Note that, for a linear estimator $\widehat{\boldsymbol{\theta}}$ such that

$$\widehat{\boldsymbol{\theta}} = \widehat{\boldsymbol{L}}\boldsymbol{r},$$

where $\widehat{\boldsymbol{L}}$ is some matrix and $\boldsymbol{r}$ is the NT-dimensional vector defined as

$$r_{N(t-1)+n} = r(\boldsymbol{s}_{t,n}, a_{t,n}, \boldsymbol{s}_{t+1,n}),$$

the variance term can be expressed in a compact form as

$$\text{Variance} = \sigma^2 \text{tr}(\boldsymbol{U}\widehat{\boldsymbol{L}}\widehat{\boldsymbol{L}}^\top),$$

where the matrix $\boldsymbol{U}$ is defined as

$$\boldsymbol{U} = \mathbb{E}_{p^{\widetilde{\pi}}(h)}\left[\frac{1}{T}\sum_{t=1}^{T}\widehat{\boldsymbol{\psi}}(\boldsymbol{s}_t, a_t; \mathcal{H}^{\widetilde{\pi}})\widehat{\boldsymbol{\psi}}(\boldsymbol{s}_t, a_t; \mathcal{H}^{\widetilde{\pi}})^\top\right]. \tag{5.1}$$

5.1.3 Estimation of Generalization Error

Since we are interested in finding a minimizer of the generalization error with respect to $\widetilde{\pi}$, the model error, which is constant, can be safely ignored in generalization error estimation. On the other hand, the bias term includes the unknown optimal parameter $\boldsymbol{\theta}^*$. Thus, it may not be possible to estimate the bias term without using reward samples. Similarly, it may not be possible to estimate the "noise" variance σ^2 included in the variance term without using reward samples.

It is known that the bias term is small enough to be neglected when the model is *approximately correct* (Sugiyama, 2006), i.e., $\boldsymbol{\theta}^{*\top}\widehat{\boldsymbol{\psi}}(\boldsymbol{s}, a)$ approximately agrees with the true function $r(\boldsymbol{s}, a)$. Then we have

$$\mathbb{E}_{\boldsymbol{\epsilon}^{\widetilde{\pi}}}\left[G(\widehat{\boldsymbol{\theta}})\right] - \text{ModelError} - \text{Bias} \propto \operatorname{tr}(\boldsymbol{U}\widehat{\boldsymbol{L}}\widehat{\boldsymbol{L}}^\top), \tag{5.2}$$

which does not require immediate reward samples for its computation. Since $\mathbb{E}_{p^{\widetilde{\pi}}(h)}$ included in $\boldsymbol{U}$ is not accessible (see Eq. (5.1)), $\boldsymbol{U}$ is replaced by its consistent estimator $\widehat{\boldsymbol{U}}$:

$$\widehat{\boldsymbol{U}} = \frac{1}{NT}\sum_{n=1}^{N}\sum_{t=1}^{T}\widehat{\boldsymbol{\psi}}(\boldsymbol{s}_{t,n}^{\widetilde{\pi}}, a_{t,n}^{\widetilde{\pi}}; \mathcal{H}^{\widetilde{\pi}})\widehat{\boldsymbol{\psi}}(\boldsymbol{s}_{t,n}^{\widetilde{\pi}}, a_{t,n}^{\widetilde{\pi}}; \mathcal{H}^{\widetilde{\pi}})^\top \widehat{w}_{t,n}.$$

Consequently, the following generalization error estimator is obtained:

$$J = \operatorname{tr}(\widehat{\boldsymbol{U}}\widehat{\boldsymbol{L}}\widehat{\boldsymbol{L}}^\top),$$

which can be computed only from $\mathcal{H}^{\widetilde{\pi}}$ and thus can be employed in the active learning scenarios. If it is possible to gather $\mathcal{H}^{\widetilde{\pi}}$ multiple times, the above J may be computed multiple times and their average is used as a generalization error estimator.

Note that the values of the generalization error estimator J and the true generalization error G are not directly comparable since irrelevant additive and multiplicative constants are ignored (see Eq. (5.2)). However, this is no problem as long as the estimator J has a similar *profile* to the true error G as a function of sampling policy $\widetilde{\pi}$ since the purpose of deriving a generalization error estimator in active learning is not to approximate the true generalization error itself, but to approximate the *minimizer* of the true generalization error with respect to sampling policy $\widetilde{\pi}$.

5.1.4 Designing Sampling Policies

Based on the generalization error estimator derived above, a sampling policy is designed as follows:

1. Prepare K candidates of sampling policy: $\{\widetilde{\pi}_k\}_{k=1}^K$.
2. Collect episodic samples without immediate rewards for each sampling-policy candidate: $\{\mathcal{H}^{\widetilde{\pi}_k}\}_{k=1}^K$.
3. Estimate $\boldsymbol{U}$ using all samples $\{\mathcal{H}^{\widetilde{\pi}_k}\}_{k=1}^K$:

$$\widehat{\boldsymbol{U}} = \frac{1}{KNT}\sum_{k=1}^{K}\sum_{n=1}^{N}\sum_{t=1}^{T}\widehat{\boldsymbol{\psi}}(\boldsymbol{s}_{t,n}^{\widetilde{\pi}_k}, a_{t,n}^{\widetilde{\pi}_k}; \{\mathcal{H}^{\widetilde{\pi}_k}\}_{k=1}^K)\widehat{\boldsymbol{\psi}}(\boldsymbol{s}_{t,n}^{\widetilde{\pi}_k}, a_{t,n}^{\widetilde{\pi}_k}; \{\mathcal{H}^{\widetilde{\pi}_k}\}_{k=1}^K)^\top \widehat{w}_{t,n}^{\widetilde{\pi}_k},$$

where $\widehat{w}_{t,n}^{\widetilde{\pi}_k}$ denotes the importance weight for the k-th sampling policy $\widetilde{\pi}_k$:

$$\widehat{w}_{t,n}^{\widetilde{\pi}_k} = \frac{\prod_{t'=1}^{t} \pi(a_{t',n}^{\widetilde{\pi}_k} | \boldsymbol{s}_{t',n}^{\widetilde{\pi}_k})}{\prod_{t'=1}^{t} \widetilde{\pi}_k(a_{t',n}^{\widetilde{\pi}_k} | \boldsymbol{s}_{t',n}^{\widetilde{\pi}_k})}.$$

4. Estimate the generalization error for each k:

$$J_k = \mathrm{tr}(\widehat{\boldsymbol{U}} \widehat{\boldsymbol{L}}^{\widetilde{\pi}_k} \widehat{\boldsymbol{L}}^{\widetilde{\pi}_k \top}),$$

where $\widehat{\boldsymbol{L}}^{\widetilde{\pi}_k}$ is defined as

$$\widehat{\boldsymbol{L}}^{\widetilde{\pi}_k} = (\widehat{\boldsymbol{\Psi}}^{\widetilde{\pi}_k \top} \widehat{\boldsymbol{W}}^{\widetilde{\pi}_k} \widehat{\boldsymbol{\Psi}}^{\widetilde{\pi}_k})^{-1} \widehat{\boldsymbol{\Psi}}^{\widetilde{\pi}_k \top} \widehat{\boldsymbol{W}}^{\widetilde{\pi}_k}.$$

$\widehat{\boldsymbol{\Psi}}^{\widetilde{\pi}_k}$ is the $NT \times B$ matrix and $\widehat{\boldsymbol{W}}^{\widetilde{\pi}_k}$ is the $NT \times NT$ diagonal matrix defined as

$$\widehat{\Psi}_{N(t-1)+n,b}^{\widetilde{\pi}_k} = \widehat{\psi}_b(\boldsymbol{s}_{t,n}^{\widetilde{\pi}_k}, a_{t,n}^{\widetilde{\pi}_k}),$$
$$\widehat{W}_{N(t-1)+n,N(t-1)+n}^{\widetilde{\pi}_k} = \widehat{w}_{t,n}^{\widetilde{\pi}_k}.$$

5. (If possible) repeat 2 to 4 several times and calculate the average for each k.

6. Determine the sampling policy as

$$\widetilde{\pi}_{\mathrm{AL}} = \underset{k=1,\ldots,K}{\mathrm{argmin}}\, J_k.$$

7. Collect training samples with immediate rewards following $\widetilde{\pi}_{\mathrm{AL}}$.

8. Learn the value function by least-squares policy iteration using the collected samples.

5.1.5 Illustration

Here, the behavior of the active learning method is illustrated on a toy 10-state chain-walk environment shown in Figure 5.1. The MDP consists of 10 states,

$$\mathcal{S} = \{s^{(i)}\}_{i=1}^{10} = \{1, 2, \ldots, 10\},$$

and 2 actions,

$$\mathcal{A} = \{a^{(i)}\}_{i=1}^{2} = \{\text{“L,” “R”}\}.$$

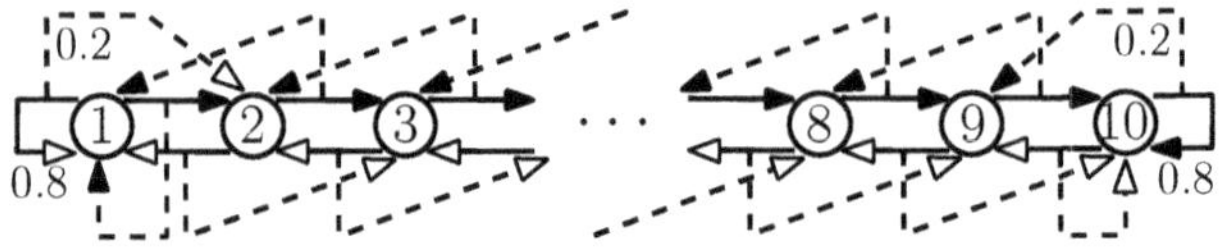

FIGURE 5.1: Ten-state chain walk. Filled and unfilled arrows indicate the transitions when taking action "R" and "L," and solid and dashed lines indicate the successful and failed transitions.

The immediate reward function is defined as

$$r(s, a, s') = f(s'),$$

where the profile of the function $f(s')$ is illustrated in Figure 5.2.

The transition probability $p(s'|s, a)$ is indicated by the numbers attached to the arrows in Figure 5.1. For example, $p(s^{(2)}|s^{(1)}, a = \text{"R"}) = 0.8$ and $p(s^{(1)}|s^{(1)}, a = \text{"R"}) = 0.2$. Thus, the agent can successfully move to the intended direction with probability 0.8 (indicated by solid-filled arrows in the figure) and the action fails with probability 0.2 (indicated by dashed-filled arrows in the figure). The discount factor γ is set at 0.9. The following 12 Gaussian basis functions $\boldsymbol{\phi}(s, a)$ are used:

$$\phi_{2(i-1)+j}(s, a) = \begin{cases} I(a = a^{(j)})\exp\left(-\dfrac{(s - c_i)^2}{2\tau^2}\right) & \\ \qquad\qquad\qquad\qquad \text{for } i = 1, \ldots, 5 \text{ and } j = 1, 2 \\ I(a = a^{(j)}) \quad \text{for } i = 6 \text{ and } j = 1, 2, \end{cases}$$

where $c_1 = 1$, $c_2 = 3$, $c_3 = 5$, $c_4 = 7$, $c_5 = 9$, and $\tau = 1.5$. $I(a = a')$ denotes the indicator function:

$$I(a = a') = \begin{cases} 1 & \text{if } a = a', \\ 0 & \text{if } a \neq a'. \end{cases}$$

Sampling policies and evaluation policies are constructed as follows. First,

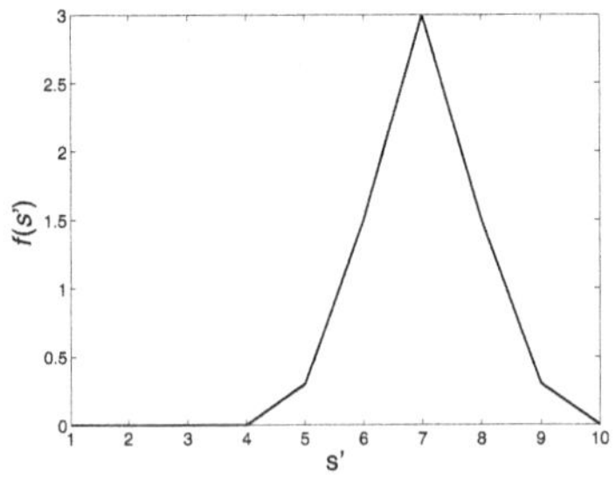

FIGURE 5.2: Profile of the function $f(s')$.

a deterministic "base" policy $\overline{\pi}$ is prepared. For example, "LLLLLRRRRR," where the i-th letter denotes the action taken at $s^{(i)}$. Let $\overline{\pi}^{\epsilon}$ be the "ϵ-greedy" version of the base policy $\overline{\pi}$, i.e., the intended action can be successfully chosen with probability $1-\epsilon/2$ and the other action is chosen with probability $\epsilon/2$. Experiments are performed for three different evaluation policies:

$$\overline{\pi}_1 : \text{“RRRRRRRRRR,”}$$
$$\overline{\pi}_2 : \text{“RRLLLLLRRR,”}$$
$$\overline{\pi}_3 : \text{“LLLLLRRRRR,”}$$

with $\epsilon = 0.1$. For each evaluation policy $\overline{\pi}_i^{0.1}$ $(i = 1, 2, 3)$, 10 candidates of the sampling policy $\{\widetilde{\pi}_i^{(k)}\}_{k=1}^{10}$ are prepared, where $\widetilde{\pi}_i^{(k)} = \overline{\pi}_i^{k/10}$. Note that $\widetilde{\pi}_i^{(1)}$ is equivalent to the evaluation policy $\overline{\pi}_i^{0.1}$.

For each sampling policy, the active learning criterion J is computed 5 times and their average is taken. The numbers of episodes and steps are set at $N = 10$ and $T = 10$, respectively. The initial-state probability $p(s)$ is set to be uniform. When the matrix inverse is computed, 10^{-3} is added to diagonal elements to avoid degeneracy. This experiment is repeated 100 times with different random seeds and the mean and standard deviation of the true generalization error and its estimate are evaluated.

The results are depicted in Figure 5.3 as functions of the index k of the sampling policies. The graphs show that the generalization error estimator overall captures the trend of the true generalization error well for all three cases.

Next, the values of the obtained generalization error G is evaluated when k is chosen so that J is minimized (active learning, AL), the evaluation policy $(k = 1)$ is used for sampling (passive learning, PL), and k is chosen optimally so that the true generalization error is minimized (optimal, OPT). Figure 5.4 shows that the active learning method compares favorably with passive learning and performs well for reducing the generalization error.

5.2 Active Policy Iteration

In Section 5.1, the unknown generalization error was shown to be accurately estimated without using immediate reward samples in one-step policy evaluation. In this section, this one-step active learning idea is extended to the framework of sample-reuse policy iteration introduced in Chapter 4, which is called *active policy iteration*. Let us denote the evaluation policy at the L-th iteration by π_L.

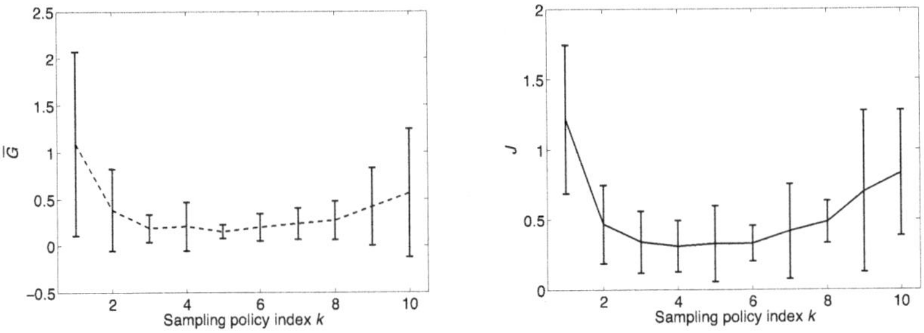

(a) $\overline{\pi}_1^{0.1}$

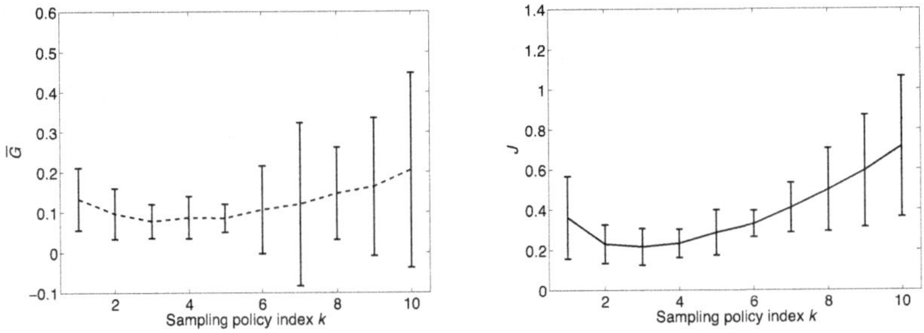

(b) $\overline{\pi}_2^{0.1}$

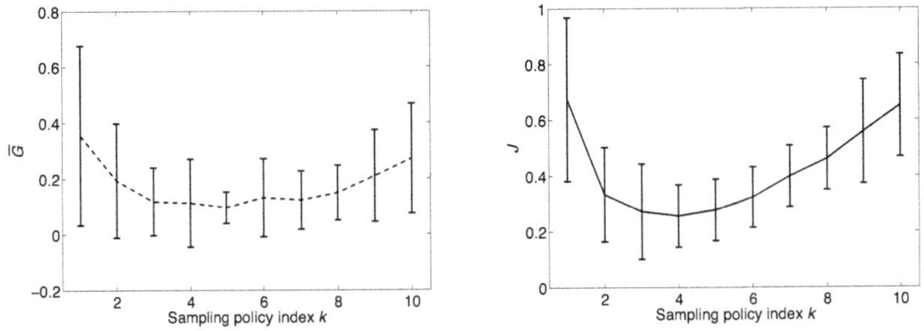

(c) $\overline{\pi}_3^{0.1}$

FIGURE 5.3: The mean and standard deviation of the true generalization error G (left) and the estimated generalization error J (right) over 100 trials.

5.2.1 Sample-Reuse Policy Iteration with Active Learning

In the original sample-reuse policy iteration, new data samples $\mathcal{H}^{\pi_l}$ are collected following the new target policy π_l for the next policy evaluation step:

$$\pi_1 \overset{\text{E}:\{\mathcal{H}^{\pi_1}\}}{\rightarrow} \widehat{Q}^{\pi_1} \overset{\text{I}}{\rightarrow} \pi_2 \overset{\text{E}:\{\mathcal{H}^{\pi_1},\mathcal{H}^{\pi_2}\}}{\rightarrow} \widehat{Q}^{\pi_2} \overset{\text{I}}{\rightarrow} \pi_3 \overset{\text{E}:\{\mathcal{H}^{\pi_1},\mathcal{H}^{\pi_2},\mathcal{H}^{\pi_3}\}}{\rightarrow} \cdots \overset{\text{I}}{\rightarrow} \pi_{L+1},$$

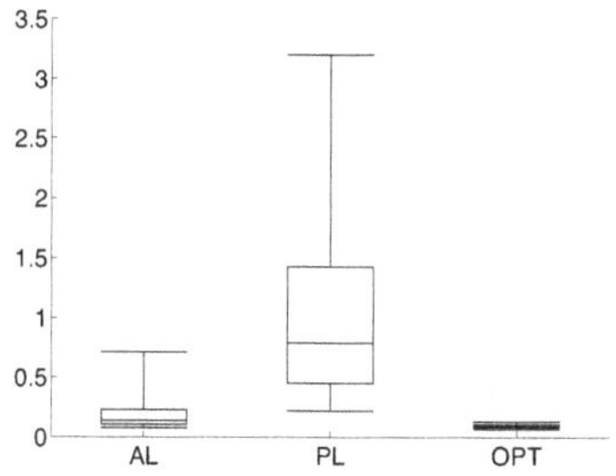

(a) $\overline{\pi}_1^{0.1}$

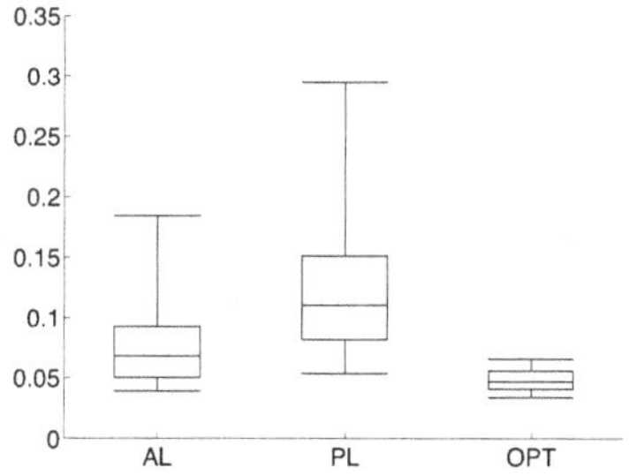

(b) $\overline{\pi}_2^{0.1}$

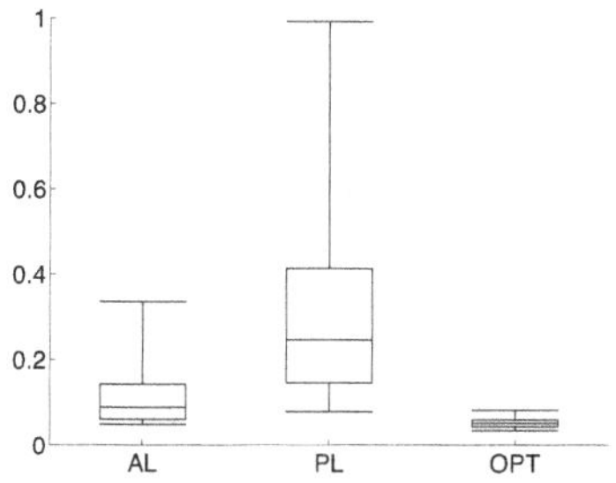

(c) $\overline{\pi}_3^{0.1}$

FIGURE 5.4: The box-plots of the values of the obtained generalization error G over 100 trials when k is chosen so that J is minimized (active learning, AL), the evaluation policy ($k = 1$) is used for sampling (passive learning, PL), and k is chosen optimally so that the true generalization error is minimized (optimal, OPT). The box-plot notation indicates the 5% quantile, 25% quantile, 50% quantile (i.e., median), 75% quantile, and 95% quantile from bottom to top.

where "E : $\{\mathcal{H}\}$" indicates policy evaluation using the data sample $\mathcal{H}$ and "I" denotes policy improvement. On the other hand, in active policy iteration, the optimized sampling policy $\widetilde{\pi}_l$ is used at each iteration:

$$\pi_1 \stackrel{\mathrm{E}:\{\mathcal{H}^{\widetilde{\pi}_1}\}}{\rightarrow} \widehat{Q}^{\pi_1} \stackrel{\mathrm{I}}{\rightarrow} \pi_2 \stackrel{\mathrm{E}:\{\mathcal{H}^{\widetilde{\pi}_1},\mathcal{H}^{\widetilde{\pi}_2}\}}{\rightarrow} \widehat{Q}^{\pi_2} \stackrel{\mathrm{I}}{\rightarrow} \pi_3 \stackrel{\mathrm{E}:\{\mathcal{H}^{\widetilde{\pi}_1},\mathcal{H}^{\widetilde{\pi}_2},\mathcal{H}^{\widetilde{\pi}_3}\}}{\rightarrow} \cdots \stackrel{\mathrm{I}}{\rightarrow} \pi_{L+1}.$$

Note that, in active policy iteration, the previously collected samples are used not only for value function approximation, but also for active learning. Thus, active policy iteration makes full use of the samples.

5.2.2 Illustration

Here, the behavior of active policy iteration is illustrated using the same 10-state chain-walk problem as Section 5.1.5 (see Figure 5.1).

The initial evaluation policy π_1 is set as

$$\pi_1(a|s) = 0.15p_{\mathrm{u}}(a) + 0.85I(a = \underset{a'}{\mathrm{argmax}}\, \widehat{Q}_0(s,a')),$$

where $p_{\mathrm{u}}(a)$ denotes the probability mass function of the uniform distribution and

$$\widehat{Q}_0(s,a) = \sum_{b=1}^{12} \phi_b(s,a).$$

Policies are updated in the l-th iteration using the ϵ-greedy rule with $\epsilon = 0.15/l$. In the sampling-policy selection step of the l-th iteration, the following four sampling-policy candidates are prepared:

$$\{\widetilde{\pi}_l^{(1)}, \widetilde{\pi}_l^{(2)}, \widetilde{\pi}_l^{(3)}, \widetilde{\pi}_l^{(4)}\} = \{\overline{\pi}_l^{0.15/l}, \overline{\pi}_l^{0.15/l+0.15}, \overline{\pi}_l^{0.15/l+0.5}, \overline{\pi}_l^{0.15/l+0.85}\},$$

where $\overline{\pi}_l$ denotes the policy obtained by greedy update using $\widehat{Q}^{\pi_{l-1}}$.

The number of iterations to learn the policy is set at 7, the number of steps is set at $T = 10$, and the number N of episodes is different in each iteration and defined as $\{N_1, \ldots, N_7\}$, where N_l $(l = 1, \ldots, 7)$ denotes the number of episodes collected in the l-th iteration. In this experiment, two types of scheduling are compared: $\{5,5,3,3,3,1,1\}$ and $\{3,3,3,3,3,3,3\}$, which are referred to as the "decreasing N" strategy and the "fixed N" strategy, respectively. The J-value calculation is repeated 5 times for active learning. The performance of the finally obtained policy π_8 is measured by the return for test samples $\{r_{t,n}^{\pi_8}\}_{t,n=1}^{T,N}$ (50 episodes with 50 steps collected following π_8):

$$\text{Performance} = \frac{1}{N}\sum_{n=1}^{N}\sum_{t=1}^{T}\gamma^{t-1} r_{t,n}^{\pi_8},$$

where the discount factor γ is set at 0.9.

The performance of passive learning (PL; the current policy is used as the sampling policy in each iteration) and active learning (AL; the best sampling policy is chosen from the policy candidates prepared in each iteration) is compared. The experiments are repeated 1000 times with different random seeds and the average performance of PL and AL is evaluated. The results are depicted in Figure 5.5, showing that AL works better than PL in both types of episode scheduling with statistical significance by the *t-test* at the significance level 1% (Henkel, 1976) for the error values obtained after the 7th iteration. Furthermore, the "decreasing N" strategy outperforms the "fixed N" strategy for both PL and AL, showing the usefulness of the "decreasing N" strategy.

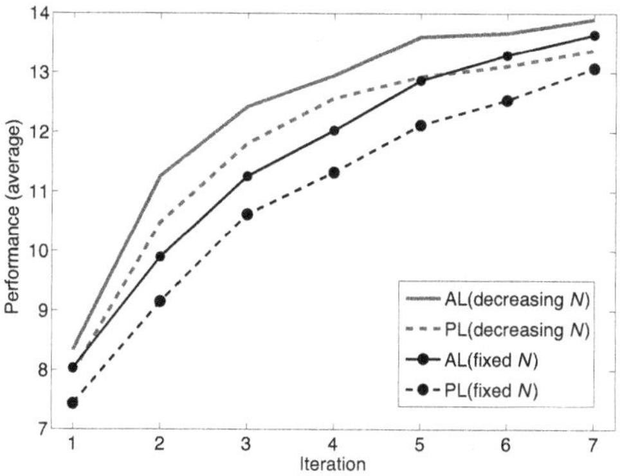

FIGURE 5.5: The mean performance over 1000 trials in the 10-state chain-walk experiment. The dotted lines denote the performance of passive learning (PL) and the solid lines denote the performance of the proposed active learning (AL) method. The error bars are omitted for clear visibility. For both the "decreasing N" and "fixed N" strategies, the performance of AL after the 7th iteration is significantly better than that of PL according to the t-test at the significance level 1% applied to the error values at the 7th iteration.

5.3 Numerical Examples

In this section, the performance of active policy iteration is evaluated using a ball-batting robot illustrated in Figure 5.6, which consists of two links and two joints. The goal of the ball-batting task is to control the robot arm so that it drives the ball as far away as possible. The state space $\mathcal{S}$ is continuous and consists of angles φ_1[rad] ($\in [0, \pi/4]$) and φ_2[rad] ($\in [-\pi/4, \pi/4]$) and angular velocities $\dot{\varphi}_1$[rad/s] and $\dot{\varphi}_2$[rad/s]. Thus, a state $\boldsymbol{s}$ ($\in \mathcal{S}$) is described by a 4-dimensional vector $\boldsymbol{s} = (\varphi_1, \dot{\varphi}_1, \varphi_2, \dot{\varphi}_2)^\top$. The action space $\mathcal{A}$ is discrete and contains two elements:

$$\mathcal{A} = \{a^{(i)}\}_{i=1}^{2} = \{(50, -35)^\top, (-50, 10)^\top\},$$

where the i-th element ($i = 1, 2$) of each vector corresponds to the torque [N · m] added to joint i.

The *open dynamics engine* (`http://ode.org/`) is used for physical calculations including the update of the angles and angular velocities, and collision detection between the robot arm, ball, and pin. The simulation time step is set at 7.5 [ms] and the next state is observed after 10 time steps. The action chosen in the current state is taken for 10 time steps. To make the experiments realistic, noise is added to actions: if action $(f_1, f_2)^\top$ is taken, the actual

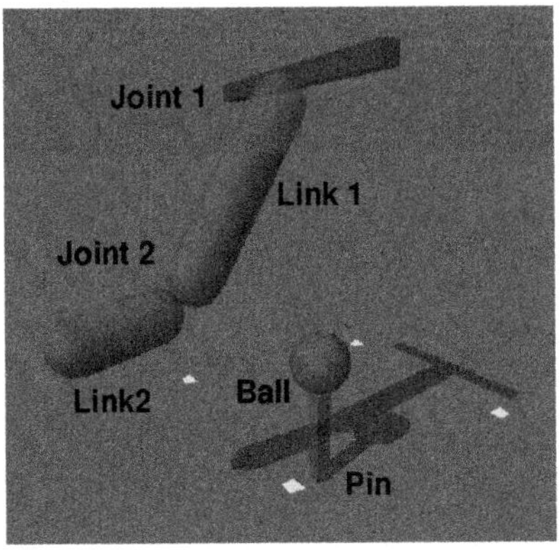

FIGURE 5.6: A ball-batting robot.

torques applied to the joints are $f_1+\varepsilon_1$ and $f_2+\varepsilon_2$, where ε_1 and ε_2 are drawn independently from the Gaussian distribution with mean 0 and variance 3.

The immediate reward is defined as the carry of the ball. This reward is given only when the robot arm collides with the ball for the first time at state $\boldsymbol{s}'$ after taking action a at current state $\boldsymbol{s}$. For value function approximation, the following 110 basis functions are used:

$$\phi_{2(i-1)+j} = \begin{cases} I(a = a^{(j)})\exp\left(-\dfrac{\| s - c_i \|^2}{2\tau^2}\right) & \\ \qquad\qquad\qquad\qquad \text{for } i = 1, \ldots, 54 \text{ and } j = 1, 2, \\ I(a = a^{(j)}) \quad \text{for } i = 55 \text{ and } j = 1, 2, \end{cases}$$

where τ is set at $3\pi/2$ and the Gaussian centers c_i $(i = 1, \ldots, 54)$ are located on the regular grid: $\{0, \pi/4\} \times \{-\pi, 0, \pi\} \times \{-\pi/4, 0, \pi/4\} \times \{-\pi, 0, \pi\}$.

For $L = 7$ and $T = 10$, the "decreasing N" strategy and the "fixed N" strategy are compared. The "decreasing N" strategy is defined by $\{10, 10, 7, 7, 7, 4, 4\}$ and the "fixed N" strategy is defined by $\{7, 7, 7, 7, 7, 7, 7\}$. The initial state is always set at $\boldsymbol{s} = (\pi/4, 0, 0, 0)^\top$, and J-calculations are repeated 5 times in the active learning method. The initial evaluation policy π_1 is set at the ϵ-greedy policy defined as

$$\pi_1(a|\boldsymbol{s}) = 0.15 p_{\mathrm{u}}(a) + 0.85 I\left(a = \underset{a'}{\mathrm{argmax}}\, \widehat{Q}_0(\boldsymbol{s}, a')\right),$$

$$\widehat{Q}_0(\boldsymbol{s}, a) = \sum_{b=1}^{110} \phi_b(\boldsymbol{s}, a).$$

Policies are updated in the l-th iteration using the ϵ-greedy rule with $\epsilon = 0.15/l$. Sampling-policy candidates are prepared in the same way as the chain-walk experiment in Section 5.2.2.

The discount factor γ is set at 1 and the performance of learned policy π_8

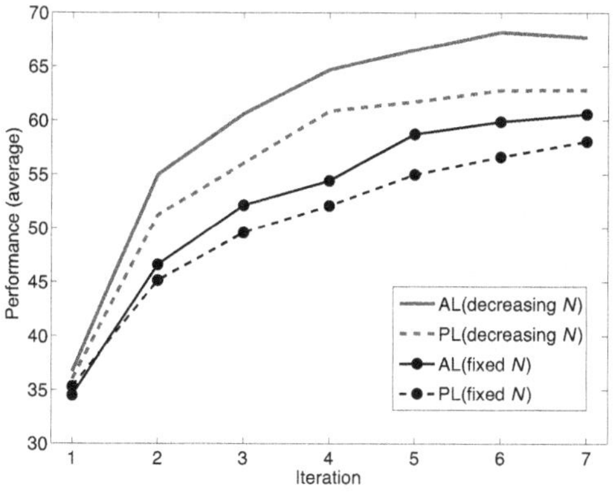

FIGURE 5.7: The mean performance over 500 trials in the ball-batting experiment. The dotted lines denote the performance of passive learning (PL) and the solid lines denote the performance of the proposed active learning (AL) method. The error bars are omitted for clear visibility. For the "decreasing N" strategy, the performance of AL after the 7th iteration is significantly better than that of PL according to the t-test at the significance level 1% for the error values at the 7th iteration.

is measured by the return for test samples $\{r_{t,n}^{\pi_8}\}_{t,n=1}^{10,20}$ (20 episodes with 10 steps collected following π_8): $\sum_{n=1}^{N}\sum_{t=1}^{T} r_{t,n}^{\pi_8}$.

The experiment is repeated 500 times with different random seeds and the average performance of each learning method is evaluated. The results, depicted in Figure 5.7, show that active learning outperforms passive learning. For the "decreasing N" strategy, the performance difference is statistically significant by the t-test at the significance level 1% for the error values after the 7th iteration.

Motion examples of the ball-batting robot trained with active learning and passive learning are illustrated in Figure 5.8 and Figure 5.9, respectively.

5.4 Remarks

When we cannot afford to collect many training samples due to high sampling costs, it is crucial to choose the most informative samples for efficiently learning the value function. In this chapter, an active learning method for optimizing data sampling strategies was introduced in the framework of sample-reuse policy iteration, and the resulting active policy iteration was demonstrated to be promising.

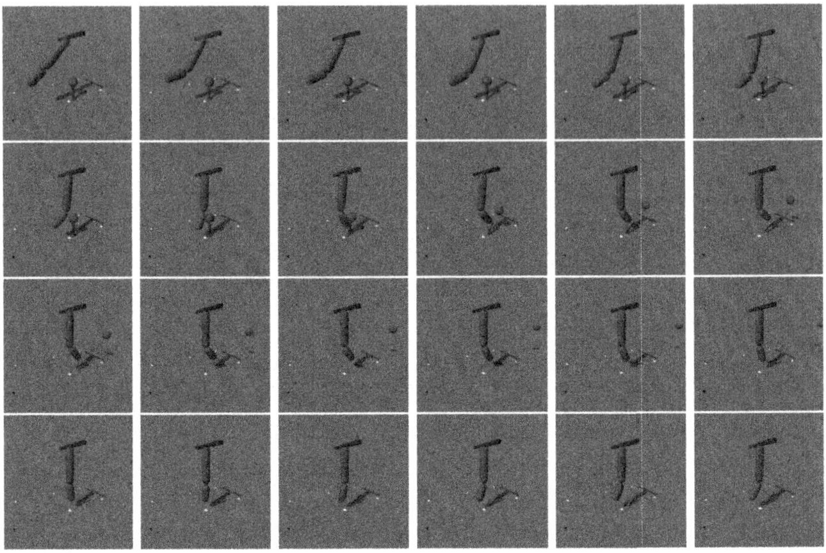

FIGURE 5.8: A motion example of the ball-batting robot trained with active learning (from left to right and top to bottom).

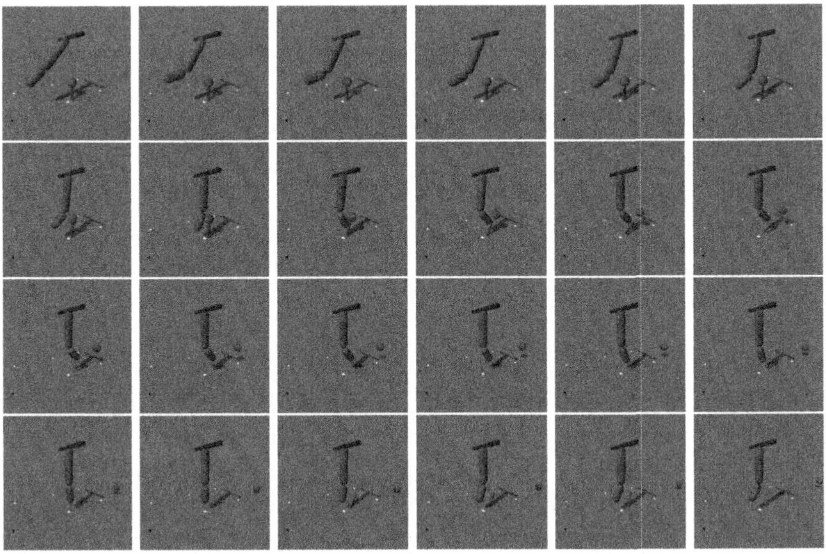

FIGURE 5.9: A motion example of the ball-batting robot trained with passive learning (from left to right and top to bottom).

Chapter 6

Robust Policy Iteration

The framework of least-squares policy iteration (LSPI) introduced in Chapter 2 is useful, thanks to its computational efficiency and analytical tractability. However, due to the squared loss, it tends to be sensitive to *outliers* in observed rewards. In this chapter, we introduce an alternative policy iteration method that employs the *absolute loss* for enhancing robustness and reliability. In Section 6.1, robustness and reliability brought by the use of the absolute loss is discussed. In Section 6.2, the policy iteration framework with the absolute loss called *least-absolute policy iteration* (LAPI) is introduced. In Section 6.3, the usefulness of LAPI is illustrated through experiments. Variations of LAPI are considered in Section 6.4, and finally this chapter is concluded in Section 6.5.

6.1 Robustness and Reliability in Policy Iteration

The basic idea of LSPI is to fit a linear model to immediate rewards under the squared loss, while the *absolute loss* is used in this chapter (see Figure 6.1). This is just replacement of loss functions, but this modification highly enhances *robustness* and *reliability*.

6.1.1 Robustness

In many robotics applications, immediate rewards are obtained through measurement such as distance sensors or computer vision. Due to intrinsic measurement noise or recognition error, the obtained rewards often deviate from the true value. In particular, the rewards occasionally contain *outliers*, which are significantly different from regular values.

Residual minimization under the squared loss amounts to obtaining the *mean* of samples $\{x_i\}_{i=1}^{m}$:

$$\underset{c}{\mathrm{argmin}}\left[\sum_{i=1}^{m}(x_i - c)^2\right] = \mathrm{mean}(\{x_i\}_{i=1}^{m}) = \frac{1}{m}\sum_{i=1}^{m} x_i.$$

If one of the values is an outlier having a very large or small value, the mean

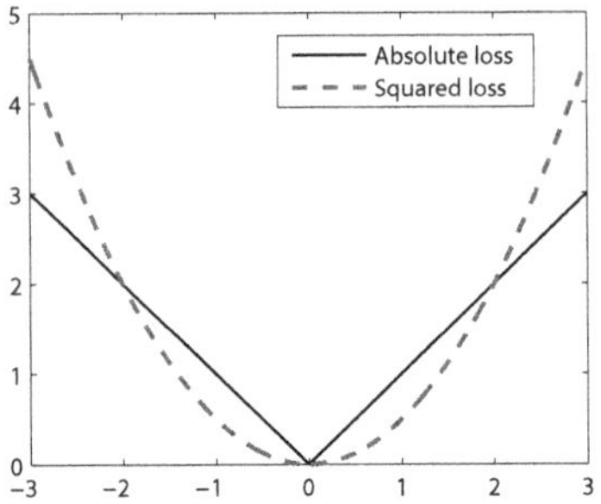

FIGURE 6.1: The absolute and squared loss functions for reducing the temporal-difference error.

would be strongly affected by this outlier. This means that *all* the values $\{x_i\}_{i=1}^m$ are responsible for the mean, and therefore even a *single* outlier observation can significantly damage the learned result.

On the other hand, residual minimization under the absolute loss amounts to obtaining the *median*:

$$\operatorname*{argmin}_c \left[\sum_{i=1}^{2n+1} |x_i - c| \right] = \mathrm{median}(\{x_i\}_{i=1}^{2n+1}) = x_{n+1},$$

where $x_1 \leq x_2 \leq \cdots \leq x_{2n+1}$. The median is influenced not by the *magnitude* of the values $\{x_i\}_{i=1}^{2n+1}$ but only by their *order*. Thus, as long as the order is kept unchanged, the median is not affected by outliers. In fact, the median is known to be the most robust estimator in light of *breakdown-point analysis* (Huber, 1981; Rousseeuw & Leroy, 1987).

Therefore, the use of the absolute loss would remedy the problem of robustness in policy iteration.

6.1.2 Reliability

In practical robot-control tasks, we often want to attain a stable performance, rather than to achieve a "dream" performance with little chance of success. For example, in the acquisition of a humanoid gait, we may want the robot to walk forward in a stable manner with high probability of success, rather than to rush very fast in a chance level.

On the other hand, we do not want to be too conservative when training robots. If we are overly concerned with unrealistic failure, no practically useful control policy can be obtained. For example, any robots can be broken in principle if they are activated for a long time. However, if we fear this fact too much, we may end up in praising a control policy that does not move the robots at all, which is obviously nonsense.

Since the squared-loss solution is not robust against outliers, it is sensitive to rare events with either positive or negative very large immediate rewards.

Consequently, the squared loss prefers an extraordinarily successful motion even if the success probability is very low. Similarly, it dislikes an unrealistic trouble even if such a terrible event may not happen in reality. On the other hand, the absolute loss solution is not easily affected by such rare events due to its robustness. Therefore, the use of the absolute loss would produce a reliable control policy even in the presence of such extreme events.

6.2 Least Absolute Policy Iteration

In this section, a policy iteration method with the absolute loss is introduced.

6.2.1 Algorithm

Instead of the squared loss, a linear model is fitted to immediate rewards under the absolute loss as

$$\min_{\boldsymbol{\theta}} \left[\sum_{t=1}^{T} \left| \boldsymbol{\theta}^\top \widehat{\boldsymbol{\psi}}(\boldsymbol{s}_t, a_t) - r_t \right| \right].$$

This minimization problem looks cumbersome due to the absolute value operator which is non-differentiable, but this minimization problem can be reduced to the following linear program (Boyd & Vandenberghe, 2004):

$$\begin{cases} \min\limits_{\boldsymbol{\theta}, \{b_t\}_{t=1}^T} & \sum\limits_{t=1}^{T} b_t \\ \text{subject to} & -b_t \leq \boldsymbol{\theta}^\top \widehat{\boldsymbol{\psi}}(\boldsymbol{s}_t, a_t) - r_t \leq b_t, \ t = 1, \ldots, T. \end{cases}$$

The number of constraints is T in the above linear program. When T is large, we may employ sophisticated optimization techniques such as *column generation* (Demiriz et al., 2002) for efficiently solving the linear programming problem. Alternatively, an approximate solution can be obtained by gradient descent or the (quasi)-Newton methods if the absolute loss is approximated by a smooth loss (see, e.g., Section 6.4.1).

The policy iteration method based on the absolute loss is called *least absolute policy iteration* (LAPI).

6.2.2 Illustration

For illustration purposes, let us consider the 4-state MDP problem described in Figure 6.2. The agent is initially located at state $s^{(0)}$ and the actions

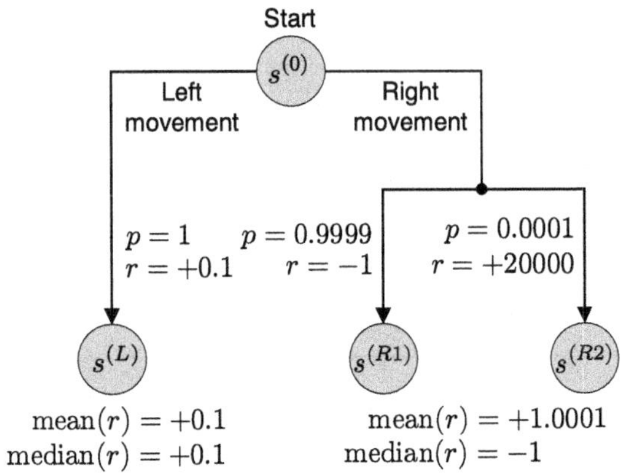

FIGURE 6.2: Illustrative MDP problem.

the agent is allowed to take are moving to the left or right state. If the left movement action is chosen, the agent always receives small positive reward $+0.1$ at $s^{(L)}$. On the other hand, if the right movement action is chosen, the agent receives negative reward -1 with probability 0.9999 at $s^{(R1)}$ or it receives very large positive reward $+20,000$ with probability 0.0001 at $s^{(R2)}$. The mean and median rewards for left movement are both $+0.1$, while the mean and median rewards for right movement are $+1.0001$ and -1, respectively.

If $Q(s^{(0)}, \text{"Left"})$ and $Q(s^{(0)}, \text{"Right"})$ are approximated by the least-squares method, it returns the mean rewards, i.e., $+0.1$ and $+1.0001$, respectively. Thus, the least-squares method prefers right movement, which is a "gambling" policy that negative reward -1 is almost always obtained at $s^{(R1)}$, but it is possible to obtain very high reward $+20,000$ with a very small probability at $s^{(R2)}$. On the other hand, if $Q(s^{(0)}, \text{"Left"})$ and $Q(s^{(0)}, \text{"Right"})$ are approximated by the least absolute method, it returns the median rewards, i.e., $+0.1$ and -1, respectively. Thus, the least absolute method prefers left movement, which is a stable policy that the agent can always receive small positive reward $+0.1$ at $s^{(L)}$.

If all the rewards in Figure 6.2 are negated, the value functions are also negated and a different interpretation can be obtained: the least-squares method is afraid of the risk of receiving very large negative reward $-20,000$ at $s^{(R2)}$ with a very low probability, and consequently it ends up in a very conservative policy that the agent always receives negative reward -0.1 at $s^{(L)}$. On the other hand, the least absolute method tries to receive positive reward $+1$ at $s^{(R1)}$ without being afraid of visiting $s^{(R2)}$ too much.

As illustrated above, the least absolute method tends to provide qualitatively different solutions from the least-squares method.

6.2.3 Properties

Here, properties of the least absolute method are investigated when the model $\widehat{Q}(\boldsymbol{s}, a)$ is *correctly specified*, i.e., there exists a parameter $\boldsymbol{\theta}^*$ such that

$$\widehat{Q}(\boldsymbol{s}, a) = Q(\boldsymbol{s}, a) \quad \text{for all } \boldsymbol{s} \text{ and } a.$$

Under the correct model assumption, when the number of samples T tends to infinity, the least absolute solution $\widehat{\boldsymbol{\theta}}$ would satisfy the following equation (Koenker, 2005):

$$\widehat{\boldsymbol{\theta}}^\top \boldsymbol{\psi}(\boldsymbol{s}, a) = \mathbb{M}_{p(\boldsymbol{s}'|\boldsymbol{s},a)} \left[r(\boldsymbol{s}, a, \boldsymbol{s}') \right] \quad \text{for all } \boldsymbol{s} \text{ and } a, \tag{6.1}$$

where $\mathbb{M}_{p(\boldsymbol{s}'|\boldsymbol{s},a)}$ denotes the conditional median of $\boldsymbol{s}'$ over $p(\boldsymbol{s}'|\boldsymbol{s}, a)$ given $\boldsymbol{s}$ and a. $\boldsymbol{\psi}(\boldsymbol{s}, a)$ is defined by

$$\boldsymbol{\psi}(\boldsymbol{s}, a) = \boldsymbol{\phi}(\boldsymbol{s}, a) - \gamma \mathbb{E}_{p(\boldsymbol{s}'|\boldsymbol{s},a)} \mathbb{E}_{\pi(a'|\boldsymbol{s}')} \left[\boldsymbol{\phi}(\boldsymbol{s}', a') \right],$$

where $\mathbb{E}_{p(\boldsymbol{s}'|\boldsymbol{s},a)}$ denotes the conditional expectation of $\boldsymbol{s}'$ over $p(\boldsymbol{s}'|\boldsymbol{s}, a)$ given $\boldsymbol{s}$ and a, and $\mathbb{E}_{\pi(a'|\boldsymbol{s}')}$ denotes the conditional expectation of a' over $\pi(a'|\boldsymbol{s}')$ given $\boldsymbol{s}'$.

From Eq. (6.1), we can obtain the following Bellman-like recursive expression:

$$\widehat{Q}(\boldsymbol{s}, a) = \mathbb{M}_{p(\boldsymbol{s}'|\boldsymbol{s},a)} \left[r(\boldsymbol{s}, a, \boldsymbol{s}') \right] + \gamma \mathbb{E}_{p(\boldsymbol{s}'|\boldsymbol{s},a)} \mathbb{E}_{\pi(a'|\boldsymbol{s}')} \left[\widehat{Q}(\boldsymbol{s}', a') \right]. \tag{6.2}$$

Note that in the case of the least-squares method where

$$\widehat{\boldsymbol{\theta}}^\top \boldsymbol{\psi}(\boldsymbol{s}, a) = \mathbb{E}_{p(\boldsymbol{s}'|\boldsymbol{s},a)} \left[r(\boldsymbol{s}, a, \boldsymbol{s}') \right]$$

is satisfied in the limit under the correct model assumption, we have

$$\widehat{Q}(\boldsymbol{s}, a) = \mathbb{E}_{p(\boldsymbol{s}'|\boldsymbol{s},a)} \left[r(\boldsymbol{s}, a, \boldsymbol{s}') \right] + \gamma \mathbb{E}_{p(\boldsymbol{s}'|\boldsymbol{s},a)} \mathbb{E}_{\pi(a'|\boldsymbol{s}')} \left[\widehat{Q}(\boldsymbol{s}', a') \right]. \tag{6.3}$$

This is the ordinary *Bellman equation*, and thus Eq. (6.2) could be regarded as an extension of the Bellman equation to the absolute loss.

From the ordinary Bellman equation (6.3), we can recover the original definition of the state-value function $Q(\boldsymbol{s}, a)$:

$$Q^\pi(\boldsymbol{s}, a) = \mathbb{E}_{p^\pi(h)} \left[\sum_{t=1}^{T} \gamma^{t-1} r(\boldsymbol{s}_t, a_t, \boldsymbol{s}_{t+1}), \middle| \boldsymbol{s}_1 = \boldsymbol{s}, a_1 = a \right],$$

where $\mathbb{E}_{p^\pi(h)}$ denotes the expectation over trajectory $h = [\boldsymbol{s}_1, a_1, \ldots, \boldsymbol{s}_T, a_T, \boldsymbol{s}_{T+1}]$ and "$|\boldsymbol{s}_1 = \boldsymbol{s}, a_1 = a$" means that the initial state $\boldsymbol{s}_1$ and the first action a_1 are fixed at $\boldsymbol{s}_1 = \boldsymbol{s}$ and $a_1 = a$, respectively. In contrast, from the absolute-loss Bellman equation (6.2), we have

$$Q'(\boldsymbol{s}, a) = \mathbb{E}_{p^\pi(h)} \left[\sum_{t=1}^{T} \gamma^{t-1} \mathbb{M}_{p(\boldsymbol{s}_{t+1}|\boldsymbol{s}_t,a_t)} \left[r(\boldsymbol{s}_t, a_t, \boldsymbol{s}_{t+1}) \right] \middle| \boldsymbol{s}_1 = \boldsymbol{s}, a_1 = a \right].$$

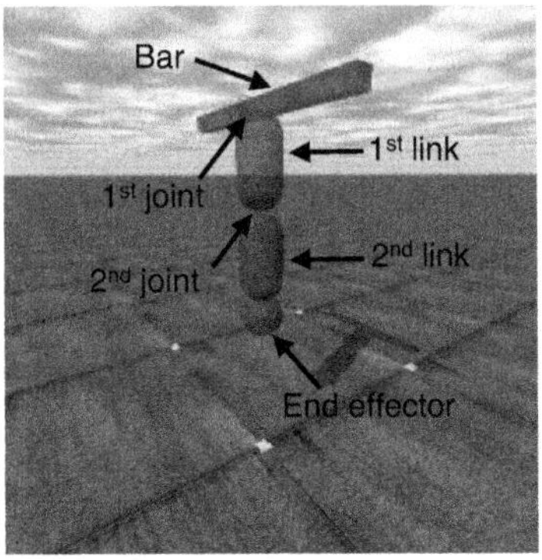

FIGURE 6.3: Illustration of the acrobot. The goal is to swing up the end effector by only controlling the second joint.

This is the value function that the least absolute method is trying to approximate, which is different from the ordinary value function. Since the discounted sum of *median* rewards — not the expected rewards — is maximized, the least absolute method is expected to be less sensitive to outliers than the least-squares method.

6.3 Numerical Examples

In this section, the behavior of LAPI is illustrated through experiments using the *acrobot* shown in Figure 6.3. The acrobot is an under-actuated system and consists of two links, two joints, and an end effector. The length of each link is 0.3 [m], and the diameter of each joint is 0.15 [m]. The diameter of the end effector is 0.10 [m], and the height of the horizontal bar is 1.2 [m]. The first joint connects the first link to the horizontal bar and is *not* controllable. The second joint connects the first link to the second link and is controllable. The end effector is attached to the tip of the second link. The control command (action) we can choose is to apply positive torque +50 [N · m], no torque 0 [N · m], or negative torque −50 [N · m] to the second joint. Note that the acrobot moves only within a plane orthogonal to the horizontal bar.

The goal is to acquire a control policy such that the end effector is swung up as high as possible. The state space consists of the angle θ_i [rad] and angular velocity $\dot{\theta}_i$ [rad/s] of the first and second joints ($i = 1, 2$). The immediate reward is given according to the height y of the center of the end effector as

$$r(\boldsymbol{s}, a, \boldsymbol{s}') = \begin{cases} 10 & \text{if } y > 1.75, \\ \exp\left(-\frac{(y-1.85)^2}{2(0.2)^2}\right) & \text{if } 1.5 < y \leq 1.75, \\ 0.001 & \text{otherwise.} \end{cases}$$

Note that $0.55 \leq y \leq 1.85$ in the current setting.

Here, suppose that the length of the links is unknown. Thus, the height y cannot be directly computed from state information. The height of the end effector is supposed to be estimated from an image taken by a camera — the end effector is detected in the image and then its vertical coordinate is computed. Due to recognition error, the estimated height is highly noisy and could contain outliers.

In each policy iteration step, 20 episodic training samples of length 150 are gathered. The performance of the obtained policy is evaluated using 50 episodic test samples of length 300. Note that the test samples are not used for learning policies. They are used only for evaluating learned policies. The policies are updated in a *soft-max* manner:

$$\pi(a|\boldsymbol{s}) \longleftarrow \frac{\exp(Q(\boldsymbol{s}, a)/\eta)}{\sum_{a' \in \mathcal{A}} \exp(Q(\boldsymbol{s}, a')/\eta)},$$

where $\eta = 10 - l + 1$ with l being the iteration number. The discounted factor is set at $\gamma = 1$, i.e., no discount. As basis functions for value function approximation, the Gaussian kernel with standard deviation π is used, where Gaussian centers are located at

$$(\theta_1, \theta_2, \dot{\theta}_1, \dot{\theta}_2) \in \{-\pi, -\tfrac{\pi}{2}, 0, \tfrac{\pi}{2}, \pi\} \times \{-\pi, 0, \pi\} \times \{-\pi, 0, \pi\} \times \{-\pi, 0, \pi\}.$$

The above 135 ($= 5 \times 3 \times 3 \times 3$) Gaussian kernels are defined for each of the three actions. Thus, 405 ($= 135 \times 3$) kernels are used in total.

Let us consider two noise environments: one is the case where no noise is added to the rewards and the other case is where Laplacian noise with mean zero and standard deviation 2 is added to the rewards with probability 0.1. Note that the tail of the Laplacian density is heavier than that of the Gaussian density (see Figure 6.4), implying that a small number of outliers tend to be included in the Laplacian noise environment. An example of the noisy training samples is shown in Figure 6.5. For each noise environment, the experiment is repeated 50 times with different random seeds and the averages of the sum of rewards obtained by LAPI and LSPI are summarized in Figure 6.6. The best method in terms of the mean value and comparable methods according to the *t-test* (Henkel, 1976) at the significance level 5% is specified by "∘."

In the noiseless case (see Figure 6.6(a)), both LAPI and LSPI improve the performance over iterations in a comparable way. On the other hand, in the noisy case (see Figure 6.6(b)), the performance of LSPI is not improved much due to outliers, while LAPI still produces a good control policy.

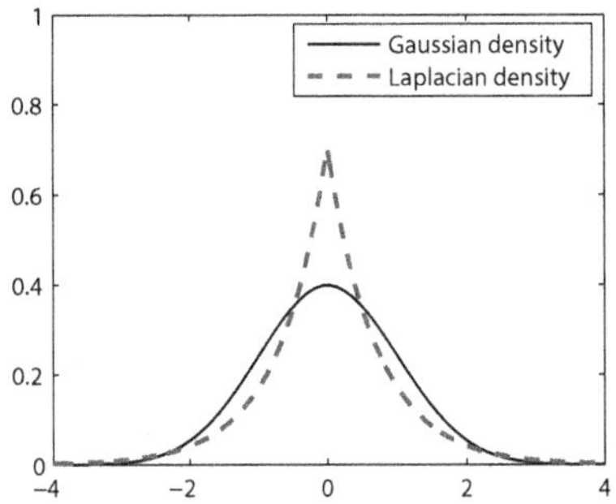

FIGURE 6.4: Probability density functions of Gaussian and Laplacian distributions.

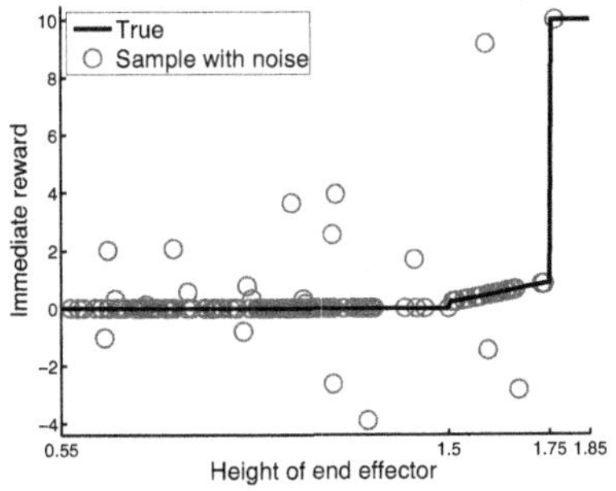

FIGURE 6.5: Example of training samples with Laplacian noise. The horizontal axis is the height of the end effector. The solid line denotes the noiseless immediate reward and "o" denotes a noisy training sample.

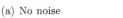

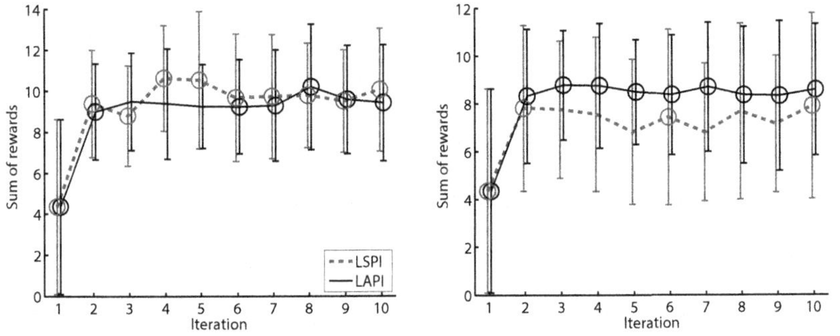

(a) No noise

(b) Laplacian noise

FIGURE 6.6: Average and standard deviation of the sum of rewards over 50 runs for the acrobot swinging-up simulation. The best method in terms of the mean value and comparable methods according to the *t-test* at the significance level 5% specified by "o."

Figure 6.7 and Figure 6.8 depict motion examples of the acrobot learned by LAPI and LSPI in the Laplacian-noise environment. When LSPI is used (Figure 6.7), the second joint is swung hard in order to lift the end effector. However, the end effector tends to stay below the horizontal bar, and therefore only a small amount of reward can be obtained by LSPI. This would be due to the existence of outliers. On the other hand, when LAPI is used (Figure 6.8), the end effector goes beyond the bar, and therefore a large amount of reward can be obtained even in the presence of outliers.

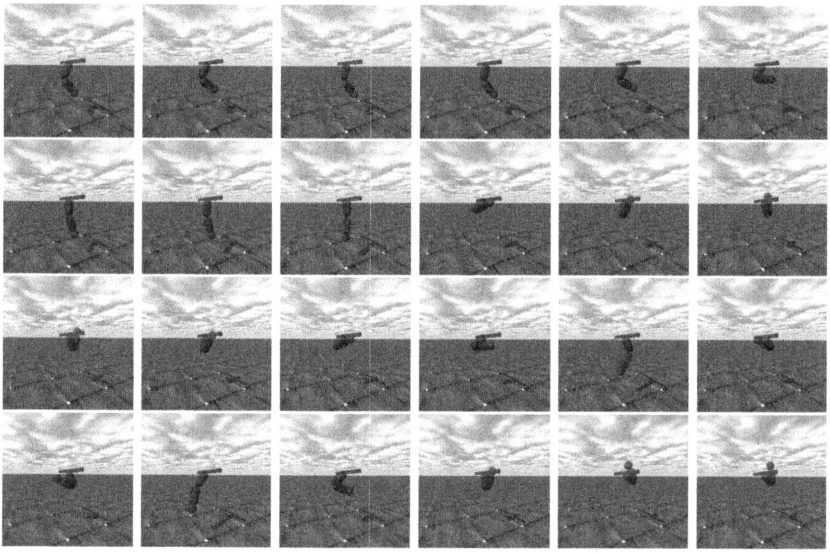

FIGURE 6.7: A motion example of the acrobot learned by LSPI in the Laplacian-noise environment (from left to right and top to bottom).

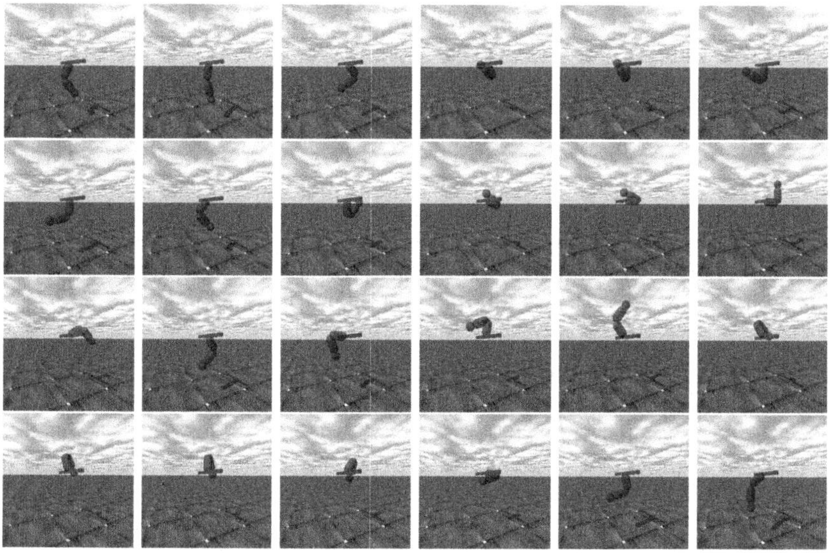

FIGURE 6.8: A motion example of the acrobot learned by LAPI in the Laplacian-noise environment (from left to right and top to bottom).

6.4 Possible Extensions

In this section, possible variations of LAPI are considered.

6.4.1 Huber Loss

Use of the *Huber loss* corresponds to making a compromise between the squared and absolute loss functions (Huber, 1981):

$$\underset{\boldsymbol{\theta}}{\operatorname{argmin}} \left[\sum_{t=1}^{T} \rho_{\kappa}^{\mathrm{HB}} \left(\boldsymbol{\theta}^{\top} \widehat{\boldsymbol{\psi}}(s_t, a_t) - r_t \right) \right],$$

where κ (≥ 0) is a threshold parameter and $\rho_{\kappa}^{\mathrm{HB}}$ is the Huber loss defined as follows (see Figure 6.9):

$$\rho_{\kappa}^{\mathrm{HB}}(x) = \begin{cases} \frac{1}{2}x^2 & \text{if } |x| \leq \kappa, \\ \kappa|x| - \frac{1}{2}\kappa^2 & \text{if } |x| > \kappa. \end{cases}$$

The Huber loss converges to the absolute loss as κ tends to zero, and it converges to the squared loss as κ tends to infinity.

The Huber loss function is rather intricate, but the solution can be obtained by solving the following convex quadratic program (Mangasarian & Musicant, 2000):

$$\begin{cases} \underset{\boldsymbol{\theta}, \{b_t, c_t\}_{t=1}^{T}}{\min} & \frac{1}{2}\sum_{t=1}^{T} b_t^2 + \kappa \sum_{t=1}^{T} c_t \\ \text{subject to} & -c_t \leq \boldsymbol{\theta}^{\top} \widehat{\boldsymbol{\psi}}(\boldsymbol{s}_t, a_t) - r_t - b_t \leq c_t, \; t = 1, \ldots, T. \end{cases}$$

Another way to obtain the solution is to use a *gradient descent method*, where the parameter $\boldsymbol{\theta}$ is updated as follows until convergence:

$$\boldsymbol{\theta} \leftarrow \boldsymbol{\theta} - \varepsilon \sum_{t=1}^{T} \Delta\rho_{\kappa}^{\mathrm{HB}}(\boldsymbol{\theta}^{\top} \widehat{\boldsymbol{\psi}}(\boldsymbol{s}_t, a_t) - r_t) \widehat{\boldsymbol{\psi}}(\boldsymbol{s}_t, a_t).$$

ε (> 0) is the learning rate and $\Delta\rho_{\kappa}^{\mathrm{HB}}$ is the derivative of $\rho_{\kappa}^{\mathrm{HB}}$ given by

$$\Delta\rho_{\kappa}^{\mathrm{HB}}(x) = \begin{cases} x & \text{if } |x| \leq \kappa, \\ \kappa & \text{if } x > \kappa, \\ -\kappa & \text{if } x < -\kappa. \end{cases}$$

In practice, the following *stochastic gradient method* (Amari, 1967) would be

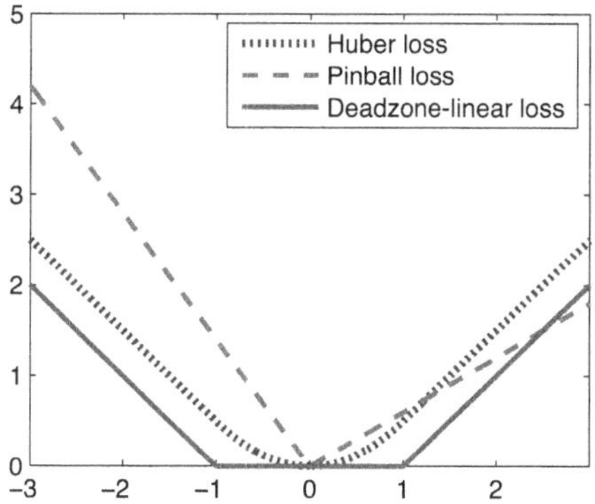

FIGURE 6.9: The Huber loss function (with $\kappa = 1$), the pinball loss function (with $\tau = 0.3$), and the deadzone-linear loss function (with $\epsilon = 1$).

more convenient. For a randomly chosen index $t \in \{1, \ldots, T\}$ in each iteration, repeat the following update until convergence:

$$\boldsymbol{\theta} \leftarrow \boldsymbol{\theta} - \varepsilon \Delta \rho_{\kappa}^{\mathrm{HB}}(\boldsymbol{\theta}^\top \widehat{\boldsymbol{\psi}}(\boldsymbol{s}_t, a_t) - r_t)\widehat{\boldsymbol{\psi}}(\boldsymbol{s}_t, a_t).$$

The plain/stochastic gradient methods also come in handy when approximating the least absolute solution, since the Huber loss function with small κ can be regarded as a smooth approximation to the absolute loss.

6.4.2 Pinball Loss

The absolute loss induces the median, which corresponds to the 50-percentile point. A similar discussion is also possible for an arbitrary percentile 100τ $(0 \le \tau \le 1)$ based on the *pinball* loss (Koenker, 2005):

$$\min_{\boldsymbol{\theta}} \left[\sum_{t=1}^{T} \rho_{\tau}^{\mathrm{PB}}(\boldsymbol{\theta}^\top \widehat{\boldsymbol{\psi}}(\boldsymbol{s}_t, a_t) - r_t) \right],$$

where $\rho_{\tau}^{\mathrm{PB}}(x)$ is the pinball loss defined by

$$\rho_{\tau}^{\mathrm{PB}}(x) = \begin{cases} 2\tau x & \text{if } x \ge 0, \\ 2(\tau - 1)x & \text{if } x < 0. \end{cases}$$

The profile of the pinball loss is depicted in Figure 6.9. When $\tau = 0.5$, the pinball loss is reduced to the absolute loss.

The solution can be obtained by solving the following linear program:

$$\begin{cases} \min\limits_{\boldsymbol{\theta}, \{b_t\}_{t=1}^{T}} & \sum\limits_{t=1}^{T} b_t \\ \text{subject to} & \dfrac{b_t}{2(\tau - 1)} \le \boldsymbol{\theta}^\top \widehat{\boldsymbol{\psi}}(\boldsymbol{s}_t, a_t) - r_t \le \dfrac{b_t}{2\tau}, \; t = 1, \ldots, T. \end{cases}$$

6.4.3 Deadzone-Linear Loss

Another variant of the absolute loss is the *deadzone-linear loss* (see Figure 6.9):

$$\min_{\boldsymbol{\theta}} \left[\sum_{t=1}^{T} \rho_{\epsilon}^{\mathrm{DL}}(\boldsymbol{\theta}^\top \widehat{\boldsymbol{\psi}}(\boldsymbol{s}_t, a_t) - r_t) \right],$$

where $\rho_{\epsilon}^{\mathrm{DL}}(x)$ is the deadzone-linear loss defined by

$$\rho_{\epsilon}^{\mathrm{DL}}(x) = \begin{cases} 0 & \text{if } |x| \le \epsilon, \\ |x| - \epsilon & \text{if } |x| > \epsilon. \end{cases}$$

That is, if the magnitude of the error is less than ϵ, no error is assessed. This loss is also called the *ϵ-insensitive loss* and used in *support vector regression* (Vapnik, 1998).

When $\epsilon = 0$, the deadzone-linear loss is reduced to the absolute loss. Thus, the deadzone-linear loss and the absolute loss are related to each other. However, the effect of the deadzone-linear loss is completely opposite to the absolute loss when $\epsilon > 0$. The influence of "good" samples (with small error) is deemphasized in the deadzone-linear loss, while the absolute loss tends to suppress the influence of "bad" samples (with large error) compared with the squared loss.

The solution can be obtained by solving the following linear program (Boyd & Vandenberghe, 2004):

$$\begin{cases} \displaystyle\min_{\boldsymbol{\theta}, \{b_t\}_{t=1}^{T}} & \displaystyle\sum_{t=1}^{T} b_t \\ \text{subject to} & -b_t - \epsilon \le \boldsymbol{\theta}^\top \widehat{\boldsymbol{\psi}}(\boldsymbol{s}_t, a_t) - r_t \le b_t + \epsilon, \\ & b_t \ge 0, \ t = 1, \ldots, T. \end{cases}$$

6.4.4 Chebyshev Approximation

The *Chebyshev approximation* minimizes the error for the "worst" sample:

$$\min_{\boldsymbol{\theta}} \left[\max_{t=1,\ldots,T} |\boldsymbol{\theta}^\top \widehat{\boldsymbol{\psi}}(\boldsymbol{s}_t, a_t) - r_t| \right].$$

This is also called the *minimax approximation*.

The solution can be obtained by solving the following linear program (Boyd & Vandenberghe, 2004):

$$\begin{cases} \displaystyle\min_{\boldsymbol{\theta}, b} & b \\ \text{subject to} & -b \le \boldsymbol{\theta}^\top \widehat{\boldsymbol{\psi}}(\boldsymbol{s}_t, a_t) - r_t \le b, \ t = 1, \ldots, T. \end{cases}$$

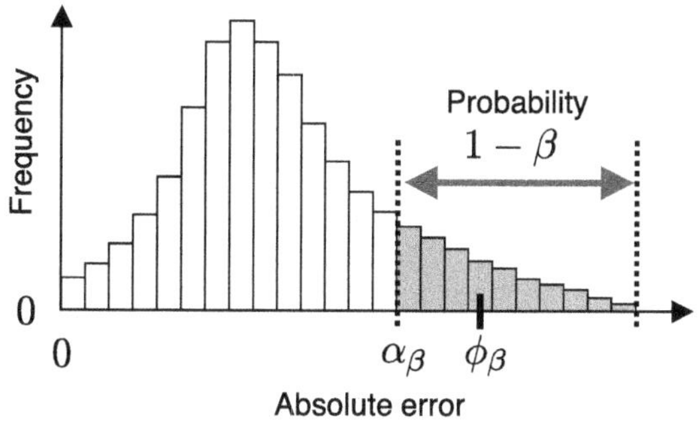

FIGURE 6.10: The conditional value-at-risk (CVaR).

6.4.5 Conditional Value-At-Risk

In the area of finance, the *conditional value-at-risk* (CVaR) is a popular risk measure (Rockafellar & Uryasev, 2002). The CVaR corresponds to the mean of the error for a set of "bad" samples (see Figure 6.10).

More specifically, let us consider the distribution of the absolute error over all training samples $\{(\boldsymbol{s}_t, a_t, r_t)\}_{t=1}^T$:

$$\Phi(\alpha|\boldsymbol{\theta}) = P\{(\boldsymbol{s}_t, a_t, r_t) \ : \ |\boldsymbol{\theta}^\top \widehat{\boldsymbol{\psi}}(\boldsymbol{s}_t, a_t) - r_t| \leq \alpha\}.$$

For $\beta \in [0, 1)$, let $\alpha_\beta(\boldsymbol{\theta})$ be the 100β percentile of the absolute error distribution:

$$\alpha_\beta(\boldsymbol{\theta}) = \min\{\alpha \mid \Phi(\alpha|\boldsymbol{\theta}) \geq \beta\}.$$

Thus, only the fraction $(1-\beta)$ of the absolute error $|\boldsymbol{\theta}^\top \widehat{\boldsymbol{\psi}}(\boldsymbol{s}_t, a_t) - r_t|$ exceeds the threshold $\alpha_\beta(\boldsymbol{\theta})$. $\alpha_\beta(\boldsymbol{\theta})$ is also referred to as the *value-at-risk* (VaR).

Let us consider the β-tail distribution of the absolute error:

$$\Phi_\beta(\alpha|\boldsymbol{\theta}) = \begin{cases} 0 & \text{if } \alpha < \alpha_\beta(\boldsymbol{\theta}), \\ \dfrac{\Phi(\alpha|\boldsymbol{\theta}) - \beta}{1-\beta} & \text{if } \alpha \geq \alpha_\beta(\boldsymbol{\theta}). \end{cases}$$

Let $\phi_\beta(\boldsymbol{\theta})$ be the mean of the β-tail distribution of the absolute temporal difference (TD) error:

$$\phi_\beta(\boldsymbol{\theta}) = \mathbb{E}_{\Phi_\beta}\left[|\boldsymbol{\theta}^\top \widehat{\boldsymbol{\psi}}(\boldsymbol{s}_t, a_t) - r_t|\right],$$

where $\mathbb{E}_{\Phi_\beta}$ denotes the expectation over the distribution Φ_β. $\phi_\beta(\boldsymbol{\theta})$ is called the CVaR. By definition, the CVaR of the absolute error is reduced to the mean absolute error if $\beta = 0$ and it converges to the worst absolute error as β tends to 1. Thus, the CVaR smoothly bridges the least absolute and Chebyshev approximation methods. CVaR is also referred to as the *expected shortfall*.

The CVaR minimization problem in the current context is formulated as

$$\min_{\boldsymbol{\theta}} \left[\mathbb{E}_{\Phi_\beta}\left[|\boldsymbol{\theta}^\top \widehat{\boldsymbol{\psi}}(\boldsymbol{s}_t, a_t) - r_t|\right]\right].$$

This optimization problem looks complicated, but the solution $\widehat{\boldsymbol{\theta}}_{\mathrm{CV}}$ can be obtained by solving the following linear program (Rockafellar & Uryasev, 2002):

$$\begin{cases} \min\limits_{\boldsymbol{\theta}, \{b_t\}_{t=1}^T, \{c_t\}_{t=1}^T, \alpha} & T(1-\beta)\alpha + \sum\limits_{t=1}^T c_t \\ \text{subject to} & -b_t \leq \boldsymbol{\theta}^\top \widehat{\boldsymbol{\psi}}(\boldsymbol{s}_t, a_t) - r_t \leq b_t, \\ & c_t \geq b_t - \alpha, \quad c_t \geq 0, \; t = 1, \ldots, T. \end{cases}$$

Note that if the definition of the absolute error is slightly changed, the CVaR minimization method amounts to minimizing the deadzone-linear loss (Takeda, 2007).

6.5 Remarks

LSPI can be regarded as regression of immediate rewards under the squared loss. In this chapter, the absolute loss was used for regression, which contributes to enhancing robustness and reliability. The least absolute method is formulated as a linear program and it can be solved efficiently by standard optimization software.

LSPI maximizes the state-action value function $Q(\boldsymbol{s}, a)$, which is the *expectation* of returns. Another way to address the robustness and reliability is to maximize other quantities such as the *median* or a *quantile* of returns. Although Bellman-like simple recursive expressions are not available for quantiles of rewards, a Bellman-like recursive equation holds for the *distribution* of the discounted sum of rewards (Morimura et al., 2010a; Morimura et al., 2010b). Developing robust reinforcement learning algorithms along this line of research would be a promising future direction.

Part III

Model-Free Policy Search

In the policy iteration approach explained in Part II, the *value function* is first estimated and then the policy is determined based on the learned value function. Policy iteration was demonstrated to work well in many real-world applications, especially in problems with discrete states and actions (Tesauro, 1994; Williams & Young, 2007; Abe et al., 2010). Although policy iteration can also handle continuous states by function approximation (Lagoudakis & Parr, 2003), continuous actions are hard to deal with due to the difficulty of finding a maximizer of the value function with respect to actions. Moreover, since policies are indirectly determined via value function approximation, misspecification of value function models can lead to an inappropriate policy even in very simple problems (Weaver & Baxter, 1999; Baxter et al., 2001). Another limitation of policy iteration especially in physical control tasks is that control policies can vary drastically in each iteration. This causes severe instability in the physical system and thus is not favorable in practice.

Policy search is an alternative approach to reinforcement learning that can overcome the limitations of policy iteration (Williams, 1992; Dayan & Hinton, 1997; Kakade, 2002). In the policy search approach, policies are directly learned so that the *return* (i.e., the discounted sum of future rewards),

$$\sum_{t=1}^{T} \gamma^{t-1} r(\boldsymbol{s}_t, a_t, \boldsymbol{s}_{t+1}),$$

is maximized.

In Part III, we focus on the framework of policy search. First, *direct policy search* methods are introduced, which try to find the policy that achieves the maximum return via gradient ascent (Chapter 7) or expectation-maximization (Chapter 8). A potential weakness of the direct policy search approach is its instability due to the randomness of stochastic policies. To overcome the instability problem, an alternative approach called *policy-prior search* is introduced in Chapter 9.

Chapter 7

Direct Policy Search by Gradient Ascent

The direct policy search approach tries to find the policy that maximizes the expected return. In this chapter, we introduce gradient-based algorithms for direct policy search. After the problem formulation in Section 7.1, the gradient ascent algorithm is introduced in Section 7.2. Then, in Section 7.3, its extention using natural gradients is described. In Section 7.4, application to computer graphics is shown. Finally, this chapter is concluded in Section 7.5.

7.1 Formulation

In this section, the problem of direct policy search is mathematically formulated.

Let us consider a Markov decision process specified by

$$(\mathcal{S}, \mathcal{A}, p(\boldsymbol{s}'|\boldsymbol{s}, a), p(\boldsymbol{s}), r, \gamma),$$

where $\mathcal{S}$ is a set of continuous states, $\mathcal{A}$ is a set of continuous actions, $p(\boldsymbol{s}'|\boldsymbol{s}, a)$ is the transition probability density from current state $\boldsymbol{s}$ to next state $\boldsymbol{s}'$ when action a is taken, $p(\boldsymbol{s})$ is the probability density of initial states, $r(\boldsymbol{s}, a, \boldsymbol{s}')$ is an immediate reward for transition from $\boldsymbol{s}$ to $\boldsymbol{s}'$ by taking action a, and $0 < \gamma \leq 1$ is the discounted factor for future rewards.

Let $\pi(a|\boldsymbol{s}, \boldsymbol{\theta})$ be a stochastic policy parameterized by $\boldsymbol{\theta}$, which represents the conditional probability density of taking action a in state $\boldsymbol{s}$. Let h be a *trajectory* of length T:

$$h = [\boldsymbol{s}_1, a_1, \ldots, \boldsymbol{s}_T, a_T, \boldsymbol{s}_{T+1}].$$

The *return* (i.e., the discounted sum of future rewards) along h is defined as

$$R(h) = \sum_{t=1}^{T} \gamma^{t-1} r(\boldsymbol{s}_t, a_t, \boldsymbol{s}_{t+1}),$$

and the expected return for policy parameter $\boldsymbol{\theta}$ is defined as

$$J(\boldsymbol{\theta}) = \mathbb{E}_{p(h|\boldsymbol{\theta})}[R(h)] = \int p(h|\boldsymbol{\theta}) R(h) \mathrm{d}h,$$

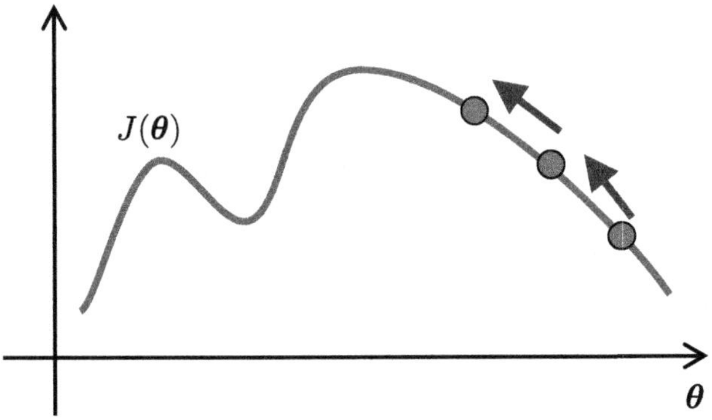

FIGURE 7.1: Gradient ascent for direct policy search.

where $\mathbb{E}_{p(h|\boldsymbol{\theta})}$ is the expectation over trajectory h drawn from $p(h|\boldsymbol{\theta})$, and $p(h|\boldsymbol{\theta})$ denotes the probability density of observing trajectory h under policy parameter $\boldsymbol{\theta}$:

$$p(h|\boldsymbol{\theta}) = p(\boldsymbol{s}_1) \prod_{t=1}^{T} p(\boldsymbol{s}_{t+1}|\boldsymbol{s}_t, a_t)\pi(a_t|\boldsymbol{s}_t, \boldsymbol{\theta}).$$

The goal of direct policy search is to find the optimal policy parameter $\boldsymbol{\theta}^*$ that maximizes the expected return $J(\boldsymbol{\theta})$:

$$\boldsymbol{\theta}^* = \underset{\boldsymbol{\theta}}{\operatorname{argmax}}\, J(\boldsymbol{\theta}).$$

However, directly maximizing $J(\boldsymbol{\theta})$ is hard since $J(\boldsymbol{\theta})$ usually involves high non-linearity with respect to $\boldsymbol{\theta}$. Below, a gradient-based algorithm is introduced to find a local maximizer of $J(\boldsymbol{\theta})$. An alternative approach based on the expectation-maximization algorithm is provided in Chapter 8.

7.2 Gradient Approach

In this section, a gradient ascent method for direct policy search is introduced (Figure 7.1).

7.2.1 Gradient Ascent

The simplest approach to finding a local maximizer of the expected return is *gradient ascent* (Williams, 1992):

$$\boldsymbol{\theta} \longleftarrow \boldsymbol{\theta} + \varepsilon \nabla_{\boldsymbol{\theta}} J(\boldsymbol{\theta}),$$

where ε is a small positive constant and $\nabla_{\boldsymbol{\theta}} J(\boldsymbol{\theta})$ denotes the gradient of expected return $J(\boldsymbol{\theta})$ with respect to policy parameter $\boldsymbol{\theta}$. The gradient $\nabla_{\boldsymbol{\theta}} J(\boldsymbol{\theta})$ is given by

$$\begin{aligned}\nabla_{\boldsymbol{\theta}} J(\boldsymbol{\theta}) &= \int \nabla_{\boldsymbol{\theta}} p(h|\boldsymbol{\theta}) R(h) \mathrm{d}h \\ &= \int p(h|\boldsymbol{\theta}) \nabla_{\boldsymbol{\theta}} \log p(h|\boldsymbol{\theta}) R(h) \mathrm{d}h \\ &= \int p(h|\boldsymbol{\theta}) \sum_{t=1}^{T} \nabla_{\boldsymbol{\theta}} \log \pi(a_t|\boldsymbol{s}_t, \boldsymbol{\theta}) R(h) \mathrm{d}h,\end{aligned}$$

where the so-called "log trick" is used:

$$\nabla_{\boldsymbol{\theta}} p(h|\boldsymbol{\theta}) = p(h|\boldsymbol{\theta}) \nabla_{\boldsymbol{\theta}} \log p(h|\boldsymbol{\theta}).$$

This expression means that the gradient $\nabla_{\boldsymbol{\theta}} J(\boldsymbol{\theta})$ is given as the expectation over $p(h|\boldsymbol{\theta})$:

$$\nabla_{\boldsymbol{\theta}} J(\boldsymbol{\theta}) = \mathbb{E}_{p(h|\boldsymbol{\theta})} \left[\sum_{t=1}^{T} \nabla_{\boldsymbol{\theta}} \log \pi(a_t|\boldsymbol{s}_t, \boldsymbol{\theta}) R(h) \right].$$

Since $p(h|\boldsymbol{\theta})$ is unknown, the expectation is approximated by the empirical average as

$$\nabla_{\boldsymbol{\theta}} \widehat{J}(\boldsymbol{\theta}) = \frac{1}{N} \sum_{n=1}^{N} \sum_{t=1}^{T} \nabla_{\boldsymbol{\theta}} \log \pi(a_{t,n}|\boldsymbol{s}_{t,n}, \boldsymbol{\theta}) R(h_n),$$

where

$$h_n = [\boldsymbol{s}_{1,n}, a_{1,n}, \ldots, \boldsymbol{s}_{T,n}, a_{T,n}, \boldsymbol{s}_{T+1,n}]$$

is an independent sample from $p(h|\boldsymbol{\theta})$. This algorithm is called *REINFORCE* (Williams, 1992), which is an acronym for "REward Increment = Nonnegative Factor × Offset Reinforcement × Characteristic Eligibility."

A popular choice for policy model $\pi(a|\boldsymbol{s}, \boldsymbol{\theta})$ is the Gaussian policy model, where policy parameter $\boldsymbol{\theta}$ consists of mean vector $\boldsymbol{\mu}$ and standard deviation σ:

$$\pi(a|\boldsymbol{s}, \boldsymbol{\mu}, \sigma) = \frac{1}{\sigma\sqrt{2\pi}} \exp\left(-\frac{(a - \boldsymbol{\mu}^\top \boldsymbol{\phi}(\boldsymbol{s}))^2}{2\sigma^2} \right). \tag{7.1}$$

Here, $\boldsymbol{\phi}(\boldsymbol{s})$ denotes the basis function. For this Gaussian policy model, the policy gradients are explicitly computed as

$$\begin{aligned}\nabla_{\boldsymbol{\mu}} \log \pi(a|\boldsymbol{s}, \boldsymbol{\mu}, \sigma) &= \frac{a - \boldsymbol{\mu}^\top \boldsymbol{\phi}(\boldsymbol{s})}{\sigma^2} \boldsymbol{\phi}(\boldsymbol{s}), \\ \nabla_{\sigma} \log \pi(a|\boldsymbol{s}, \boldsymbol{\mu}, \sigma) &= \frac{(a - \boldsymbol{\mu}^\top \boldsymbol{\phi}(\boldsymbol{s}))^2 - \sigma^2}{\sigma^3}.\end{aligned}$$

As shown above, the gradient ascent algorithm for direct policy search is very simple to implement. Furthermore, the property that policy parameters are gradually updated in the gradient ascent algorithm is preferable when reinforcement learning is applied to the control of a vulnerable physical system such as a humanoid robot, because sudden policy change can damage the system. However, the variance of policy gradients tends to be large in practice (Peters & Schaal, 2006; Sehnke et al., 2010), which can result in slow and unstable convergence.

7.2.2 Baseline Subtraction for Variance Reduction

Baseline subtraction is a useful technique to reduce the variance of gradient estimators. Technically, baseline subtraction can be viewed as the method of *control variates* (Fishman, 1996), which is an effective approach to reducing the variance of Monte Carlo integral estimators.

The basic idea of baseline subtraction is that an unbiased estimator $\widehat{\eta}$ is still unbiased if a zero-mean random variable m multiplied by a constant ξ is subtracted:

$$\widehat{\eta}_\xi = \widehat{\eta} - \xi m.$$

The constant ξ, which is called a *baseline*, may be chosen so that the variance of $\widehat{\eta}_\xi$ is minimized. By baseline subtraction, a more stable estimator than the original $\widehat{\eta}$ can be obtained.

A policy gradient estimator with baseline ξ subtracted is given by

$$\begin{aligned}\nabla_{\boldsymbol{\theta}} \widehat{J}^{\xi}(\boldsymbol{\theta}) &= \nabla_{\boldsymbol{\theta}} \widehat{J}(\boldsymbol{\theta}) - \xi \sum_{t=1}^{T} \nabla_{\boldsymbol{\theta}} \log \pi(a_{t,n}|\boldsymbol{s}_{t,n}, \boldsymbol{\theta}) \\ &= \frac{1}{N} \sum_{n=1}^{N} (R(h_n) - \xi) \sum_{t=1}^{T} \nabla_{\boldsymbol{\theta}} \log \pi(a_{t,n}|\boldsymbol{s}_{t,n}, \boldsymbol{\theta}),\end{aligned}$$

where the expectation of $\nabla_{\boldsymbol{\theta}} \log \pi(a|\boldsymbol{s}, \boldsymbol{\theta})$ is zero:

$$\begin{aligned}\mathbb{E}[\nabla_{\boldsymbol{\theta}} \log \pi(a|\boldsymbol{s}, \boldsymbol{\theta})] &= \int \pi(a|\boldsymbol{s}, \boldsymbol{\theta}) \nabla_{\boldsymbol{\theta}} \log \pi(a|\boldsymbol{s}, \boldsymbol{\theta}) \mathrm{d}a \\ &= \int \nabla_{\boldsymbol{\theta}} \pi(a|\boldsymbol{s}, \boldsymbol{\theta}) \mathrm{d}a \\ &= \nabla_{\boldsymbol{\theta}} \int \pi(a|\boldsymbol{s}, \boldsymbol{\theta}) \mathrm{d}a = \nabla_{\boldsymbol{\theta}} 1 = 0.\end{aligned}$$

The optimal baseline is defined as the minimizer of the variance of the gradient estimator with respect to the baseline (Greensmith et al., 2004; Weaver & Tao, 2001):

$$\xi^* = \underset{\xi}{\operatorname{argmin}} \, \mathbf{Var}_{p(h|\boldsymbol{\theta})}[\nabla_{\boldsymbol{\theta}} \widehat{J}^{\xi}(\boldsymbol{\theta})],$$

where $\mathbf{Var}_{p(h|\boldsymbol{\theta})}$ denotes the trace of the covariance matrix:

$$\begin{aligned}\mathbf{Var}_{p(h|\boldsymbol{\theta})}[\boldsymbol{\zeta}] &= \mathrm{tr}\Big(\mathbb{E}_{p(h|\boldsymbol{\theta})}\big[(\boldsymbol{\zeta} - \mathbb{E}_{p(h|\boldsymbol{\theta})}[\boldsymbol{\zeta}])(\boldsymbol{\zeta} - \mathbb{E}_{p(h|\boldsymbol{\theta})}[\boldsymbol{\zeta}])^\top\big]\Big) \\ &= \mathbb{E}_{p(h|\boldsymbol{\theta})}\Big[\|\boldsymbol{\zeta} - \mathbb{E}_{p(h|\boldsymbol{\theta})}[\boldsymbol{\zeta}]\|^2\Big].\end{aligned}$$

It was shown in Peters and Schaal (2006) that the optimal baseline ξ^* is given as

$$\xi^* = \frac{\mathbb{E}_{p(h|\boldsymbol{\theta})}[R(h)\|\sum_{t=1}^{T} \nabla_{\boldsymbol{\theta}} \log \pi(a_t|\boldsymbol{s}_t, \boldsymbol{\theta})\|^2]}{\mathbb{E}_{p(h|\boldsymbol{\theta})}[\|\sum_{t=1}^{T} \nabla_{\boldsymbol{\theta}} \log \pi(a_t|\boldsymbol{s}_t, \boldsymbol{\theta})\|^2]}.$$

In practice, the expectations are approximated by sample averages.

7.2.3 Variance Analysis of Gradient Estimators

Here, the variance of gradient estimators is theoretically investigated for the Gaussian policy model (7.1) with $\boldsymbol{\phi}(\boldsymbol{s}) = \boldsymbol{s}$. See Zhao et al. (2012) for technical details.

In the theoretical analysis, subsets of the following assumptions are considered:

Assumption (A): $r(\boldsymbol{s}, a, \boldsymbol{s}') \in [-\beta, \beta]$ for $\beta > 0$.

Assumption (B): $r(\boldsymbol{s}, a, \boldsymbol{s}') \in [\alpha, \beta]$ for $0 < \alpha < \beta$.

Assumption (C): For $\delta > 0$, there exist two series $\{c_t\}_{t=1}^{T}$ and $\{d_t\}_{t=1}^{T}$ such that $\|\boldsymbol{s}_t\| \geq c_t$ and $\|\boldsymbol{s}_t\| \leq d_t$ hold with probability at least $1 - \frac{\delta}{2N}$, respectively, over the choice of sample paths.

Note that Assumption (B) is stronger than Assumption (A). Let

$$\zeta(T) = C_T \alpha^2 - D_T \beta^2/(2\pi),$$

where

$$C_T = \sum_{t=1}^{T} c_t^2 \quad \text{and} \quad D_T = \sum_{t=1}^{T} d_t^2.$$

First, the variance of gradient estimators is analyzed.

Theorem 7.1 *Under Assumptions (A) and (C), the following upper bound holds with probability at least* $1 - \delta/2$*:*

$$\mathbf{Var}_{p(h|\boldsymbol{\theta})}\Big[\nabla_{\boldsymbol{\mu}} \widehat{J}(\boldsymbol{\mu}, \sigma)\Big] \leq \frac{D_T \beta^2 (1 - \gamma^T)^2}{N\sigma^2(1-\gamma)^2}.$$

Under Assumption (A), it holds that

$$\mathbf{Var}_{p(h|\boldsymbol{\theta})}\Big[\nabla_{\sigma} \widehat{J}(\boldsymbol{\mu}, \sigma)\Big] \leq \frac{2T\beta^2 (1 - \gamma^T)^2}{N\sigma^2(1-\gamma)^2}.$$

The above upper bounds are monotone increasing with respect to trajectory length T.

For the variance of $\nabla_{\boldsymbol{\mu}}\widehat{J}(\boldsymbol{\mu}, \sigma)$, the following lower bound holds (its upper bound has not been derived yet):

Theorem 7.2 *Under Assumptions (B) and (C), the following lower bound holds with probability at least* $1 - \delta$*:*

$$\mathbf{Var}_{p(h|\boldsymbol{\theta})}\left[\nabla_{\boldsymbol{\mu}}\widehat{J}(\boldsymbol{\mu}, \sigma)\right] \geq \frac{(1-\gamma^T)^2}{N\sigma^2(1-\gamma)^2}\zeta(T).$$

This lower bound is non-trivial if $\zeta(T) > 0$, which can be fulfilled, e.g., if α and β satisfy

$$2\pi C_T \alpha^2 > D_T \beta^2.$$

Next, the contribution of the optimal baseline is investigated. It was shown (Greensmith et al., 2004; Weaver & Tao, 2001) that the excess variance for an arbitrary baseline ξ is given by

$$\mathbf{Var}_{p(h|\boldsymbol{\theta})}[\nabla_{\boldsymbol{\theta}}\widehat{J}^{\xi}(\boldsymbol{\theta})] - \mathbf{Var}_{p(h|\boldsymbol{\theta})}[\nabla_{\boldsymbol{\theta}}\widehat{J}^{\xi^*}(\boldsymbol{\theta})]$$
$$= \frac{(\xi - \xi^*)^2}{N}\mathbb{E}_{p(h|\boldsymbol{\theta})}\left[\left\|\sum_{t=1}^{T}\nabla_{\boldsymbol{\theta}}\log\pi(a_t|\boldsymbol{s}_t, \boldsymbol{\theta})\right\|^2\right].$$

Based on this expression, the following theorem can be obtained.

Theorem 7.3 *Under Assumptions (B) and (C), the following bounds hold with probability at least* $1 - \delta$*:*

$$\frac{C_T\alpha^2(1-\gamma^T)^2}{N\sigma^2(1-\gamma)^2} \leq \mathbf{Var}_{p(h|\boldsymbol{\theta})}[\nabla_{\boldsymbol{\mu}}\widehat{J}(\boldsymbol{\mu}, \sigma)] - \mathbf{Var}_{p(h|\boldsymbol{\theta})}[\nabla_{\boldsymbol{\mu}}\widehat{J}^{\xi^*}(\boldsymbol{\mu}, \sigma)]$$
$$\leq \frac{\beta^2(1-\gamma^T)^2 D_T}{N\sigma^2(1-\gamma)^2}.$$

This theorem shows that the lower bound of the excess variance is positive and monotone increasing with respect to the trajectory length T. This means that the variance is always reduced by optimal baseline subtraction and the amount of variance reduction is monotone increasing with respect to the trajectory length T. Note that the upper bound is also monotone increasing with respect to the trajectory length T.

Finally, the variance of gradient estimators with the optimal baseline is investigated:

Theorem 7.4 *Under Assumptions (B) and (C), it holds that*

$$\mathbf{Var}_{p(h|\boldsymbol{\theta})}[\nabla_{\boldsymbol{\mu}}\widehat{J}^{\xi^*}(\boldsymbol{\mu}, \sigma)] \leq \frac{(1-\gamma^T)^2}{N\sigma^2(1-\gamma)^2}(\beta^2 D_T - \alpha^2 C_T),$$

where the inequality holds with probability at least $1 - \delta$*.*

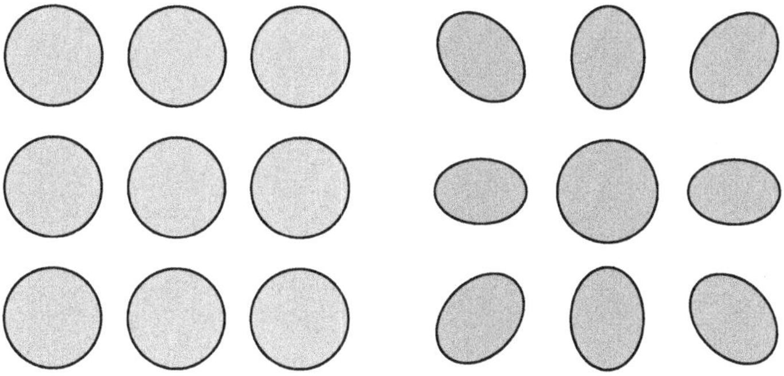

(a) Ordinary gradients (b) Natural gradients

FIGURE 7.2: Ordinary and natural gradients. Ordinary gradients treat all dimensions equally, while natural gradients take the Riemannian structure into account.

This theorem shows that the upper bound of the variance of the gradient estimators with the optimal baseline is still monotone increasing with respect to the trajectory length T. Thus, when the trajectory length T is large, the variance of the gradient estimators can still be large even with the optimal baseline.

In Chapter 9, another gradient approach will be introduced for overcoming this large-variance problem.

7.3 Natural Gradient Approach

The gradient-based policy parameter update used in the REINFORCE algorithm is performed under the *Euclidean metric*. In this section, we show another useful choice of the metric for gradient-based policy search.

7.3.1 Natural Gradient Ascent

Use of the Euclidean metric implies that all dimensions of the policy parameter vector $\boldsymbol{\theta}$ are treated equally (Figure 7.2(a)). However, since a policy parameter $\boldsymbol{\theta}$ specifies a conditional probability density $\pi(a|\boldsymbol{s}, \boldsymbol{\theta})$, use of the Euclidean metric in the parameter space does not necessarily mean all dimensions are treated equally in the space of conditional probability densities. Thus, a small change in the policy parameter $\boldsymbol{\theta}$ can cause a big change in the conditional probability density $\pi(a|\boldsymbol{s}, \boldsymbol{\theta})$ (Kakade, 2002).

Figure 7.3 describes the Gaussian densities with mean $\mu = -5, 0, 5$ and standard deviation $\sigma = 1, 2$. This shows that if the standard deviation is

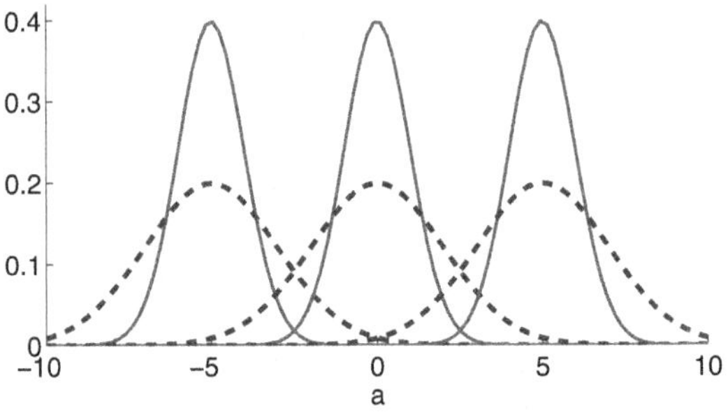

FIGURE 7.3: Gaussian densities with different means and standard deviations. If the standard deviation is doubled (from the solid lines to dashed lines), the difference in mean should also be doubled to maintain the same overlapping level.

doubled, the difference in mean should also be doubled to maintain the same overlapping level. Thus, it is "natural" to compute the distance between two Gaussian densities parameterized with (μ, σ) and $(\mu + \Delta\mu, \sigma)$ not by $\Delta\mu$, but by $\Delta\mu/\sigma$.

Gradients that treat all dimensions equally in the space of probability densities are called *natural gradients* (Amari, 1998; Amari & Nagaoka, 2000). The ordinary gradient is defined as the steepest ascent direction under the Euclidean metric (Figure 7.2(a)):

$$\nabla_{\boldsymbol{\theta}} J(\boldsymbol{\theta}) = \operatorname*{argmax}_{\Delta\boldsymbol{\theta}} J(\boldsymbol{\theta} + \Delta\boldsymbol{\theta}) \quad \text{subject to } \Delta\boldsymbol{\theta}^\top \Delta\boldsymbol{\theta} \leq \epsilon,$$

where ϵ is a small positive number. On the other hand, the natural gradient is defined as the steepest ascent direction under the *Riemannian metric* (Figure 7.2(b)):

$$\widetilde{\nabla}_{\boldsymbol{\theta}} J(\boldsymbol{\theta}) = \operatorname*{argmax}_{\Delta\boldsymbol{\theta}} J(\boldsymbol{\theta} + \Delta\boldsymbol{\theta}) \quad \text{subject to } \Delta\boldsymbol{\theta}^\top \boldsymbol{R}_{\boldsymbol{\theta}} \Delta\boldsymbol{\theta} \leq \epsilon,$$

where $\boldsymbol{R}_{\boldsymbol{\theta}}$ is the Riemannian metric, which is a positive definite matrix. The solution of the above optimization problem is given by

$$\widetilde{\nabla}_{\boldsymbol{\theta}} J(\boldsymbol{\theta}) = \boldsymbol{R}_{\boldsymbol{\theta}}^{-1} \nabla_{\boldsymbol{\theta}} J(\boldsymbol{\theta}).$$

Thus, the ordinary gradient $\nabla_{\boldsymbol{\theta}} J(\boldsymbol{\theta})$ is modified by the inverse Riemannian metric $\boldsymbol{R}_{\boldsymbol{\theta}}^{-1}$ in the natural gradient.

A standard distance metric in the space of probability densities is the *Kullback–Leibler (KL) divergence* (Kullback & Leibler, 1951). The KL divergence from density p to density q is defined as

$$\mathrm{KL}(p \| q) = \int p(\boldsymbol{\theta}) \log \frac{p(\boldsymbol{\theta})}{q(\boldsymbol{\theta})} \mathrm{d}\boldsymbol{\theta}.$$

$\mathrm{KL}(p\|q)$ is always non-negative and zero if and only if $p = q$. Thus, smaller $\mathrm{KL}(p\|q)$ means that p and q are "closer." However, note that the KL divergence is not symmetric, i.e., $\mathrm{KL}(p\|q) \neq \mathrm{KL}(q\|p)$ in general.

For small $\Delta\boldsymbol{\theta}$, the KL divergence from $p(h|\boldsymbol{\theta})$ to $p(h|\boldsymbol{\theta} + \Delta\boldsymbol{\theta})$ can be approximated by

$$\Delta\boldsymbol{\theta}^\top \boldsymbol{F}_{\boldsymbol{\theta}} \Delta\boldsymbol{\theta},$$

where $\boldsymbol{F}_{\boldsymbol{\theta}}$ is the *Fisher information matrix*:

$$\boldsymbol{F}_{\boldsymbol{\theta}} = \mathbb{E}_{p(h|\boldsymbol{\theta})}[\nabla_{\boldsymbol{\theta}} \log p(h|\boldsymbol{\theta}) \nabla_{\boldsymbol{\theta}} \log p(h|\boldsymbol{\theta})^\top].$$

Thus, $\boldsymbol{F}_{\boldsymbol{\theta}}$ is the Riemannian metric induced by the KL divergence.

Then the update rule of the policy parameter $\boldsymbol{\theta}$ based on the natural gradient is given by

$$\boldsymbol{\theta} \longleftarrow \boldsymbol{\theta} + \varepsilon \widehat{\boldsymbol{F}}_{\boldsymbol{\theta}}^{-1} \nabla_{\boldsymbol{\theta}} J(\boldsymbol{\theta}),$$

where ε is a small positive constant and $\widehat{\boldsymbol{F}}_{\boldsymbol{\theta}}$ is a sample approximation of $\boldsymbol{F}_{\boldsymbol{\theta}}$:

$$\widehat{\boldsymbol{F}}_{\boldsymbol{\theta}} = \frac{1}{N} \sum_{n=1}^{N} \nabla_{\boldsymbol{\theta}} \log p(h_n|\boldsymbol{\theta}) \nabla_{\boldsymbol{\theta}} \log p(h_n|\boldsymbol{\theta})^\top.$$

Under mild regularity conditions, the Fisher information matrix $\boldsymbol{F}_{\boldsymbol{\theta}}$ can be expressed as

$$\boldsymbol{F}_{\boldsymbol{\theta}} = -\mathbb{E}_{p(h|\boldsymbol{\theta})}[\nabla^2_{\boldsymbol{\theta}} \log p(h|\boldsymbol{\theta})],$$

where $\nabla^2_{\boldsymbol{\theta}} \log p(h|\boldsymbol{\theta})$ denotes the *Hessian matrix* of $\log p(h|\boldsymbol{\theta})$. That is, the (b, b')-th element of $\nabla^2_{\boldsymbol{\theta}} \log p(h|\boldsymbol{\theta})$ is given by $\frac{\partial^2}{\partial\theta_b \partial\theta_{b'}} \log p(h|\boldsymbol{\theta})$. This means that the natural gradient takes the *curvature* into account, by which the convergence behavior at flat plateaus and steep ridges tends to be improved. On the other hand, a potential weakness of natural gradients is that computation of the inverse Riemannian metric tends to be numerically unstable (Deisenroth et al., 2013).

7.3.2 Illustration

Let us illustrate the difference between ordinary and natural gradients numerically.

Consider one-dimensional real-valued state space $\mathcal{S} = \mathbb{R}$ and one-dimensional real-valued action space $\mathcal{A} = \mathbb{R}$. The transition dynamics is linear and deterministic as $s' = s + a$, and the reward function is quadratic as $r = 0.5s^2 - 0.05a$. The discount factor is set at $\gamma = 0.95$. The Gaussian policy model,

$$\pi(a|s, \mu, \sigma) = \frac{1}{\sigma\sqrt{2\pi}} \exp\left(-\frac{(a - \mu s)^2}{2\sigma^2}\right),$$

is employed, which contains the mean parameter μ and the standard deviation parameter σ. The optimal policy parameters in this setup are given by $(\mu^*, \sigma^*) \approx (-0.912, 0)$.

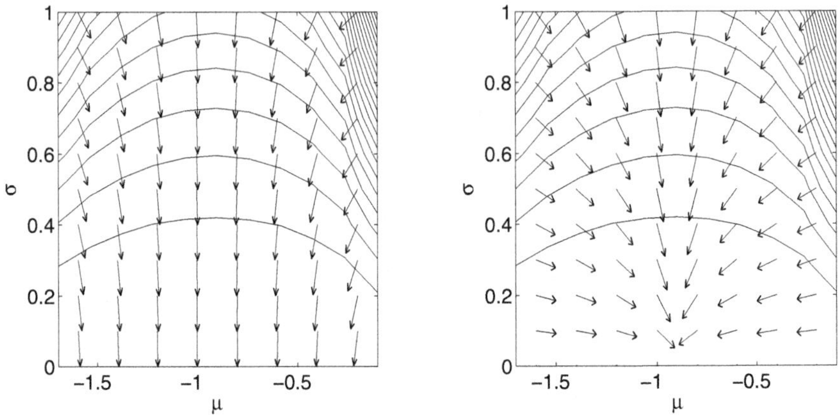

(a) Ordinary gradients (b) Natural gradients

FIGURE 7.4: Numerical illustrations of ordinary and natural gradients.

Figure 7.4 shows numerical comparison of ordinary and natural gradients for the Gaussian policy. The contour lines and the arrows indicate the expected return surface and the gradient directions, respectively. The graphs show that the ordinary gradients tend to strongly reduce the standard deviation parameter σ without really updating the mean parameter μ. This means that the stochasticity of the policy is lost quickly and thus the agent becomes less exploratory. Consequently, once σ gets closer to zero, the solution is at a flat plateau along the direction of μ and thus policy updates in μ are very slow. On the other hand, the natural gradients reduce both the mean parameter μ and the standard deviation parameter σ in a balanced way. As a result, convergence gets much faster than the ordinary gradient method.

7.4 Application in Computer Graphics: Artist Agent

Oriental ink painting, which is also called *sumie*, is one of the most distinctive painting styles and has attracted artists around the world. Major challenges in sumie simulation are to abstract complex scene information and reproduce smooth and natural brush strokes. Reinforcement learning is useful to automatically generate such smooth and natural strokes (Xie et al., 2013). In this section, the REINFORCE algorithm explained in Section 7.2 is applied to sumie agent training.

7.4.1 Sumie Painting

Among various techniques of *non-photorealistic rendering* (Gooch & Gooch, 2001), *stroke-based painterly rendering* synthesizes an image from a source image in a desired painting style by placing discrete strokes (Hertzmann, 2003). Such an algorithm simulates the common practice of human painters who create paintings with brush strokes.

Western painting styles such as water-color, pastel, and oil painting overlay strokes onto multiple layers, while oriental ink painting uses a few expressive strokes produced by soft brush tufts to convey significant information about a target scene. The appearance of the stroke in oriental ink painting is therefore determined by the shape of the object to paint, the path and posture of the brush, and the distribution of pigments in the brush.

Drawing smooth and natural strokes in arbitrary shapes is challenging since an optimal brush trajectory and the posture of a brush footprint are different for each shape. Existing methods can efficiently map brush texture by deformation onto a user-given trajectory line or the shape of a target stroke (Hertzmann, 1998; Guo & Kunii, 2003). However, the geometrical process of morphing the entire texture of a brush stroke into the target shape leads to undesirable effects such as unnatural foldings and creased appearances at corners or curves.

Here, a soft-tuft brush is treated as a reinforcement learning agent, and the REINFORCE algorithm is used to automatically draw artistic strokes. More specifically, given any closed contour that represents the shape of a desired single stroke without overlap, the agent moves the brush on the canvas to fill the given shape from a start point to an end point with stable poses along a smooth continuous movement trajectory (see Figure 7.5).

In oriental ink painting, there are several different brush styles that characterize the paintings. Below, two representative styles called the *upright brush style* and the *oblique brush style* are considered (see Figure 7.6). In the upright brush style, the tip of the brush should be located on the medial axis of the expected stroke shape, and the bottom of the brush should be tangent to both sides of the boundary. On the other hand, in the oblique brush style, the tip of the brush should touch one side of the boundary and the bottom of the brush should be tangent to the other side of the boundary. The choice of the upright brush style and the oblique brush style is exclusive and a user is asked to choose one of the styles in advance.

7.4.2 Design of States, Actions, and Immediate Rewards

Here, specific design of states, actions, and immediate rewards tailored to the sumie agent is described.

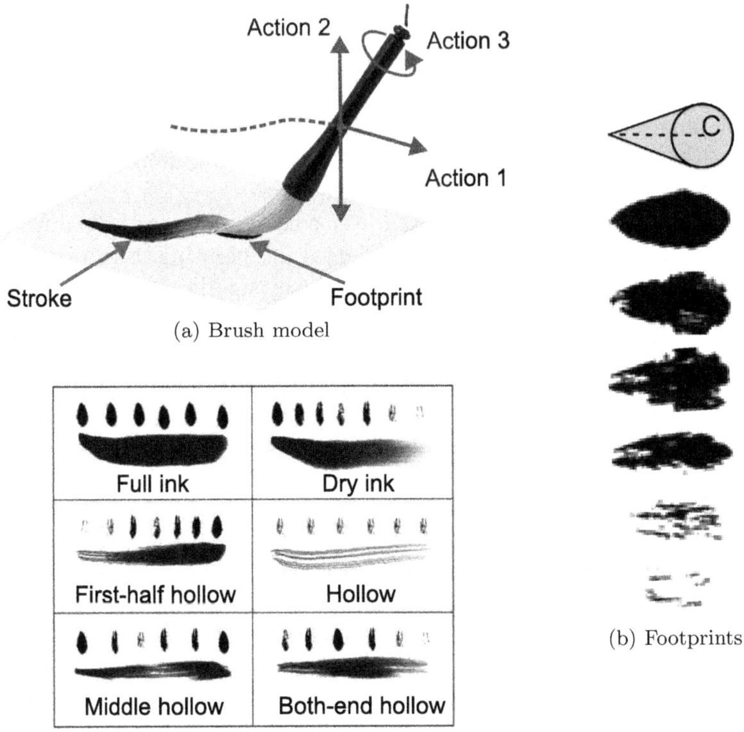

(a) Brush model

(b) Footprints

(c) Basic stroke styles

FIGURE 7.5: Illustration of the brush agent and its path. (a) A stroke is generated by moving the brush with the following 3 actions: Action 1 is regulating the direction of the brush movement, Action 2 is pushing down/lifting up the brush, and Action 3 is rotating the brush handle. Only Action 1 is determined by reinforcement learning, and Action 2 and Action 3 are determined based on Action 1. (b) The top symbol illustrates the brush agent, which consists of a tip Q and a circle with center C and radius r. Others illustrate footprints of a real brush with different ink quantities. (c) There are 6 basic stroke styles: full ink, dry ink, first-half hollow, hollow, middle hollow, and both-end hollow. Small footprints on the top of each stroke show the interpolation order.

7.4.2.1 States

The *global* measurement (i.e., the pose configuration of a footprint under the global Cartesian coordinate) and the *local* measurement (i.e., the pose and the locomotion information of the brush agent relative to the surrounding environment) are used as states. Here, only the local measurement is used to calculate a reward and a policy, by which the agent can learn the drawing policy that is generalizable to new shapes. Below, the local measurement is regarded as state $\boldsymbol{s}$ and the global measurement is dealt with only implicitly.

FIGURE 7.6: Upright brush style (left) and oblique brush style (right).

The local state-space design consists of two components: a current surrounding shape and an upcoming shape. More specifically, state vector $\boldsymbol{s}$ consists of the following six features:

$$\boldsymbol{s} = (\omega, \phi, d, \kappa_1, \kappa_2, l)^\top.$$

Each feature is defined as follows (see Figures 7.7):

- $\omega \in (-\pi, \pi]$: The angle of the velocity vector of the brush agent relative to the medial axis.
- $\phi \in (-\pi, \pi]$: The heading direction of the brush agent relative to the medial axis.
- $d \in [-2, 2]$: The ratio of offset distance δ from the center C of the brush agent to the nearest point P on the medial axis $\mathcal{M}$ over the radius r of the brush agent ($|d| = \delta/r$). d takes a positive/negative value when the center of the brush agent is on the left-/right-hand side of the medial axis:
  - d takes the value 0 when the center of the brush agent is on the medial axis.
  - d takes a value in $[-1, 1]$ when the brush agent is inside the boundaries.
  - The value of d is in $[-2, -1)$ or in $(1, 2]$ when the brush agent goes over the boundary of one side.

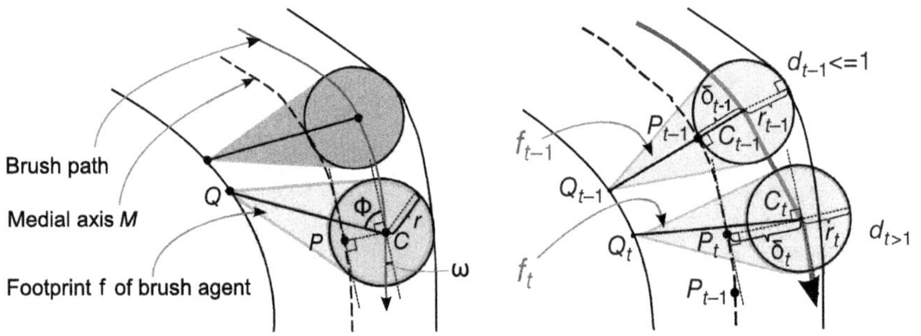

FIGURE 7.7: Illustration of the design of states. Left: The brush agent consists of a tip Q and a circle with center C and radius r. Right: The ratio d of the offset distance δ over the radius r. Footprint f_{t-1} is inside the drawing area, and the circle with center C_{t-1} and the tip Q_{t-1} touch the boundary on each side. In this case, $\delta_{t-1} \leq r_{t-1}$ and $d_{t-1} \in [0,1]$. On the other hand, f_t goes over the boundary, and then $\delta_t > r_t$ and $d_t > 1$. Note that d is restricted to be in $[-2,2]$, and P is the nearest point on medial axis $\mathcal{M}$ to C.

Note that the center of the agent is restricted within the shape. Therefore, the extreme values of d are ± 2 when the center of the agent is on the boundary.

- $\kappa_1, \kappa_2 \in (-1,1)$: κ_1 provides the current surrounding information on the point P_t, whereas κ_2 provides the upcoming shape information on point P_{t+1}:

$$\kappa_i = \frac{2}{\pi} \arctan\left(0.05/\sqrt{r_i'}\right),$$

  where r_i' is the radius of the curve. More specifically, the value takes 0/negative/positive when the shape is straight/left-curved/right-curved, and the larger its absolute value is, the tighter the curve is.

- $l \in \{0,1\}$: A binary label that indicates whether the agent moves to a region covered by the previous footprints or not. $l=0$ means that the agent moves to a region covered by the previous footprint. Otherwise, $l=1$ means that it moves to an uncovered region.

7.4.2.2 Actions

To generate elegant brush strokes, the brush agent should move inside given boundaries properly. Here, the following actions are considered to control the brush (see Figure 7.5(a)):

- Action 1: Movement of the brush on the canvas paper.
- Action 2: Scaling up/down of the footprint.

- Action 3: Rotation of the heading direction of the brush.

Since properly covering the whole desired region is the most important in terms of the visual quality, the movement of the brush (Action 1) is regarded as the primary action. More specifically, Action 1 takes a value in $(-\pi, -\pi]$ that indicates the offset turning angle of the motion direction relative to the medial axis of an expected stroke shape. In practical applications, the agent should be able to deal with arbitrary strokes in various scales. To achieve stable performance in different scales, the velocity is adaptively changed as $r/3$, where r is the radius of the current footprint.

Action 1 is determined by the Gaussian policy function trained by the REINFORCE algorithm, and Action 2 and Action 3 are determined as follows.

- Oblique brush stroke style: The tip of the agent is set to touch one side of the boundary, and the bottom of the agent is set to be tangent to the other side of the boundary.
- Upright brush stroke style: The tip of the agent is chosen to travel along the medial axis of the shape.

If it is not possible to satisfy the above constraints by adjusting Action 2 and Action 3, the new footprint will simply be the same posture as the previous one.

7.4.2.3 Immediate Rewards

The immediate reward function measures the quality of the brush agent's movement after taking an action at each time step. The reward is designed to reflect the following two aspects:

- The distance between the center of the brush agent and the nearest point on the medial axis of the shape at the current time step: This detects whether the agent moves out of the region or travels backward from the correct direction.
- Change of the local configuration of the brush agent after executing an action: This detects whether the agent moves smoothly.

These two aspects are formalized by defining the reward function as follows:

$$r(\boldsymbol{s}_t, a_t, \boldsymbol{s}_{t+1}) = \begin{cases} 0 & \text{if } f_t = f_{t+1} \text{ or } l_{t+1} = 0, \\ \dfrac{2 + |\kappa_1(t)| + |\kappa_2(t)|}{E^{(t)}_{\text{location}} + E^{(t)}_{\text{posture}}} & \text{otherwise,} \end{cases}$$

where f_t and f_{t+1} are the footprints at time steps t and $t+1$, respectively. This reward design implies that the immediate reward is zero when the brush is blocked by a boundary as $f_t = f_{t+1}$ or the brush is going backward to a region that has already been covered by previous footprints. $\kappa_1(t)$ and $\kappa_2(t)$ are the values of κ_1 and κ_2 at time step t. $|\kappa_1(t)| + |\kappa_2(t)|$ adaptively increases the immediate reward depending on the curvatures $\kappa_1(t)$ and $\kappa_2(t)$ of the medial axis.

$E^{(t)}_{\text{location}}$ measures the quality of the location of the brush agent with respect to the medial axis, defined by

$$E^{(t)}_{\text{location}} = \begin{cases} \tau_1 |\omega_t| + \tau_2(|d_t| + 5) & d_t \in [-2, -1) \cup (1, 2], \\ \tau_1 |\omega_t| + \tau_2 |d_t| & d_t \in [-1, 1], \end{cases}$$

where d_t is the value of d at time step t. τ_1 and τ_2 are weight parameters, which are chosen depending on the brush style: $\tau_1 = \tau_2 = 0.5$ for the upright brush style and $\tau_1 = 0.1$ and $\tau_2 = 0.9$ for the oblique brush style. Since d_t contains information about whether the agent goes over the boundary or not, as illustrated in Figure 7.7, the penalty $+5$ is added to E_{location} when the agent goes over the boundary of the shape.

$E^{(t)}_{\text{posture}}$ measures the quality of the posture of the brush agent based on neighboring footprints, defined by

$$E^{(t)}_{\text{posture}} = \Delta\omega_t/3 + \Delta\phi_t/3 + \Delta d_t/3,$$

where $\Delta\omega_t$, $\Delta\phi_t$, and Δd_t are changes in angle ω of the velocity vector, heading direction ϕ, and ratio d of the offset distance, respectively. The notation Δx_t denotes the normalized squared change between x_{t-1} and x_t defined by

$$\Delta x_t = \begin{cases} 1 & \text{if } x_t = x_{t-1} = 0, \\ \dfrac{(x_t - x_{t-1})^2}{(|x_t| + |x_{t-1}|)^2} & \text{otherwise.} \end{cases}$$

7.4.2.4 Training and Test Sessions

A naive way to train an agent is to use an entire stroke shape as a training sample. However, this has several drawbacks, e.g., collecting many training samples is costly and generalization to new shapes is hard. To overcome these limitations, the agent is trained based on *partial* shapes, not the entire shapes (Figure 7.8(a)). This allows us to generate various partial shapes from a single entire shape, which significantly increases the number and variation of training samples. Another merit is that the generalization ability to new shapes can be enhanced, because even when the entire profile of a new shape is quite different from that of training data, the new shape may contain similar partial shapes. Figure 7.8(c) illustrates 8 examples of 80 digitized real single brush strokes that are commonly used in oriental ink painting. Boundaries are extracted as the shape information and are arranged in a queue for training (see Figure 7.8(b)).

In the training session, the initial position of the first episode is chosen to be the start point of the medial axis, and the direction to move is chosen to be

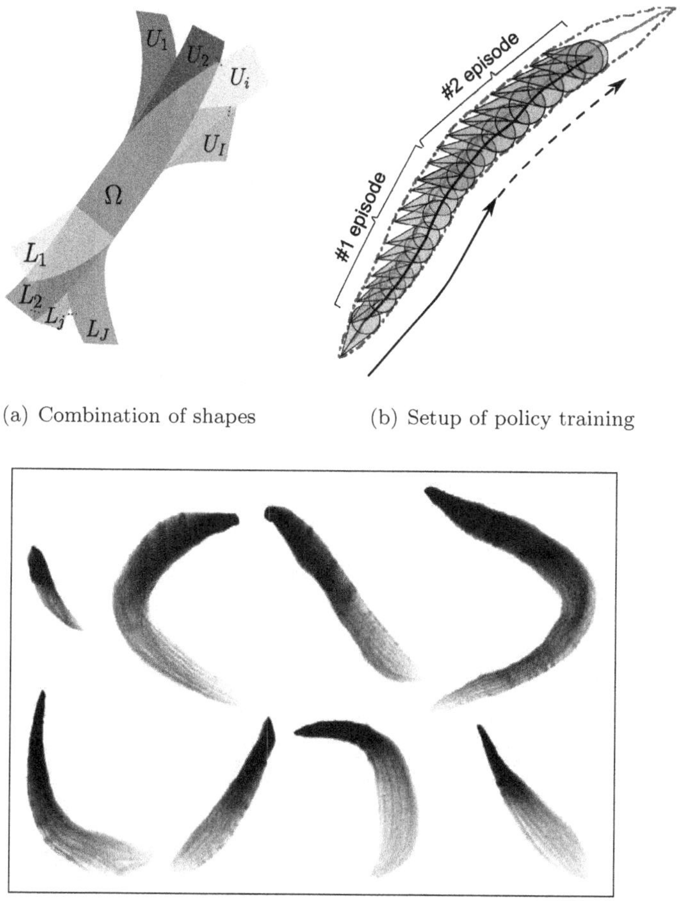

(a) Combination of shapes

(b) Setup of policy training

(c) Training shapes

FIGURE 7.8: Policy training scheme. (a) Each entire shape is composed of one of the upper regions U_i, the common region Ω, and one of the lower regions L_j. (b) Boundaries are extracted as the shape information and are arranged in a queue for training. (c) Eight examples of 80 digitized real single brush strokes that are commonly used in oriental ink painting are illustrated.

the goal point, as illustrated in Figure 7.8(b). In the first episode, the initial footprint is set at the start point of the shape. Then, in the following episodes, the initial footprint is set at either the last footprint in the previous episode or the start point of the shape, depending on whether the agent moved well or was blocked by the boundary in the previous episode.

After learning a drawing policy, the brush agent applies the learned policy to covering given boundaries with smooth strokes. The location of the agent is

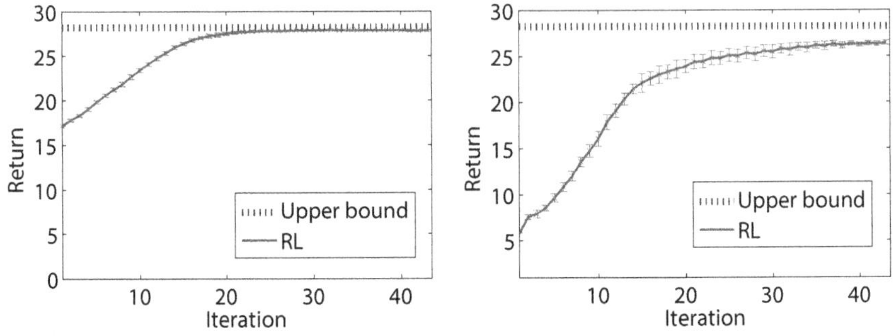

FIGURE 7.9: Average and standard deviation of returns obtained by the reinforcement learning (RL) method over 10 trials and the upper limit of the return value.

initialized at the start point of a new shape. The agent then sequentially selects actions based on the learned policy and makes transitions until it reaches the goal point.

7.4.3 Experimental Results

First, the performance of the reinforcement learning (RL) method is investigated. Policies are separately trained by the REINFORCE algorithm for the upright brush style and the oblique brush style using 80 single strokes as training data (see Figure 7.8(c)). The parameters of the initial policy are set at

$$\boldsymbol{\theta} = (\boldsymbol{\mu}^\top, \sigma)^\top = (0, 0, 0, 0, 0, 0, 2)^\top,$$

where the first six elements correspond to the Gaussian mean and the last element is the Gaussian standard deviation. The agent collects $N = 300$ episodic samples with trajectory length $T = 32$. The discounted factor is set at $\gamma = 0.99$.

The average and standard deviations of the return for 300 training episodic samples over 10 trials are plotted in Figure 7.9. The graphs show that the average returns sharply increase in an early stage and approach the optimal values (i.e., receiving the maximum immediate reward, $+1$, for all steps).

Next, the performance of the RL method is compared with that of the *dynamic programming* (DP) method (Xie et al., 2011), which involves discretization of continuous state space. In Figure 7.10, the experimental results obtained by DP with different numbers of footprint candidates in each step of the DP search are plotted together with the result obtained by RL. This shows that the execution time of the DP method increases significantly as the number of footprint candidates increases. In the DP method, the best return

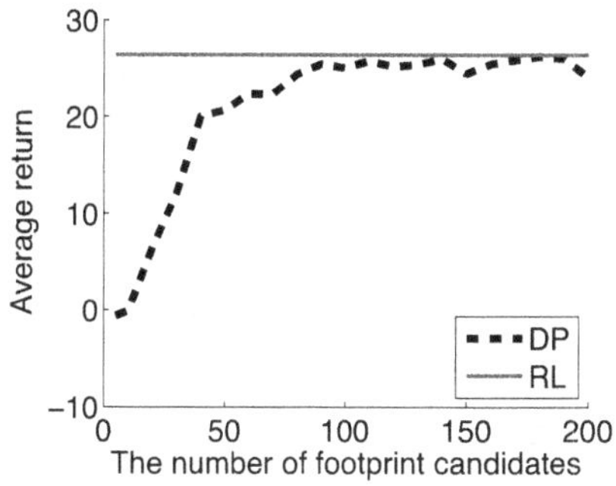

(a) Average return

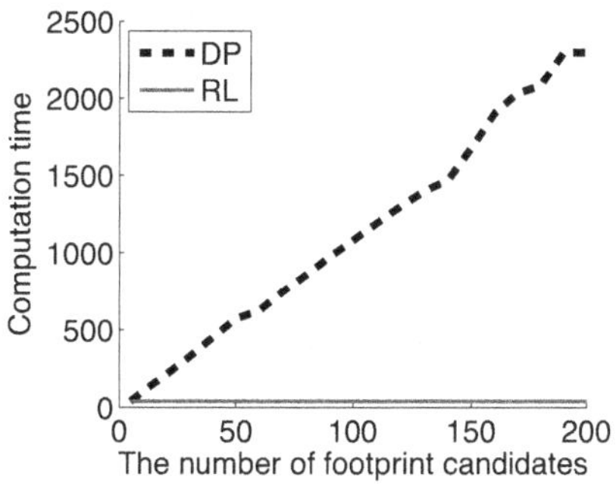

(b) Computation time

FIGURE 7.10: Average return and computation time for reinforcement learning (RL) and dynamic programming (DP).

value 26.27 is achieved when the number of footprint candidates is set at 180. Although this maximum value is comparable to the return obtained by the RL method (26.44), RL is about 50 times faster than the DP method. Figure 7.11 shows some exemplary strokes generated by RL (the top two rows) and DP (the bottom two rows). This shows that the agent trained by RL is able to draw nice strokes with stable poses after the 30th policy update iteration (see also Figure 7.9). On the other hand, as illustrated in Figure 7.11, the DP results for 5, 60, and 100 footprint candidates are unacceptably poor. Given that the DP method requires manual tuning of the number of footprint candidates at each step for each input shape, the RL method is demonstrated to be promising.

The RL method is further applied to more realistic shapes, illustrated in Figure 7.12. Although the shapes are not included in the training samples, the RL method can produce smooth and natural brush strokes for various unlearned shapes. More results are illustrated in Figure 7.13, showing that the RL method is promising in photo conversion into the sumie style.

7.5 Remarks

In this chapter, gradient-based algorithms for direct policy search are introduced. These gradient-based methods are suitable for controlling vulnerable physical systems such as humanoid robots, thanks to the nature of gradient methods that parameters are updated gradually. Furthermore, direct policy search can handle continuous actions in a straightforward way, which is an advantage over policy iteration, explained in Part II.

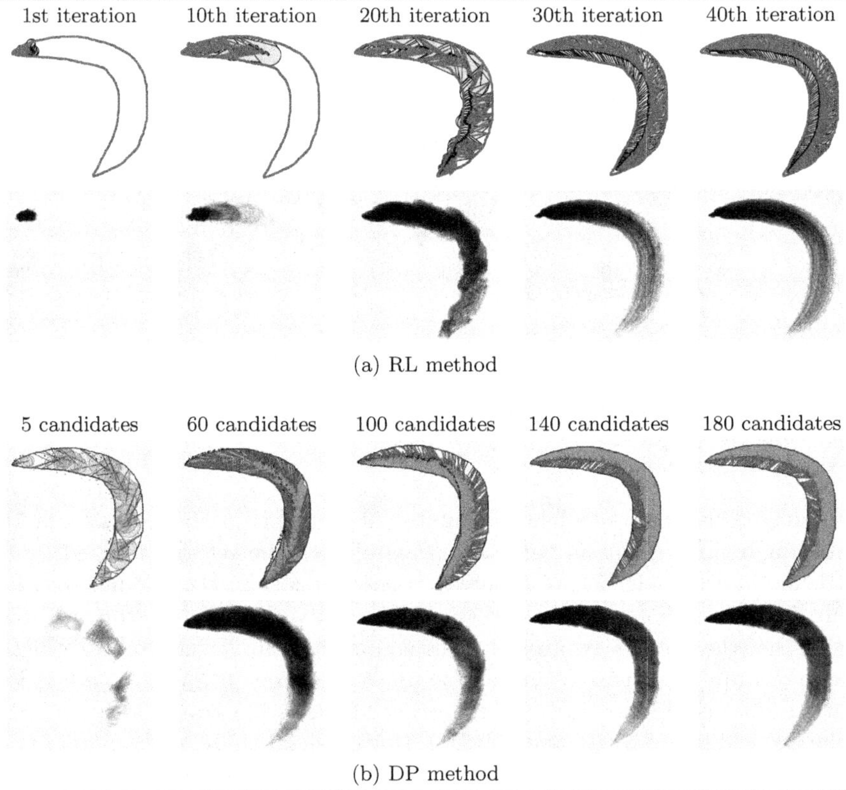

FIGURE 7.11: Examples of strokes generated by RL and DP. The top two rows show the RL results over policy update iterations, while the bottom two rows show the DP results for different numbers of footprint candidates. The line segment connects the center and the tip of a footprint, and the circle denotes the bottom circle of the footprint.

The gradient-based method was successfully applied to automatic sumie painting generation. Considering *local* measurements in state design was shown to be useful, which allowed a brush agent to learn a general drawing policy that is independent of a specific entire shape. Another important factor was to train the brush agent on *partial* shapes, not the entire shapes. This contributed highly to enhancing the generalization ability to new shapes, because even when a new shape is quite different from training data as a whole, it often contains similar partial shapes. In this kind of real-world applications manually designing immediate reward functions is often time consuming and difficult. The use of *inverse reinforcement learning* (Abbeel & Ng, 2004) would be a promising approach for this purpose. In particular, in the con-

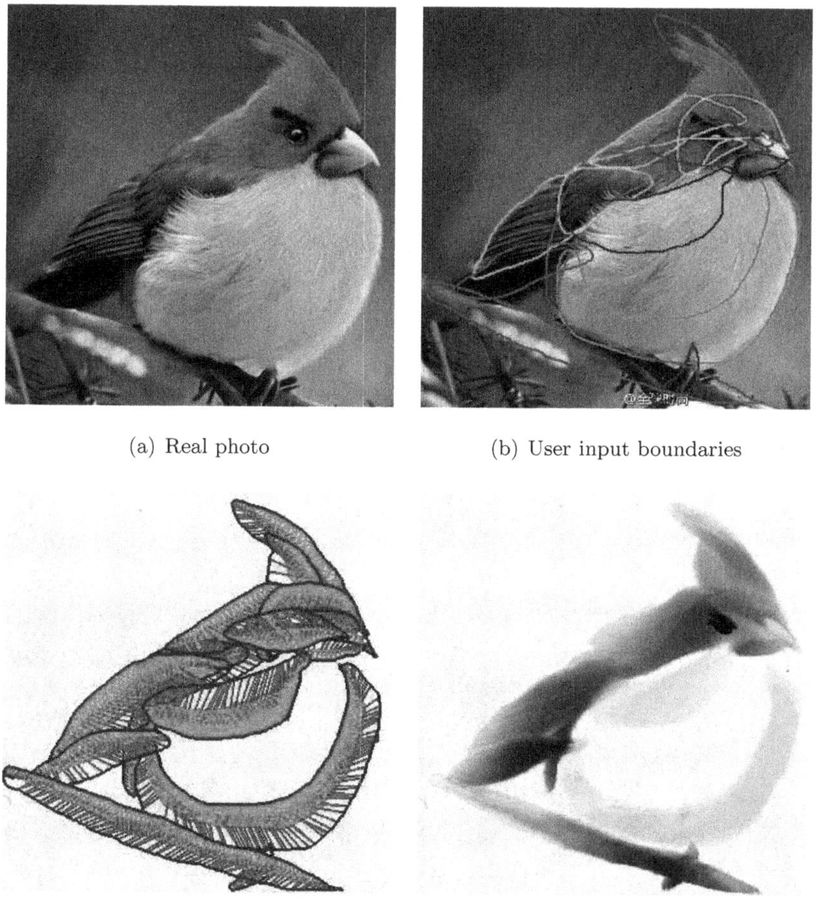

(a) Real photo

(b) User input boundaries

(c) Trajectories estimated by RL

(d) Rendering results

FIGURE 7.12: Results on new shapes.

text of sumie drawing, such data-driven design of reward functions will allow automatic learning of the *style* of a particular artist from his/her drawings.

A practical weakness of the gradient-based approach is that the step size of gradient ascent is often difficult to choose. In Chapter 8, a step-size-free method of direct policy search based on the expectation-maximization algorithm will be introduced. Another critical problem of direct policy search is that policy update is rather unstable due to the stochasticity of policies. Although variance reduction by baseline subtraction can mitigate this problem to some extent, the instability problem is still critical in practice. The natural gradient method could be an alternative, but computing the inverse Riemannian metric tends to be unstable. In Chapter 9, another gradient approach that can address the instability problem will be introduced.

FIGURE 7.13: Photo conversion into the sumie style.

Chapter 8

Direct Policy Search by Expectation-Maximization

Gradient-based direct policy search methods introduced in Chapter 7 are useful particularly in controlling continuous systems. However, appropriately choosing the step size of gradient ascent is often difficult in practice. In this chapter, we introduce another direct policy search method based on the expectation-maximization (EM) algorithm that does not contain the step size parameter. In Section 8.1, the main idea of the EM-based method is described, which is expected to converge faster because policies are more aggressively updated than the gradient-based approach. In practice, however, direct policy search often requires a large number of samples to obtain a stable policy update estimator. To improve the stability when the sample size is small, reusing previously collected samples is a promising approach. In Section 8.2, the sample-reuse technique that has been successfully used to improve the performance of policy iteration (see Chapter 4) is applied to the EM-based method. Then its experimental performance is evaluated in Section 8.3 and this chapter is concluded in Section 8.4.

8.1 Expectation-Maximization Approach

The gradient-based optimization algorithms introduced in Section 7.2 gradually update policy parameters over iterations. Although this is advantageous when controlling a physical system, it requires many iterations until convergence. In this section, the *expectation-maximization* (EM) algorithm (Dempster et al., 1977) is used to cope with this problem.

The basic idea of EM-based policy search is to iteratively update the policy parameter $\boldsymbol{\theta}$ by maximizing a lower bound of the expected return $J(\boldsymbol{\theta})$:

$$J(\boldsymbol{\theta}) = \int p(h|\boldsymbol{\theta})R(h)\mathrm{d}h.$$

To derive a lower bound of $J(\boldsymbol{\theta})$, *Jensen's inequality* (Bishop, 2006) is utilized:

$$\int q(h)f(g(h))\mathrm{d}h \geq f\left(\int q(h)g(h)\mathrm{d}h\right),$$

where q is a probability density, f is a convex function, and g is a non-negative function. For $f(t) = -\log t$, Jensen's inequality yields

$$\int q(h) \log g(h) \mathrm{d}h \leq \log \int q(h) g(h) \mathrm{d}h. \tag{8.1}$$

Assume that the return $R(h)$ is nonnegative. Let $\widetilde{\boldsymbol{\theta}}$ be the current policy parameter during the optimization procedure, and q and g in Eq. (8.1) are set as

$$q(h) = \frac{p(h|\widetilde{\boldsymbol{\theta}})R(h)}{J(\widetilde{\boldsymbol{\theta}})} \quad \text{and} \quad g(h) = \frac{p(h|\boldsymbol{\theta})}{p(h|\widetilde{\boldsymbol{\theta}})}.$$

Then the following lower bound holds for all $\boldsymbol{\theta}$:

$$\begin{aligned}
\log \frac{J(\boldsymbol{\theta})}{J(\widetilde{\boldsymbol{\theta}})} &= \log \int \frac{p(h|\boldsymbol{\theta})R(h)}{J(\widetilde{\boldsymbol{\theta}})} \mathrm{d}h \\
&= \log \int \frac{p(h|\widetilde{\boldsymbol{\theta}})R(h)}{J(\widetilde{\boldsymbol{\theta}})} \frac{p(h|\boldsymbol{\theta})}{p(h|\widetilde{\boldsymbol{\theta}})} \mathrm{d}h \\
&\geq \int \frac{p(h|\widetilde{\boldsymbol{\theta}})R(h)}{J(\widetilde{\boldsymbol{\theta}})} \log \frac{p(h|\boldsymbol{\theta})}{p(h|\widetilde{\boldsymbol{\theta}})} \mathrm{d}h.
\end{aligned}$$

This yields

$$\log J(\boldsymbol{\theta}) \geq \log \widetilde{J}(\boldsymbol{\theta}),$$

where

$$\log \widetilde{J}(\boldsymbol{\theta}) = \int \frac{R(h)p(h|\widetilde{\boldsymbol{\theta}})}{J(\widetilde{\boldsymbol{\theta}})} \log \frac{p(h|\boldsymbol{\theta})}{p(h|\widetilde{\boldsymbol{\theta}})} \mathrm{d}h + \log J(\widetilde{\boldsymbol{\theta}}).$$

In the EM approach, the parameter $\boldsymbol{\theta}$ is iteratively updated by maximizing the lower bound $\widetilde{J}(\boldsymbol{\theta})$:

$$\widehat{\boldsymbol{\theta}} = \underset{\boldsymbol{\theta}}{\operatorname{argmax}} \widetilde{J}(\boldsymbol{\theta}).$$

Since $\log \widetilde{J}(\widetilde{\boldsymbol{\theta}}) = \log J(\widetilde{\boldsymbol{\theta}})$, the lower bound $\widetilde{J}$ touches the target function J at the current solution $\widetilde{\boldsymbol{\theta}}$:

$$\widetilde{J}(\widetilde{\boldsymbol{\theta}}) = J(\widetilde{\boldsymbol{\theta}}).$$

Thus, monotone non-decrease of the expected return is guaranteed:

$$J(\widehat{\boldsymbol{\theta}}) \geq J(\widetilde{\boldsymbol{\theta}}).$$

This update is iterated until convergence (see Figure 8.1).

Let us employ the Gaussian policy model defined as

$$\pi(a|\boldsymbol{s}, \boldsymbol{\theta}) = \pi(a|\boldsymbol{s}, \boldsymbol{\mu}, \sigma)$$

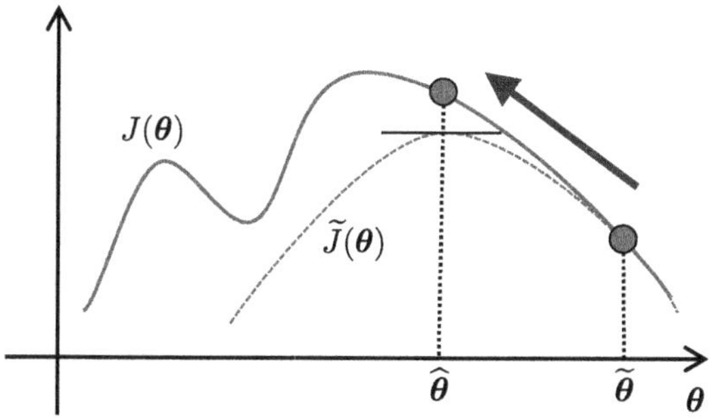

FIGURE 8.1: Policy parameter update in the EM-based policy search. The policy parameter $\boldsymbol{\theta}$ is updated iteratively by maximizing the lower bound $\widetilde{J}(\boldsymbol{\theta})$, which touches the true expected return $J(\boldsymbol{\theta})$ at the current solution $\widetilde{\boldsymbol{\theta}}$.

$$= \frac{1}{\sigma\sqrt{2\pi}} \exp\left(-\frac{(a - \boldsymbol{\mu}^\top \boldsymbol{\phi}(\boldsymbol{s}))^2}{2\sigma^2}\right),$$

where $\boldsymbol{\theta} = (\boldsymbol{\mu}^\top, \sigma)^\top$ and $\boldsymbol{\phi}(\boldsymbol{s})$ denotes the basis function.

The maximizer $\widehat{\boldsymbol{\theta}} = (\widehat{\boldsymbol{\mu}}^\top, \widehat{\sigma})^\top$ of the lower bound $\widetilde{J}(\boldsymbol{\theta})$ can be analytically obtained as

$$\begin{aligned}
\widehat{\boldsymbol{\mu}} &= \left(\int p(h|\widetilde{\boldsymbol{\theta}})R(h)\sum_{t=1}^{T}\boldsymbol{\phi}(\boldsymbol{s}_t)\boldsymbol{\phi}(\boldsymbol{s}_t)^\top \mathrm{d}h\right)^{-1}\left(\int p(h|\widetilde{\boldsymbol{\theta}})R(h)\sum_{t=1}^{T}a_t\boldsymbol{\phi}(\boldsymbol{s}_t)\mathrm{d}h\right)\\
&\approx \left(\sum_{n=1}^{N}R(h_n)\sum_{t=1}^{T}\boldsymbol{\phi}(\boldsymbol{s}_{t,n})\boldsymbol{\phi}(\boldsymbol{s}_{t,n})^\top\right)^{-1}\left(\sum_{n=1}^{N}R(h_n)\sum_{t=1}^{T}a_{t,n}\boldsymbol{\phi}(\boldsymbol{s}_{t,n})\right),\\
\widehat{\sigma}^2 &= \left(\int p(h|\widetilde{\boldsymbol{\theta}})R(h)\mathrm{d}h\right)^{-1}\left(\int p(h|\widetilde{\boldsymbol{\theta}})R(h)\frac{1}{T}\sum_{t=1}^{T}(a_t - \widehat{\boldsymbol{\mu}}^\top\boldsymbol{\phi}(\boldsymbol{s}_t))^2\mathrm{d}h\right)\\
&\approx \left(\sum_{n=1}^{N}R(h_n)\right)^{-1}\left(\sum_{n=1}^{N}R(h_n)\frac{1}{T}\sum_{t=1}^{T}(a_{t,n} - \widehat{\boldsymbol{\mu}}^\top\boldsymbol{\phi}(\boldsymbol{s}_{t,n}))^2\right),
\end{aligned}$$

where the expectation over h is approximated by the average over roll-out samples $\mathcal{H} = \{h_n\}_{n=1}^{N}$ from the current policy $\widetilde{\boldsymbol{\theta}}$:

$$h_n = [\boldsymbol{s}_{1,n}, a_{1,n}, \ldots, \boldsymbol{s}_{T,n}, a_{T,n}].$$

Note that EM-based policy search for Gaussian models is called *reward-weighted regression* (RWR) (Peters & Schaal, 2007).

8.2 Sample Reuse

In practice, a large number of samples is needed to obtain a stable policy update estimator in the EM-based policy search. In this section, the sample-reuse technique is applied to the EM method to cope with the instability problem.

8.2.1 Episodic Importance Weighting

The original RWR method is an *on-policy* algorithm that uses data drawn from the current policy. On the other hand, the situation called *off-policy* reinforcement learning is considered here, where the *sampling policy* for collecting data samples is different from the target policy. More specifically, N trajectory samples are gathered following the policy π_ℓ in the ℓ-th policy update iteration:

$$\mathcal{H}^{\pi_\ell} = \{h_1^{\pi_\ell}, \dots, h_N^{\pi_\ell}\},$$

where each trajectory sample $h_n^{\pi_\ell}$ is given as

$$h_n^{\pi_\ell} = [\boldsymbol{s}_{1,n}^{\pi_\ell}, a_{1,n}^{\pi_\ell}, \dots, \boldsymbol{s}_{T,n}^{\pi_\ell}, a_{T,n}^{\pi_\ell}, \boldsymbol{s}_{T+1,n}^{\pi_\ell}].$$

We want to utilize all these samples to improve the current policy.

Suppose that we are currently at the L-th policy update iteration. If the policies $\{\pi_\ell\}_{\ell=1}^{L}$ remain unchanged over the RWR updates, just using the plain update rules provided in Section 8.1 gives a consistent estimator $\widehat{\boldsymbol{\theta}}_{L+1}^{\mathrm{NIW}} = (\widehat{\boldsymbol{\mu}}_{L+1}^{\mathrm{NIW}\top}, \widehat{\sigma}_{L+1}^{\mathrm{NIW}})^\top$, where

$$\begin{aligned}
\widehat{\boldsymbol{\mu}}_{L+1}^{\mathrm{NIW}} &= \left(\sum_{\ell=1}^{L}\sum_{n=1}^{N} R(h_n^{\pi_\ell}) \sum_{t=1}^{T} \boldsymbol{\phi}(\boldsymbol{s}_{t,n}^{\pi_\ell})\boldsymbol{\phi}(\boldsymbol{s}_{t,n}^{\pi_\ell})^\top\right)^{-1} \\
&\quad \times \left(\sum_{\ell=1}^{L}\sum_{n=1}^{N} R(h_n^{\pi_\ell}) \sum_{t=1}^{T} a_{t,n}^{\pi_\ell}\boldsymbol{\phi}(\boldsymbol{s}_{t,n}^{\pi_\ell})\right), \\
(\widehat{\sigma}_{L+1}^{\mathrm{NIW}})^2 &= \left(\sum_{\ell=1}^{L}\sum_{n=1}^{N} R(h_n^{\pi_\ell})\right)^{-1} \\
&\quad \times \left(\sum_{\ell=1}^{L}\sum_{n=1}^{N} R(h_n^{\pi_\ell}) \frac{1}{T}\sum_{t=1}^{T} \left(a_{t,n}^{\pi_\ell} - \widehat{\boldsymbol{\mu}}_{L+1}^{\mathrm{NIW}\top}\boldsymbol{\phi}(\boldsymbol{s}_{t,n}^{\pi_\ell})\right)^2\right).
\end{aligned}$$

The superscript "NIW" stands for "no importance weight." However, since policies are updated in each RWR iteration, data samples $\{\mathcal{H}^{\pi_\ell}\}_{\ell=1}^{L}$ collected over iterations generally follow different probability distributions induced by different policies. Therefore, naive use of the above update rules will result in an inconsistent estimator.

In the same way as the discussion in Chapter 4, *importance sampling* can be used to cope with this problem. The basic idea of importance sampling is to weight the samples drawn from a different distribution to match the target distribution. More specifically, from i.i.d. (*independent and identically distributed*) samples $\{h_n^{\pi_\ell}\}_{n=1}^N$ following $p(h|\boldsymbol{\theta}_\ell)$, the expectation of a function $g(h)$ over another probability density function $p(h|\boldsymbol{\theta}_L)$ can be estimated in a consistent manner by the *importance-weighted average*:

$$\begin{aligned}\frac{1}{N}\sum_{n=1}^N g(h_n^{\pi_\ell})\frac{p(h_n^{\pi_\ell}|\boldsymbol{\theta}_L)}{p(h_n^{\pi_\ell}|\boldsymbol{\theta}_\ell)} &\stackrel{N\to\infty}{\longrightarrow} \mathbb{E}_{p(h|\boldsymbol{\theta}_\ell)}\left[g(h)\frac{p(h|\boldsymbol{\theta}_L)}{p(h|\boldsymbol{\theta}_\ell)}\right]\\ &= \int g(h)\frac{p(h|\boldsymbol{\theta}_L)}{p(h|\boldsymbol{\theta}_\ell)}p(h|\boldsymbol{\theta}_\ell)\mathrm{d}h = \int g(h)p(h|\boldsymbol{\theta}_L)\mathrm{d}h\\ &= \mathbb{E}_{p(h|\boldsymbol{\theta}_L)}\left[g(h)\right].\end{aligned}$$

The ratio of two densities $p(h|\boldsymbol{\theta}_L)/p(h|\boldsymbol{\theta}_\ell)$ is called the *importance weight* for trajectory h.

This importance sampling technique can be employed in RWR to obtain a consistent estimator $\widehat{\boldsymbol{\theta}}_{L+1}^{\mathrm{EIW}} = (\widehat{\boldsymbol{\mu}}_{L+1}^{\mathrm{EIW}\top}, \widehat{\sigma}_{L+1}^{\mathrm{EIW}})^\top$, where

$$\begin{aligned}\widehat{\boldsymbol{\mu}}_{L+1}^{\mathrm{EIW}} &= \left(\sum_{\ell=1}^L\sum_{n=1}^N R(h_n^{\pi_\ell})w^{(L,\ell)}(h)\sum_{t=1}^T \boldsymbol{\phi}(\boldsymbol{s}_{t,n}^{\pi_\ell})\boldsymbol{\phi}(\boldsymbol{s}_{t,n}^{\pi_\ell})^\top\right)^{-1}\\ &\quad\times\left(\sum_{\ell=1}^L\sum_{n=1}^N R(h_n^{\pi_\ell})w^{(L,\ell)}(h)\sum_{t=1}^T a_{t,n}^{\pi_\ell}\boldsymbol{\phi}(\boldsymbol{s}_{t,n}^{\pi_\ell})\right),\\ (\widehat{\sigma}_{L+1}^{\mathrm{EIW}})^2 &= \left(\sum_{\ell=1}^L\sum_{n=1}^N R(h_n^{\pi_\ell})w^{(L,\ell)}(h_n^{\pi_\ell})\right)^{-1}\\ &\quad\times\left(\sum_{\ell=1}^L\sum_{n=1}^N R(h_n^{\pi_\ell})w^{(L,\ell)}(h_n^{\pi_\ell})\frac{1}{T}\sum_{t=1}^T\left(a_{t,n}^{\pi_\ell}-\widehat{\boldsymbol{\mu}}_{L+1}^{\mathrm{EIW}\top}\boldsymbol{\phi}(\boldsymbol{s}_{t,n}^{\pi_\ell})\right)^2\right).\end{aligned}$$

Here, $w^{(L,\ell)}(h)$ denotes the importance weight defined by

$$w^{(L,\ell)}(h) = \frac{p(h|\boldsymbol{\theta}_L)}{p(h|\boldsymbol{\theta}_\ell)}.$$

The superscript "EIW" stands for "episodic importance weight."

$p(h|\boldsymbol{\theta}_L)$ and $p(h|\boldsymbol{\theta}_\ell)$ denote the probability density of observing trajectory

$$h = [\boldsymbol{s}_1, a_1, \ldots, \boldsymbol{s}_T, a_T, \boldsymbol{s}_{T+1}]$$

under policy parameters $\boldsymbol{\theta}_L$ and $\boldsymbol{\theta}_\ell$, which can be explicitly written as

$$p(h|\boldsymbol{\theta}_L) = p(\boldsymbol{s}_1)\prod_{t=1}^T p(\boldsymbol{s}_{t+1}|\boldsymbol{s}_t, a_t)\pi(a_t|\boldsymbol{s}_t, \boldsymbol{\theta}_L),$$

$$p(h|\boldsymbol{\theta}_\ell) = p(\boldsymbol{s}_1)\prod_{t=1}^{T} p(\boldsymbol{s}_{t+1}|\boldsymbol{s}_t, a_t)\pi(a_t|\boldsymbol{s}_t, \boldsymbol{\theta}_\ell).$$

The two probability densities $p(h|\boldsymbol{\theta}_L)$ and $p(h|\boldsymbol{\theta}_\ell)$ both contain unknown probability densities $p(\boldsymbol{s}_1)$ and $\{p(\boldsymbol{s}_{t+1}|\boldsymbol{s}_t, a_t)\}_{t=1}^{T}$. However, since they cancel out in the importance weight, it can be computed without the knowledge of $p(\boldsymbol{s})$ and $p(\boldsymbol{s}'|\boldsymbol{s}, a)$ as

$$w^{(L,\ell)}(h) = \frac{\prod_{t=1}^{T}\pi(a_t|\boldsymbol{s}_t, \boldsymbol{\theta}_L)}{\prod_{t=1}^{T}\pi(a_t|\boldsymbol{s}_t, \boldsymbol{\theta}_\ell)}.$$

Although the importance-weighted estimator $\widehat{\boldsymbol{\theta}}_{L+1}^{\mathrm{EIW}}$ is guaranteed to be consistent, it tends to have large variance (Shimodaira, 2000; Sugiyama & Kawanabe, 2012). Therefore, the importance-weighted estimator tends to be unstable when the number of episodes N is rather small.

8.2.2 Per-Decision Importance Weight

Since the reward at the t-th step does not depend on future state-action transitions after the t-th step, an episodic importance weight can be decomposed into stepwise importance weights (Precup et al., 2000). For instance, the expected return $J(\boldsymbol{\theta}_L)$ can be expressed as

$$\begin{aligned} J(\boldsymbol{\theta}_L) &= \int R(h)p(h|\boldsymbol{\theta}_L)\mathrm{d}h \\ &= \int \Big(\sum_{t=1}^{T}\gamma^{t-1}r(\boldsymbol{s}_t, a_t, \boldsymbol{s}_{t+1})\Big)w^{(L,\ell)}(h)p(h|\boldsymbol{\theta}_\ell)\mathrm{d}h \\ &= \int \Big(\sum_{t=1}^{T}\gamma^{t-1}r(\boldsymbol{s}_t, a_t, \boldsymbol{s}_{t+1})w_t^{(L,\ell)}(h)\Big)p(h|\boldsymbol{\theta}_\ell)\mathrm{d}h, \end{aligned}$$

where $w_t^{(L,\ell)}(h)$ is the t-step importance weight, called the *per-decision importance weight* (PIW), defined as

$$w_t^{(L,\ell)}(h) = \frac{\prod_{t'=1}^{t}\pi(a_{t'}|\boldsymbol{s}_{t'}, \boldsymbol{\theta}_L)}{\prod_{t'=1}^{t}\pi(a_{t'}|\boldsymbol{s}_{t'}, \boldsymbol{\theta}_\ell)}.$$

Here, the PIW idea is applied to RWR and a more stable algorithm is developed. A slight complication is that the policy update formula given in Section 8.2.1 contains double sums over T steps, e.g.,

$$R(h)\sum_{t'=1}^{T}\phi(\boldsymbol{s}_{t'})\phi(\boldsymbol{s}_{t'}) = \sum_{t,t'=1}^{T}\gamma^{t-1}r(\boldsymbol{s}_t, a_t, \boldsymbol{s}_{t+1})\phi(\boldsymbol{s}_{t'})\phi(\boldsymbol{s}_{t'}).$$

In this case, the summand

$$\gamma^{t-1}r(\boldsymbol{s}_t, a_t, \boldsymbol{s}_{t+1})\phi(\boldsymbol{s}_{t'})\phi(\boldsymbol{s}_{t'})$$

does not depend on future state-action pairs after the $\max(t,t')$-th step. Thus, the episodic importance weight for

$$\gamma^{t-1} r(\boldsymbol{s}_t, a_t, \boldsymbol{s}_{t+1}) \phi(\boldsymbol{s}_{t'}) \phi(\boldsymbol{s}_{t'})$$

can be simplified to the per-decision importance weight $w^{(L,\ell)}_{\max(t,t')}$. Consequently, the PIW-based policy update rules are given as

$$\begin{aligned}
\widehat{\boldsymbol{\mu}}^{\mathrm{PIW}}_{L+1} &= \left(\sum_{\ell=1}^{L} \sum_{n=1}^{N} \sum_{t,t'=1}^{T} \gamma^{t-1} r_{t,n} \boldsymbol{\phi}(\boldsymbol{s}^{\pi_\ell}_{t',n}) \boldsymbol{\phi}(\boldsymbol{s}^{\pi_\ell}_{t',n})^\top w^{(L,\ell)}_{\max(t,t')}(h^{\pi_\ell}_n) \right)^{-1} \\
&\quad \times \left(\sum_{\ell=1}^{L} \sum_{n=1}^{N} \sum_{t,t'=1}^{T} \gamma^{t-1} r_{t,n} a^{\pi_\ell}_{t',n} \boldsymbol{\phi}(\boldsymbol{s}^{\pi_\ell}_{t',n}) w^{(L,\ell)}_{\max(t,t')}(h^{\pi_\ell}_n) \right), \\
(\widehat{\sigma}^{\mathrm{PIW}}_{L+1})^2 &= \left(\sum_{\ell=1}^{L} \sum_{n=1}^{N} \sum_{t=1}^{T} \gamma^{t-1} r_{t,n} w^{(L,\ell)}_{t}(h^{\pi_\ell}_n) \right)^{-1} \\
&\quad \times \left(\frac{1}{T} \sum_{\ell=1}^{L} \sum_{n=1}^{N} \sum_{t,t'=1}^{T} \gamma^{t-1} r_{t,n} \left(a^{\pi_\ell}_{t',n} - \widehat{\boldsymbol{\mu}}^{\mathrm{PIW}\top}_{L+1} \boldsymbol{\phi}(\boldsymbol{s}^{\pi_\ell}_{t',n}) \right)^2 w^{(L,\ell)}_{\max(t,t')}(h^{\pi_\ell}_n) \right),
\end{aligned}$$

where

$$r_{t,n} = r(\boldsymbol{s}_{t,n}, a_{t,n}, \boldsymbol{s}_{t+1,n}).$$

This PIW estimator $\widehat{\boldsymbol{\theta}}^{\mathrm{PIW}}_{L+1} = (\widehat{\boldsymbol{\mu}}^{\mathrm{PIW}\top}_{L+1}, \widehat{\sigma}^{\mathrm{PIW}}_{L+1})^\top$ is consistent and potentially more stable than the plain EIW estimator $\widehat{\boldsymbol{\theta}}^{\mathrm{EIW}}_{L+1}$.

8.2.3 Adaptive Per-Decision Importance Weighting

To more actively control the stability of the PIW estimator, the *adaptive per-decision importance weight* (AIW) is employed. More specifically, an importance weight $w^{(L,\ell)}_{\max(t,t')}(h)$ is "flattened" by *flattening parameter* $\nu \in [0,1]$ as $\left(w^{(L,\ell)}_{\max(t,t')}(h)\right)^\nu$, i.e., the ν-th power of the per-decision importance weight. Then we have $\widehat{\boldsymbol{\theta}}^{\mathrm{AIW}}_{L+1} = (\widehat{\boldsymbol{\mu}}^{\mathrm{AIW}\top}_{L+1}, \widehat{\sigma}^{\mathrm{AIW}}_{L+1})^\top$, where

$$\begin{aligned}
\widehat{\boldsymbol{\mu}}^{\mathrm{AIW}}_{L+1} &= \left(\sum_{\ell=1}^{L} \sum_{n=1}^{N} \sum_{t,t'=1}^{T} \gamma^{t-1} r_{t,n} \boldsymbol{\phi}(\boldsymbol{s}^{\pi_\ell}_{t',n}) \boldsymbol{\phi}(\boldsymbol{s}^{\pi_\ell}_{t',n})^\top \left(w^{(L,\ell)}_{\max(t,t')}(h^{\pi_\ell}_n) \right)^\nu \right)^{-1} \\
&\quad \times \left(\sum_{\ell=1}^{L} \sum_{n=1}^{N} \sum_{t,t'=1}^{T} \gamma^{t-1} r_{t,n} a^{\pi_\ell}_{t',n} \boldsymbol{\phi}(\boldsymbol{s}^{\pi_\ell}_{t',n}) \left(w^{(L,\ell)}_{\max(t,t')}(h^{\pi_\ell}_n) \right)^\nu \right), \\
(\widehat{\sigma}^{\mathrm{AIW}}_{L+1})^2 &= \left(\sum_{\ell=1}^{L} \sum_{n=1}^{N} \sum_{t=1}^{T} \gamma^{t-1} r_{t,n} \left(w^{(L,\ell)}_{t}(h^{\pi_\ell}_n) \right)^\nu \right)^{-1}
\end{aligned}$$

$$\times \left(\frac{1}{T} \sum_{\ell=1}^{L} \sum_{n=1}^{N} \sum_{t,t'=1}^{T} \gamma^{t-1} r_{t,n} \left(a_{t',n}^{\pi_\ell} - \widehat{\boldsymbol{\mu}}_{L+1}^{\mathrm{AIW}\top} \boldsymbol{\phi}(\boldsymbol{s}_{t',n}^{\pi_\ell}) \right)^2 \left(w_{\max(t,t')}^{(L,\ell)}(h_n^{\pi_\ell}) \right)^{\nu} \right).$$

When $\nu = 0$, AIW is reduced to NIW. Therefore, it is relatively stable, but not consistent. On the other hand, when $\nu = 1$, AIW is reduced to PIW. Therefore, it is consistent, but rather unstable. In practice, an intermediate ν often produces a better estimator. Note that the value of the flattening parameter can be different in each iteration, i.e., ν may be replaced by ν_ℓ. However, for simplicity, a single common value ν is considered here.

8.2.4 Automatic Selection of Flattening Parameter

The flattening parameter allows us to control the trade-off between consistency and stability. Here, we show how the value of the flattening parameter can be optimally chosen using data samples.

The goal of policy search is to find the optimal policy that maximizes the expected return $J(\boldsymbol{\theta})$. Therefore, the optimal flattening parameter value ν_L^* at the L-th iteration is given by

$$\nu_L^* = \underset{\nu}{\mathrm{argmax}}\, J(\widehat{\boldsymbol{\theta}}_{L+1}^{\mathrm{AIW}}(\nu)).$$

Directly obtaining ν_L^* requires the computation of the expected return $J(\widehat{\boldsymbol{\theta}}_{L+1}^{\mathrm{AIW}}(\nu))$ for each candidate of ν. To this end, data samples following $\pi(a|\boldsymbol{s}; \widehat{\boldsymbol{\theta}}_{L+1}^{\mathrm{AIW}}(\nu))$ are needed for each ν, which is prohibitively expensive. To reuse samples generated by previous policies, a variation of cross-validation called *importance-weighted cross-validation* (IWCV) (Sugiyama et al., 2007) is employed.

The basic idea of IWCV is to split the training dataset $\mathcal{H}^{\pi_{1:L}} = \{\mathcal{H}^{\pi_\ell}\}_{\ell=1}^{L}$ into an "estimation part" and a "validation part." Then the policy parameter $\widehat{\boldsymbol{\theta}}_{L+1}^{\mathrm{AIW}}(\nu)$ is learned from the estimation part and its expected return $J(\widehat{\boldsymbol{\theta}}^{\mathrm{AIW}}(\nu))$ is approximated using the importance-weighted loss for the validation part. As pointed out in Section 8.2.1, importance weighting tends to be unstable when the number N of episodes is small. For this reason, per-decision importance weighting is used for cross-validation. Below, how IWCV is applied to the selection of the flattening parameter ν in the current context is explained in more detail.

Let us divide the training dataset $\mathcal{H}^{\pi_{1:L}} = \{\mathcal{H}^{\pi_\ell}\}_{\ell=1}^{L}$ into K disjoint subsets $\{\mathcal{H}_k^{\pi_{1:L}}\}_{k=1}^{K}$ of the same size, where each $\mathcal{H}_k^{\pi_{1:L}}$ contains N/K episodic samples from every $\mathcal{H}^{\pi_\ell}$. For simplicity, we assume that N is divisible by K, i.e., N/K is an integer. $K = 5$ will be used in the experiments later.

Let $\widehat{\boldsymbol{\theta}}_{L+1,k}^{\mathrm{AIW}}(\nu)$ be the policy parameter learned from $\{\mathcal{H}_{k'}^{\pi_{1:L}}\}_{k' \neq k}$ (i.e., all data without $\mathcal{H}_k^{\pi_{1:L}}$) by AIW estimation. The expected return of $\widehat{\boldsymbol{\theta}}_{L+1,k}^{\mathrm{AIW}}(\nu)$ is estimated using the PIW estimator from $\mathcal{H}_k^{\pi_{1:L}}$ as

$$\widehat{J}_{\mathrm{IWCV}}^k(\widehat{\boldsymbol{\theta}}_{L+1,k}^{\mathrm{AIW}}(\nu)) = \frac{1}{\eta} \sum_{h \in \mathcal{H}_k^{\pi_{1:L}}} \sum_{t=1}^{T} \gamma^{t-1} r(\boldsymbol{s}_t, a_t, \boldsymbol{s}_{t+1}) w_t^{(L,\ell)}(h),$$

where η is a normalization constant. An ordinary choice is $\eta = LN/K$, but a more stable variant given by

$$\eta = \sum_{h \in \mathcal{H}_k^{\pi_{1:L}}} w_t^{(L,\ell)}(h)$$

is often preferred in practice (Precup et al., 2000).

The above procedure is repeated for all $k = 1, \ldots, K$, and the average score,

$$\widehat{J}_{\mathrm{IWCV}}(\widehat{\boldsymbol{\theta}}_{L+1}^{\mathrm{AIW}}(\nu)) = \frac{1}{K} \sum_{k=1}^{K} \widehat{J}_{\mathrm{IWCV}}^k(\widehat{\boldsymbol{\theta}}_{L+1,k}^{\mathrm{AIW}}(\nu)),$$

is computed. This is the K-fold IWCV estimator of $J(\widehat{\boldsymbol{\theta}}_{L+1}^{\mathrm{AIW}}(\nu))$, which was shown to be almost unbiased (Sugiyama et al., 2007).

This K-fold IWCV score is computed for each candidate value of the flattening parameter ν and the one that maximizes the IWCV score is chosen:

$$\widehat{\nu}_{\mathrm{IWCV}} = \underset{\nu}{\mathrm{argmax}}\, \widehat{J}_{\mathrm{IWCV}}(\widehat{\boldsymbol{\theta}}_{L+1}^{\mathrm{AIW}}(\nu)).$$

This IWCV scheme can also be used for choosing the basis functions $\boldsymbol{\phi}(\boldsymbol{s})$ in the Gaussian policy model.

Note that when the importance weights $w_{\max(t,t')}^{(L,\ell)}$ are all one (i.e., no importance weighting), the above IWCV procedure is reduced to the ordinary CV procedure. The use of IWCV is essential here since the target policy $\pi(a|\boldsymbol{s}, \widehat{\boldsymbol{\theta}}_{L+1}^{\mathrm{AIW}}(\nu))$ is usually different from the previous policies used for collecting the data samples $\mathcal{H}^{\pi_{1:L}}$. Therefore, the expected return estimated using ordinary CV, $\widehat{J}_{\mathrm{CV}}(\widehat{\boldsymbol{\theta}}_{L+1}^{\mathrm{AIW}}(\nu))$, would be heavily biased.

8.2.5 Reward-Weighted Regression with Sample Reuse

So far, we have introduced AIW to control the stability of the policy-parameter update and IWCV to automatically choose the flattening parameter based on the estimated expected return. The policy search algorithm that combines these two methods is called *reward-weighted regression with sample reuse* (RRR).

In each iteration ($L = 1, 2, \ldots$) of RRR, episodic data samples $\mathcal{H}^{\pi_L}$ are collected following the current policy $\pi(a|\boldsymbol{s}, \boldsymbol{\theta}_L^{\mathrm{AIW}})$, the flattening parameter ν is chosen so as to maximize the expected return $\widehat{J}_{\mathrm{IWCV}}(\nu)$ estimated by IWCV using $\{\mathcal{H}^{\pi_\ell}\}_{\ell=1}^{L}$, and then the policy parameter is updated to $\boldsymbol{\theta}_{L+1}^{\mathrm{AIW}}$ using $\{\mathcal{H}^{\pi_\ell}\}_{\ell=1}^{L}$.

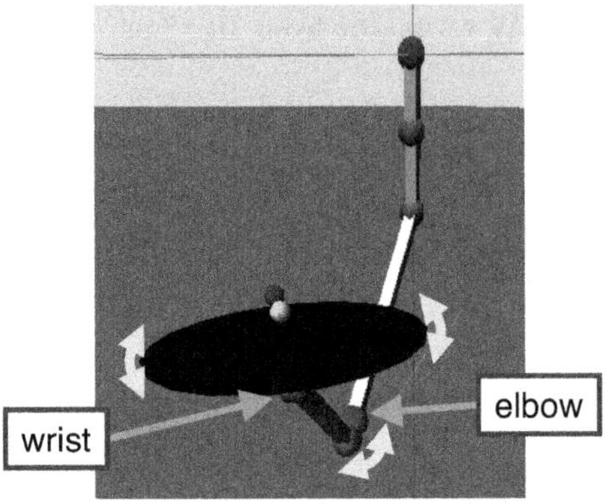

FIGURE 8.2: Ball balancing using a robot arm simulator. Two joints of the robots are controlled to keep the ball in the middle of the tray.

8.3 Numerical Examples

The performance of RRR is experimentally evaluated on a ball-balancing task using a robot arm simulator (Schaal, 2009).

As illustrated in Figure 8.2, a 7-degree-of-freedom arm is mounted on the ceiling upside down, which is equipped with a circular tray of radius 0.24 [m] at the end effector. The goal is to control the joints of the robot so that the ball is brought to the middle of the tray. However, the difficulty is that the angle of the tray cannot be controlled directly, which is a typical restriction in real-world joint-motion planning based on feedback from the environment (e.g., the state of the ball).

To simplify the problem, only two joints are controlled here: the wrist angle α_{roll} and the elbow angle α_{pitch}. All the remaining joints are fixed. Control of the wrist and elbow angles would roughly correspond to changing the *roll* and *pitch* angles of the tray, but not directly.

Two separate control subsystems are designed here, each of which is in charge of controlling the roll and pitch angles. Each subsystem has its own policy parameter $\boldsymbol{\theta}$, state space $\mathcal{S}$, and action space $\mathcal{A}$. The state space $\mathcal{S}$ is continuous and consists of $(x, \dot{x})$, where x [m] is the position of the ball on the tray along each axis and $\dot{x}$ [m/s] is the velocity of the ball. The action space $\mathcal{A}$ is continuous and corresponds to the target angle a [rad] of the joint. The reward function is defined as

$$r(\boldsymbol{s}, a, \boldsymbol{s}') = \exp\left(-\frac{5(x')^2 + (\dot{x}')^2 + a^2}{2(0.24/2)^2}\right),$$

where the number 0.24 in the denominator comes from the radius of the tray.

Below, how the control system is designed is explained in more detail.

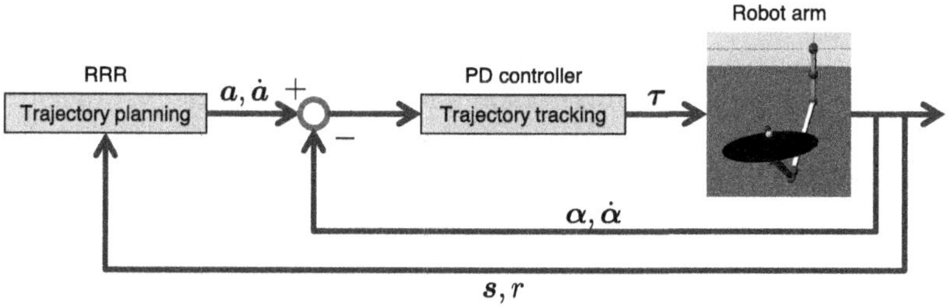

FIGURE 8.3: The block diagram of the robot-arm control system for ball balancing. The control system has two feedback loops, i.e., joint-trajectory planning by RRR and trajectory tracking by a high-gain proportional-derivative (PD) controller.

As illustrated in Figure 8.3, the control system has two feedback loops for trajectory planning using an RRR controller and trajectory tracking using a high-gain *proportional-derivative* (PD) controller (Siciliano & Khatib, 2008). The RRR controller outputs the target joint angle obtained by the current policy at every 0.2 [s]. Nine Gaussian kernels are used as basis functions $\phi(\boldsymbol{s})$ with the kernel centers $\{\boldsymbol{c}_b\}_{b=1}^{9}$ located over the state space at

$$(x, \dot{x}) \in \{(-0.2, -0.4), (-0.2, 0), (-0.1, 0.4), (0, -0.4), (0, 0), (0, 0.4), (0.1, -0.4), (0.2, 0), (0.2, 0.4)\}.$$

The Gaussian width is set at $\sigma_{\text{basis}} = 0.1$. Based on the discrete-time target angles obtained by RRR, the desired joint trajectory in the continuous time domain is linearly interpolated as

$$a_{t,u} = a_t + u\dot{a}_t,$$

where u is the time from the last output a_t of RRR at the t-th step. $\dot{a}_t$ is the angular velocity computed by

$$\dot{a}_t = \frac{a_t - a_{t-1}}{0.2},$$

where a_0 is the initial angle of a joint. The angular velocity is assumed to be constant during the 0.2 [s] cycle of trajectory planning.

On the other hand, the PD controller converts desired joint trajectories to motor torques as

$$\boldsymbol{\tau}_{t,u} = \boldsymbol{\mu}_{\text{p}} * (\boldsymbol{a}_{t,u} - \boldsymbol{\alpha}_{t,u}) + \boldsymbol{\mu}_{\text{d}} * (\dot{\boldsymbol{a}}_t - \dot{\boldsymbol{\alpha}}_{t,u}),$$

where $\boldsymbol{\tau}$ is the 2-dimensional vector consisting of the torque applied to the wrist and elbow joints. $\boldsymbol{a} = (a_{\text{pitch}}, a_{\text{roll}})^\top$ and $\dot{\boldsymbol{a}} = (\dot{a}_{\text{pitch}}, \dot{a}_{\text{roll}})^\top$ are the 2-dimensional vectors consisting of the desired angles and velocities. $\boldsymbol{\alpha} =$

$(\alpha_{\text{pitch}}, \alpha_{\text{roll}})^\top$ and $\dot{\boldsymbol{\alpha}} = (\dot{\alpha}_{\text{pitch}}, \dot{\alpha}_{\text{roll}})^\top$ are the 2-dimensional vectors consisting of the current joint angles and velocities. $\boldsymbol{\mu}_{\text{p}}$ and $\boldsymbol{\mu}_{\text{d}}$ are the 2-dimensional vectors consisting of the proportional and derivative gains. "$*$" denotes the element-wise product. Since the control cycle of the robot arm is 0.002 [s], the PD controller is applied 100 times (i.e., $t = 0.002, 0.004, \ldots, 0.198, 0.2$) in each RRR cycle.

Figure 8.4 depicts a desired trajectory of the wrist joint generated by a random policy and an actual trajectory obtained using the high-gain PD controller described above. The graphs show that the desired trajectory is followed by the robot arm reasonably well.

The policy parameter $\boldsymbol{\theta}_L$ is learned through the RRR iterations. The initial policy parameters $\boldsymbol{\theta}_1 = (\boldsymbol{\mu}_1^\top, \sigma_1)^\top$ are set manually as

$$\boldsymbol{\mu}_1 = (-0.5, -0.5, 0, -0.5, 0, 0, 0, 0, 0)^\top \quad \text{and} \quad \sigma_1 = 0.1,$$

so that a wide range of states and actions can be safely explored in the first iteration. The initial position of the ball is randomly selected as $x \in [-0.05, 0.05]$. The dataset collected in each iteration consists of 10 episodes with 20 steps. The duration of an episode is 4 [s] and the sampling cycle by RRR is 0.2 [s].

Three scenarios are considered here:

- **NIW:** Sample reuse with $\nu = 0$.
- **PIW:** Sample reuse with $\nu = 1$.
- **RRR:** Sample reuse with ν chosen by IWCV from $\{0, 0.25, 0.5, 0.75, 1\}$ in each iteration.

The discount factor is set at $\gamma = 0.99$. Figure 8.5 depicts the averaged expected return over 10 trials as a function of the number of policy update iterations. The expected return in each trial is computed from 20 test episodic samples that have not been used for training. The graph shows that RRR nicely improves the performance over iterations. On the other hand, the performance for $\nu = 0$ is saturated after the 3rd iteration, and the performance for $\nu = 1$ is improved in the beginning but suddenly goes down at the 5th iteration. The result for $\nu = 1$ indicates that a large change in policies causes severe instability in sample reuse.

Figure 8.6 and Figure 8.7 depict examples of trajectories of the wrist angle α_{roll}, the elbow angle α_{pitch}, resulting ball movement x, and reward r for policies obtained by NIW ($\nu = 0$) and RRR (ν is chosen by IWCV) after the 10th iteration. By the policy obtained by NIW, the ball goes through the middle of the tray, i.e., $(x_{\text{roll}}, x_{\text{pitch}}) = (0, 0)$, and does not stop. On the other hand, the policy obtained by RRR successfully guides the ball to the middle of the tray along the roll axis, although the movement along the pitch axis looks similar to that by NIW. Motion examples by RRR with ν chosen by IWCV are illustrated in Figure 8.8.

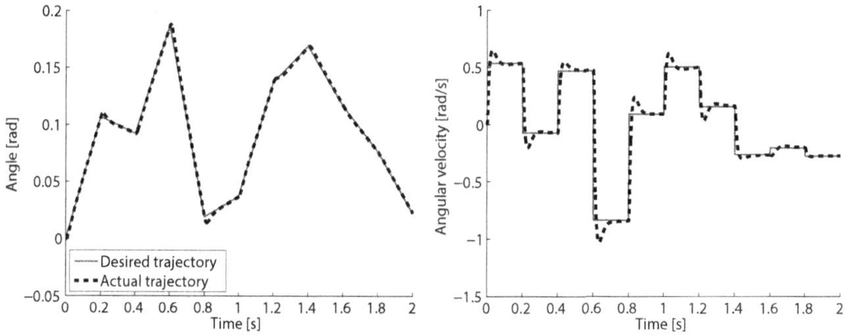

(a) Trajectory in angles (b) Trajectory in angular velocities

FIGURE 8.4: An example of desired and actual trajectories of the wrist joint in the realistic ball-balancing task. The target joint angle is determined by a random policy at every 0.2 [s], and then a linearly interpolated angle and constant velocity are tracked using the proportional-derivative (PD) controller in the cycle of 0.002 [s].

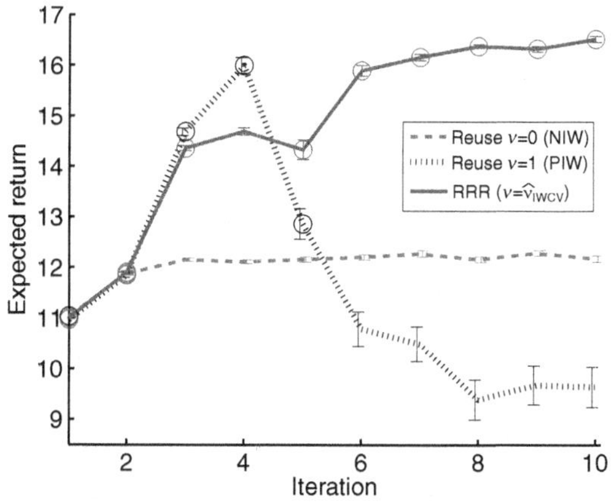

FIGURE 8.5: The performance of learned policies when $\nu = 0$ (NIW), $\nu = 1$ (PIW), and ν is chosen by IWCV (RRR) in ball balancing using a simulated robot-arm system. The performance is measured by the return averaged over 10 trials. The symbol "$\circ$" indicates that the method is the best or comparable to the best one in terms of the expected return by the *t-test* at the significance level 5%, performed at each iteration. The error bars indicate 1/10 of a standard deviation.

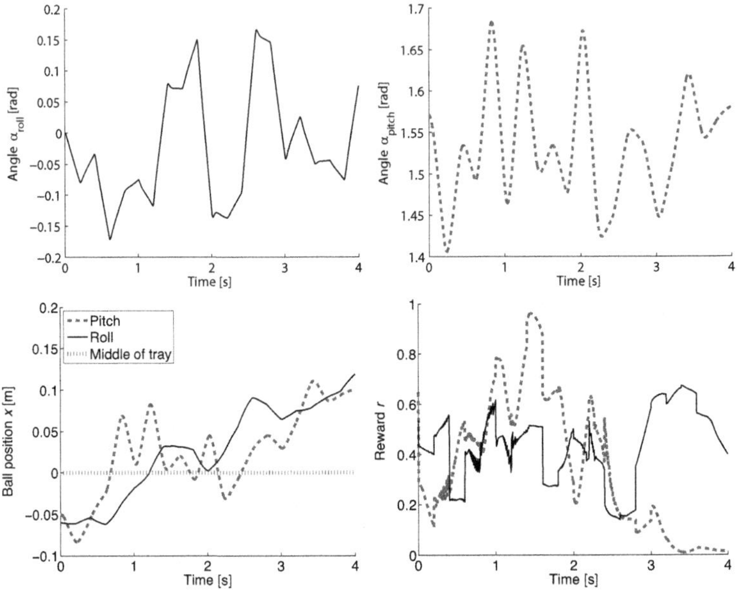

FIGURE 8.6: Typical examples of trajectories of wrist angle α_{roll}, elbow angle α_{pitch}, resulting ball movement x, and reward r for policies obtained by NIW ($\nu = 0$) at the 10th iteration in the ball-balancing task.

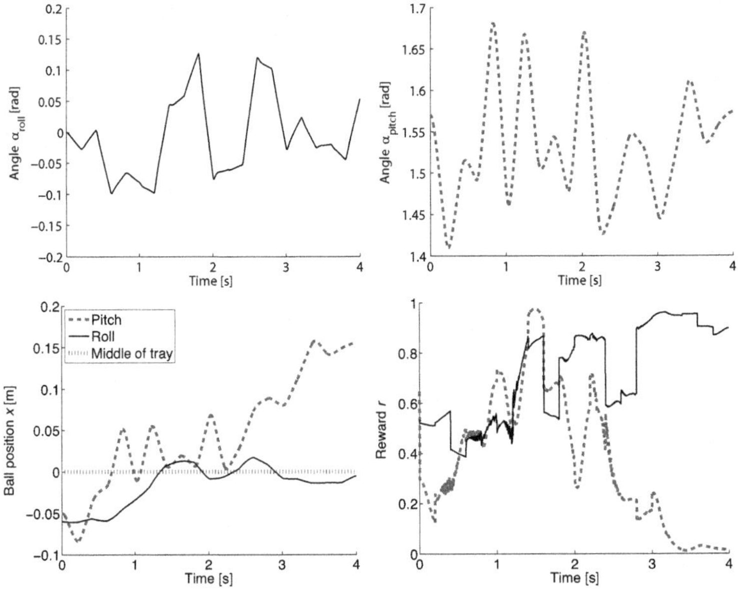

FIGURE 8.7: Typical examples of trajectories of wrist angle α_{roll}, elbow angle α_{pitch}, resulting ball movement x, and reward r for policies obtained by RRR (ν is chosen by IWCV) at the 10th iteration in the ball-balancing task.

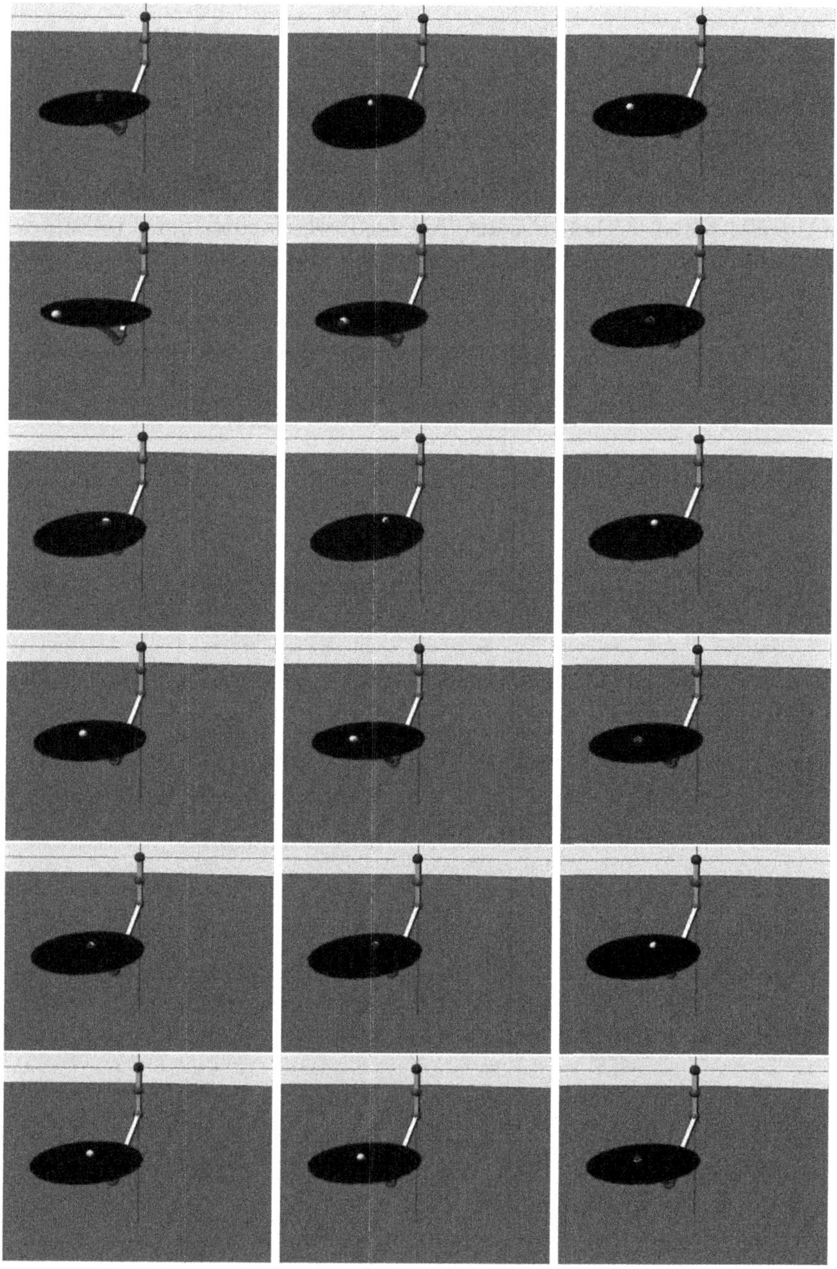

FIGURE 8.8: Motion examples of ball balancing by RRR (from left to right and top to bottom).

8.4 Remarks

A direct policy search algorithm based on expectation-maximization (EM) iteratively maximizes the lower-bound of the expected return. The EM-based approach does not include the step size parameter, which is an advantage over the gradient-based approach introduced in Chapter 7. A sample-reuse variant of the EM-based method was also provided, which contributes to improving the stability of the algorithm in small-sample scenarios.

In practice, however, the EM-based approach is still rather instable even if it is combined with the sample-reuse technique. In Chapter 9, another policy search approach will be introduced to further improve the stability of policy updates.

Chapter 9

Policy-Prior Search

The direct policy search methods explained in Chapter 7 and Chapter 8 are useful in solving problems with continuous actions such as robot control. However, they tend to suffer from instability of policy update. In this chapter, we introduce an alternative policy search method called *policy-prior search*, which is adopted in the PGPE (*policy gradients with parameter-based exploration*) method (Sehnke et al., 2010). The basic idea is to use deterministic policies to remove excessive randomness and introduce useful stochasticity by considering a *prior distribution* for policy parameters.

After formulating the problem of policy-prior search in Section 9.1, a gradient-based algorithm is introduced in Section 9.2, including its improvement using baseline subtraction, theoretical analysis, and experimental evaluation. Then, in Section 9.3, a sample-reuse variant is described and its performance is theoretically analyzed and experimentally investigated using a humanoid robot. Finally, this chapter is concluded in Section 9.4.

9.1 Formulation

In this section, the policy search problem is formulated based on *policy priors*.

The basic idea is to use a deterministic policy and introduce stochasticity by drawing policy parameters from a prior distribution. More specifically, policy parameters are randomly determined following the prior distribution at the beginning of each trajectory, and thereafter action selection is deterministic (Figure 9.1). Note that transitions are generally stochastic, and thus trajectories are also stochastic even though the policy is deterministic. Thanks to this per-trajectory formulation, the variance of gradient estimators in policy-prior search does not increase with respect to the trajectory length, which allows us to overcome the critical drawback of direct policy search.

Policy-prior search uses a deterministic policy with typically a linear architecture:

$$\pi(a|\boldsymbol{s}, \boldsymbol{\theta}) = \delta(a = \boldsymbol{\theta}^\top \boldsymbol{\phi}(\boldsymbol{s})),$$

where $\delta(\cdot)$ is the *Dirac delta function* and $\boldsymbol{\phi}(\boldsymbol{s})$ is the basis function. The policy

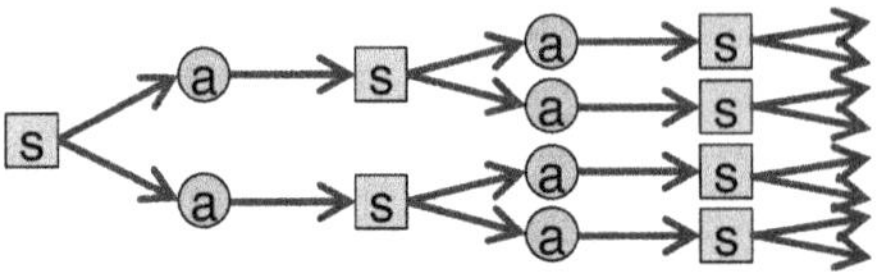

(a) Stochastic policy

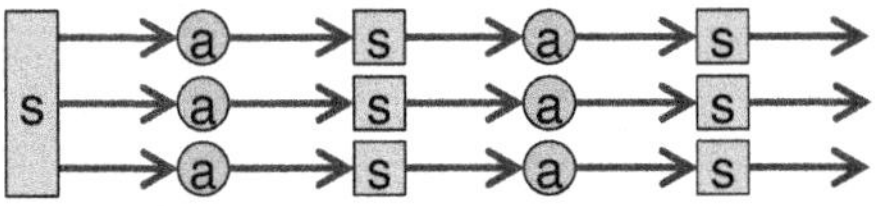

(b) Deterministic policy with prior

FIGURE 9.1: Illustration of the stochastic policy and the deterministic policy with a prior under deterministic transition. The number of possible trajectories is exponential with respect to the trajectory length when stochastic policies are used, while it does not grow when deterministic policies drawn from a prior distribution are used.

parameter $\boldsymbol{\theta}$ is drawn from a prior distribution $p(\boldsymbol{\theta}|\boldsymbol{\rho})$ with *hyper-parameter* $\boldsymbol{\rho}$.

The expected return in policy-prior search is defined in terms of the expectations over both trajectory h and policy parameter $\boldsymbol{\theta}$ as a function of hyper-parameter $\boldsymbol{\rho}$:

$$J(\boldsymbol{\rho}) = \mathbb{E}_{p(h|\boldsymbol{\theta})p(\boldsymbol{\theta}|\boldsymbol{\rho})}[R(h)] = \iint p(h|\boldsymbol{\theta})p(\boldsymbol{\theta}|\boldsymbol{\rho})R(h)\mathrm{d}h\mathrm{d}\boldsymbol{\theta},$$

where $\mathbb{E}_{p(h|\boldsymbol{\theta})p(\boldsymbol{\theta}|\boldsymbol{\rho})}$ denotes the expectation over trajectory h and policy parameter $\boldsymbol{\theta}$ drawn from $p(h|\boldsymbol{\theta})p(\boldsymbol{\theta}|\boldsymbol{\rho})$. In policy-prior search, the hyper-parameter $\boldsymbol{\rho}$ is optimized so that the expected return $J(\boldsymbol{\rho})$ is maximized. Thus, the optimal hyper-parameter $\boldsymbol{\rho}^*$ is given by

$$\boldsymbol{\rho}^* = \underset{\boldsymbol{\rho}}{\mathrm{argmax}}\, J(\boldsymbol{\rho}).$$

9.2 Policy Gradients with Parameter-Based Exploration

In this section, a gradient-based algorithm for policy-prior search is given.

9.2.1 Policy-Prior Gradient Ascent

Here, a gradient method is used to find a local maximizer of the expected return J with respect to hyper-parameter $\boldsymbol{\rho}$:

$$\boldsymbol{\rho} \longleftarrow \boldsymbol{\rho} + \varepsilon \nabla_{\boldsymbol{\rho}} J(\boldsymbol{\rho}),$$

where ε is a small positive constant and $\nabla_{\boldsymbol{\rho}} J(\boldsymbol{\rho})$ is the derivative of J with respect to $\boldsymbol{\rho}$:

$$\begin{aligned}
\nabla_{\boldsymbol{\rho}} J(\boldsymbol{\rho}) &= \iint p(h|\boldsymbol{\theta}) \nabla_{\boldsymbol{\rho}} p(\boldsymbol{\theta}|\boldsymbol{\rho}) R(h) \mathrm{d}h \mathrm{d}\boldsymbol{\theta} \\
&= \iint p(h|\boldsymbol{\theta}) p(\boldsymbol{\theta}|\boldsymbol{\rho}) \nabla_{\boldsymbol{\rho}} \log p(\boldsymbol{\theta}|\boldsymbol{\rho}) R(h) \mathrm{d}h \mathrm{d}\boldsymbol{\theta} \\
&= \mathbb{E}_{p(h|\boldsymbol{\theta})p(\boldsymbol{\theta}|\boldsymbol{\rho})} [\nabla_{\boldsymbol{\rho}} \log p(\boldsymbol{\theta}|\boldsymbol{\rho}) R(h)],
\end{aligned}$$

where the logarithmic derivative,

$$\nabla_{\boldsymbol{\rho}} \log p(\boldsymbol{\theta}|\boldsymbol{\rho}) = \frac{\nabla_{\boldsymbol{\rho}} p(\boldsymbol{\theta}|\boldsymbol{\rho})}{p(\boldsymbol{\theta}|\boldsymbol{\rho})},$$

was used in the derivation. The expectations over h and $\boldsymbol{\theta}$ are approximated by the empirical averages:

$$\nabla_{\boldsymbol{\rho}} \widehat{J}(\boldsymbol{\rho}) = \frac{1}{N} \sum_{n=1}^{N} \nabla_{\boldsymbol{\rho}} \log p(\boldsymbol{\theta}_n|\boldsymbol{\rho}) R(h_n), \tag{9.1}$$

where each trajectory sample h_n is drawn independently from $p(h|\boldsymbol{\theta}_n)$ and parameter $\boldsymbol{\theta}_n$ is drawn from $p(\boldsymbol{\theta}|\boldsymbol{\rho})$. Thus, in policy-prior search, samples are pairs of $\boldsymbol{\theta}$ and h:

$$\mathcal{H} = \{(\boldsymbol{\theta}_1, h_1), \ldots, (\boldsymbol{\theta}_N, h_N)\}.$$

As the prior distribution for policy parameter $\boldsymbol{\theta} = (\theta_1, \ldots, \theta_B)^\top$, where B is the dimensionality of the basis vector $\boldsymbol{\phi}(\boldsymbol{s})$, the independent Gaussian distribution is a standard choice. For this Gaussian prior, the hyper-parameter $\boldsymbol{\rho}$ consists of prior means $\boldsymbol{\eta} = (\eta_1, \ldots, \eta_B)^\top$ and prior standard deviations $\boldsymbol{\tau} = (\tau_1, \ldots, \tau_B)^\top$:

$$p(\boldsymbol{\theta}|\boldsymbol{\eta}, \boldsymbol{\tau}) = \prod_{b=1}^{B} \frac{1}{\tau_b \sqrt{2\pi}} \exp\left(-\frac{(\theta_b - \eta_b)^2}{2\tau_b^2}\right). \tag{9.2}$$

Then the derivatives of log-prior $\log p(\boldsymbol{\theta}|\boldsymbol{\eta}, \boldsymbol{\tau})$ with respect to η_b and τ_b are given as

$$\begin{aligned}
\nabla_{\eta_b} \log p(\boldsymbol{\theta}|\boldsymbol{\eta}, \boldsymbol{\tau}) &= \frac{\theta_b - \eta_b}{\tau_b^2}, \\
\nabla_{\tau_b} \log p(\boldsymbol{\theta}|\boldsymbol{\eta}, \boldsymbol{\tau}) &= \frac{(\theta_b - \eta_b)^2 - \tau_b^2}{\tau_b^3}.
\end{aligned}$$

By substituting these derivatives into Eq. (9.1), the policy-prior gradients with respect to $\boldsymbol{\eta}$ and $\boldsymbol{\tau}$ can be approximated.

9.2.2 Baseline Subtraction for Variance Reduction

As explained in Section 7.2.2, subtraction of a *baseline* can reduce the variance of gradient estimators. Here, a baseline subtraction method for policy-prior search is described.

For a *baseline* ξ, a modified gradient estimator is given by

$$\nabla_{\boldsymbol{\rho}} \widehat{J}^{\xi}(\boldsymbol{\rho}) = \frac{1}{N} \sum_{n=1}^{N} (R(h_n) - \xi) \nabla_{\boldsymbol{\rho}} \log p(\boldsymbol{\theta}_n | \boldsymbol{\rho}).$$

Let ξ^* be the optimal baseline that minimizes the variance of the gradient:

$$\xi^* = \underset{\xi}{\operatorname{argmin}} \, \mathbf{Var}_{p(h|\boldsymbol{\theta})p(\boldsymbol{\theta}|\boldsymbol{\rho})} [\nabla_{\boldsymbol{\rho}} \widehat{J}^{\xi}(\boldsymbol{\rho})],$$

where $\mathbf{Var}_{p(h|\boldsymbol{\theta})p(\boldsymbol{\theta}|\boldsymbol{\rho})}$ denotes the trace of the covariance matrix:

$$\begin{aligned}
&\mathbf{Var}_{p(h|\boldsymbol{\theta})p(\boldsymbol{\theta}|\boldsymbol{\rho})}[\boldsymbol{\zeta}] \\
&= \operatorname{tr}\Big(\mathbb{E}_{p(h|\boldsymbol{\theta})p(\boldsymbol{\theta}|\boldsymbol{\rho})}\big[(\boldsymbol{\zeta} - \mathbb{E}_{p(h|\boldsymbol{\theta})p(\boldsymbol{\theta}|\boldsymbol{\rho})}[\boldsymbol{\zeta}])(\boldsymbol{\zeta} - \mathbb{E}_{p(h|\boldsymbol{\theta})p(\boldsymbol{\theta}|\boldsymbol{\rho})}[\boldsymbol{\zeta}])^{\top}\big]\Big) \\
&= \mathbb{E}_{p(h|\boldsymbol{\theta})p(\boldsymbol{\theta}|\boldsymbol{\rho})}\Big[\|\boldsymbol{\zeta} - \mathbb{E}_{p(h|\boldsymbol{\theta})p(\boldsymbol{\theta}|\boldsymbol{\rho})}[\boldsymbol{\zeta}]\|^2\Big].
\end{aligned}$$

It was shown in Zhao et al. (2012) that the optimal baseline for policy-prior search is given by

$$\xi^* = \frac{\mathbb{E}_{p(h|\boldsymbol{\theta})p(\boldsymbol{\theta}|\boldsymbol{\rho})}[R(h)\|\nabla_{\boldsymbol{\rho}} \log p(\boldsymbol{\theta}|\boldsymbol{\rho})\|^2]}{\mathbb{E}_{p(\boldsymbol{\theta}|\boldsymbol{\rho})}[\|\nabla_{\boldsymbol{\rho}} \log p(\boldsymbol{\theta}|\boldsymbol{\rho})\|^2]},$$

where $\mathbb{E}_{p(\boldsymbol{\theta}|\boldsymbol{\rho})}$ denotes the expectation over policy parameter $\boldsymbol{\theta}$ drawn from $p(\boldsymbol{\theta}|\boldsymbol{\rho})$. In practice, the expectations are approximated by the sample averages.

9.2.3 Variance Analysis of Gradient Estimators

Here the variance of gradient estimators is theoretically investigated for the independent Gaussian prior (9.2) with $\boldsymbol{\phi}(\boldsymbol{s}) = \boldsymbol{s}$. See Zhao et al. (2012) for technical details.

Below, subsets of the following assumptions are considered (which are the same as the ones used in Section 7.2.3):

Assumption (A): $r(\boldsymbol{s}, a, \boldsymbol{s}') \in [-\beta, \beta]$ for $\beta > 0$.

Assumption (B): $r(\boldsymbol{s}, a, \boldsymbol{s}') \in [\alpha, \beta]$ for $0 < \alpha < \beta$.

Assumption (C): For $\delta > 0$, there exist two series $\{c_t\}_{t=1}^{T}$ and $\{d_t\}_{t=1}^{T}$ such that

$$\|\boldsymbol{s}_t\| \geq c_t \quad \text{and} \quad _t\| \leq d_t$$

hold with probability at least $1 - \frac{\delta}{2N}$, respectively, over the choice of sample paths.

Note that Assumption (B) is stronger than Assumption (A).

Let

$$G = \sum_{b=1}^{B} \tau_b^{-2}.$$

First, the variance of gradient estimators in policy-prior search is analyzed:

Theorem 9.1 *Under Assumption (A), the following upper bounds hold:*

$$\mathbf{Var}_{p(h|\boldsymbol{\theta})p(\boldsymbol{\theta}|\boldsymbol{\rho})}\left[\nabla_{\boldsymbol{\eta}}\widehat{J}(\boldsymbol{\eta},\boldsymbol{\tau})\right] \leq \frac{\beta^2(1-\gamma^T)^2 G}{N(1-\gamma)^2} \leq \frac{\beta^2 G}{N(1-\gamma)^2},$$

$$\mathbf{Var}_{p(h|\boldsymbol{\theta})p(\boldsymbol{\theta}|\boldsymbol{\rho})}\left[\nabla_{\boldsymbol{\tau}}\widehat{J}(\boldsymbol{\eta},\boldsymbol{\tau})\right] \leq \frac{2\beta^2(1-\gamma^T)^2 G}{N(1-\gamma)^2} \leq \frac{2\beta^2 G}{N(1-\gamma)^2}.$$

The second upper bounds are independent of the trajectory length T, while the upper bounds for direct policy search (Theorem 7.1 in Section 7.2.3) are monotone increasing with respect to the trajectory length T. Thus, gradient estimation in policy-prior search is expected to be more reliable than that in direct policy search when the trajectory length T is large.

The following theorem more explicitly compares the variance of gradient estimators in direct policy search and policy-prior search:

Theorem 9.2 *In addition to Assumptions (B) and (C), assume that*

$$\zeta(T) = C_T\alpha^2 - D_T\beta^2/(2\pi)$$

is positive and monotone increasing with respect to T, where

$$C_T = \sum_{t=1}^{T} c_t^2 \quad \textit{and} \quad D_T = \sum_{t=1}^{T} d_t^2.$$

If there exists T_0 such that

$$\zeta(T_0) \geq \beta^2 G\sigma^2,$$

then it holds that

$$\mathbf{Var}_{p(h|\boldsymbol{\theta})p(\boldsymbol{\theta}|\boldsymbol{\rho})}[\nabla_{\boldsymbol{\mu}}\widehat{J}(\boldsymbol{\theta})] > \mathbf{Var}_{p(h|\boldsymbol{\theta})p(\boldsymbol{\theta}|\boldsymbol{\rho})}[\nabla_{\boldsymbol{\eta}}\widehat{J}(\boldsymbol{\eta},\boldsymbol{\tau})]$$

for all $T > T_0$, with probability at least $1-\delta$.

The above theorem means that policy-prior search is more favorable than direct policy search in terms of the variance of gradient estimators of the mean, if trajectory length T is large.

Next, the contribution of the optimal baseline to the variance of the gradient estimator with respect to mean parameter $\boldsymbol{\eta}$ is investigated. It was shown in Zhao et al. (2012) that the excess variance for a baseline ξ is given by

$$\mathbf{Var}_{p(h|\boldsymbol{\theta})p(\boldsymbol{\theta}|\boldsymbol{\rho})}[\nabla_{\boldsymbol{\rho}}\widehat{J}^{\xi}(\boldsymbol{\rho})] - \mathbf{Var}_{p(h|\boldsymbol{\theta})p(\boldsymbol{\theta}|\boldsymbol{\rho})}[\nabla_{\boldsymbol{\rho}}\widehat{J}^{\xi^*}(\boldsymbol{\rho})]$$

$$= \frac{(\xi - \xi^*)^2}{N} \mathbb{E}_{p(h|\boldsymbol{\theta})p(\boldsymbol{\theta}|\boldsymbol{\rho})} \left[\|\nabla_{\boldsymbol{\rho}} \log p(\boldsymbol{\theta}|\boldsymbol{\rho})\|^2 \right].$$

Based on this expression, the following theorem holds.

Theorem 9.3 *If $r(\boldsymbol{s}, a, \boldsymbol{s}') \geq \alpha > 0$, the following lower bound holds:*

$$\mathbf{Var}_{p(h|\boldsymbol{\theta})p(\boldsymbol{\theta}|\boldsymbol{\rho})}[\nabla_{\boldsymbol{\eta}} \widehat{J}(\boldsymbol{\eta}, \boldsymbol{\tau})] - \mathbf{Var}_{p(h|\boldsymbol{\theta})p(\boldsymbol{\theta}|\boldsymbol{\rho})}[\nabla_{\boldsymbol{\eta}} \widehat{J}^{\xi^*}(\boldsymbol{\eta}, \boldsymbol{\tau})] \geq \frac{\alpha^2(1-\gamma^T)^2 G}{N(1-\gamma)^2}.$$

Under Assumption (A), the following upper bound holds:

$$\mathbf{Var}_{p(h|\boldsymbol{\theta})p(\boldsymbol{\theta}|\boldsymbol{\rho})}[\nabla_{\boldsymbol{\eta}} \widehat{J}(\boldsymbol{\eta}, \boldsymbol{\tau})] - \mathbf{Var}_{p(h|\boldsymbol{\theta})p(\boldsymbol{\theta}|\boldsymbol{\rho})}[\nabla_{\boldsymbol{\eta}} \widehat{J}^{\xi^*}(\boldsymbol{\eta}, \boldsymbol{\tau})] \leq \frac{\beta^2(1-\gamma^T)^2 G}{N(1-\gamma)^2}.$$

The above theorem shows that the lower bound of the excess variance is positive and monotone increasing with respect to the trajectory length T. This means that the variance is always reduced by subtracting the optimal baseline and the amount of variance reduction is monotone increasing with respect to the trajectory length T. Note that the upper bound is also monotone increasing with respect to the trajectory length T.

Finally, the variance of the gradient estimator with the optimal baseline is investigated:

Theorem 9.4 *Under Assumptions (B) and (C), the following upper bound holds with probability at least $1 - \delta$:*

$$\mathbf{Var}_{p(h|\boldsymbol{\theta})p(\boldsymbol{\theta}|\boldsymbol{\rho})}[\nabla_{\boldsymbol{\eta}} \widehat{J}^{\xi^*}(\boldsymbol{\eta}, \boldsymbol{\tau})] \leq \frac{(1-\gamma^T)^2}{N(1-\gamma)^2}(\beta^2 - \alpha^2)G \leq \frac{(\beta^2 - \alpha^2)G}{N(1-\gamma)^2}.$$

The second upper bound is independent of the trajectory length T, while Theorem 7.4 in Section 7.2.3 showed that the upper bound of the variance of gradient estimators with the optimal baseline in direct policy search is monotone increasing with respect to trajectory length T. Thus, when trajectory length T is large, policy-prior search is more favorable than direct policy search in terms of the variance of the gradient estimator with respect to the mean even when optimal baseline subtraction is applied.

9.2.4 Numerical Examples

Here, the performance of the direct policy search and policy-prior search algorithms are experimentally compared.

9.2.4.1 Setup

Let the state space $\mathcal{S}$ be one-dimensional and continuous, and the initial state is randomly chosen following the standard normal distribution. The action space $\mathcal{A}$ is also set to be one-dimensional and continuous. The transition dynamics of the environment is set at

$$s_{t+1} = s_t + a_t + \varepsilon,$$

TABLE 9.1: Variance and bias of estimated parameters.

(a) Trajectory length $T = 10$

Method	Variance		Bias	
	μ, η	σ, τ	μ, η	σ, τ
REINFORCE	13.257	26.917	-0.310	-1.510
REINFORCE-OB	0.091	0.120	0.067	0.129
PGPE	0.971	1.686	-0.069	0.132
PGPE-OB	0.037	0.069	-0.016	0.051

(b) Trajectory length $T = 50$

Method	Variance		Bias	
	μ, η	σ, τ	μ, η	σ, τ
REINFORCE	188.386	278.310	-1.813	-5.175
REINFORCE-OB	0.545	0.900	-0.299	-0.201
PGPE	1.657	3.372	-0.105	-0.329
PGPE-OB	0.085	0.182	0.048	-0.078

where $\varepsilon \sim \mathcal{N}(0, 0.5^2)$ is stochastic noise and $\mathcal{N}(\mu, \sigma^2)$ denotes the normal distribution with mean μ and variance σ^2. The immediate reward is defined as

$$r = \exp\left(-s^2/2 - a^2/2\right) + 1,$$

which is bounded as $1 < r \leq 2$. The length of the trajectory is set at $T = 10$ or 50, the discount factor is set at $\gamma = 0.9$, and the number of episodic samples is set at $N = 100$.

9.2.4.2 Variance and Bias

First, the variance and the bias of gradient estimators of the following methods are investigated:

- **REINFORCE:** REINFORCE (gradient-based direct policy search) without a baseline (Williams, 1992).
- **REINFORCE-OB:** REINFORCE with optimal baseline subtraction (Peters & Schaal, 2006).
- **PGPE:** PGPE (gradient-based policy-prior search) without a baseline (Sehnke et al., 2010).
- **PGPE-OB:** PGPE with optimal baseline subtraction (Zhao et al., 2012).

Table 9.1 summarizes the variance of gradient estimators over 100 runs, showing that the variance of REINFORCE is overall larger than PGPE. A notable difference between REINFORCE and PGPE is that the variance of REINFORCE significantly grows as the trajectory length T increases, whereas that of PGPE is not influenced that much by T. This agrees well with the theoretical analyses given in Section 7.2.3 and Section 9.2.3. Optimal baseline subtraction (REINFORCE-OB and PGPE-OB) is shown to contribute highly to reducing the variance, especially when trajectory length T is large, which also agrees well with the theoretical analysis.

The bias of the gradient estimator of each method is also investigated. Here, gradients estimated with $N = 1000$ are regarded as true gradients, and the bias of gradient estimators is computed. The results are also included in Table 9.1, showing that introduction of baselines does not increase the bias; rather, it tends to reduce the bias.

9.2.4.3 Variance and Policy Hyper-Parameter Change through Entire Policy-Update Process

Next, the variance of gradient estimators is investigated when policy hyper-parameters are updated over iterations. If the deviation parameter σ takes a negative value during the policy-update process, it is set at 0.05. In this experiment, the variance is computed from 50 runs for $T = 20$ and $N = 10$, and policies are updated over 50 iterations. In order to evaluate the variance in a stable manner, the above experiments are repeated 20 times with random choice of initial mean parameter μ from $[-3.0, -0.1]$, and the average variance of gradient estimators is investigated with respect to mean parameter μ over 20 trials. The results are plotted in Figure 9.2. Figure 9.2(a) compares the variance of REINFORCE with/without baselines, whereas Figure 9.2(b) compares the variance of PGPE with/without baselines. These graphs show that introduction of baselines contributes highly to the reduction of the variance over iterations.

Let us illustrate how parameters are updated by PGPE-OB over 50 iterations for $N = 10$ and $T = 10$. The initial mean parameter is set at $\eta = -1.6$, -0.8, or -0.1, and the initial deviation parameter is set at $\tau = 1$. Figure 9.3 depicts the contour of the expected return and illustrates trajectories of parameter updates over iterations by PGPE-OB. In the graph, the maximum of the return surface is located at the middle bottom, and PGPE-OB leads the solutions to a maximum point rapidly.

9.2.4.4 Performance of Learned Policies

Finally, the return obtained by each method is evaluated. The trajectory length is fixed at $T = 20$, and the maximum number of policy-update iterations is set at 50. Average returns over 20 runs are investigated as functions of the number of episodic samples N. Figure 9.4(a) shows the results when initial mean parameter μ is chosen randomly from $[-1.6, -0.1]$, which tends to perform well. The graph shows that PGPE-OB performs the best, especially when $N < 5$; then REINFORCE-OB follows with a small margin. The

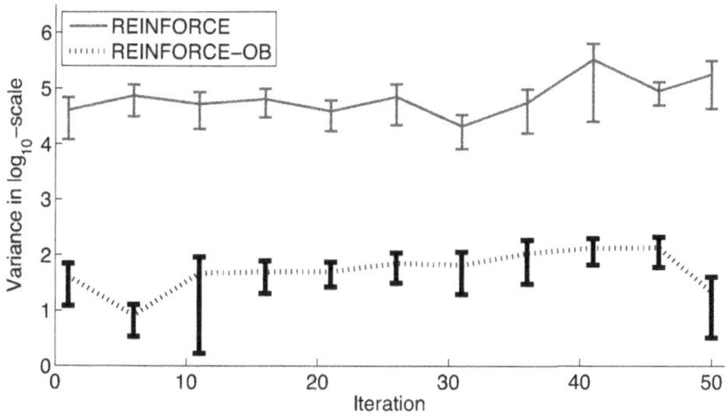

(a) REINFORCE and REINFORCE-OB

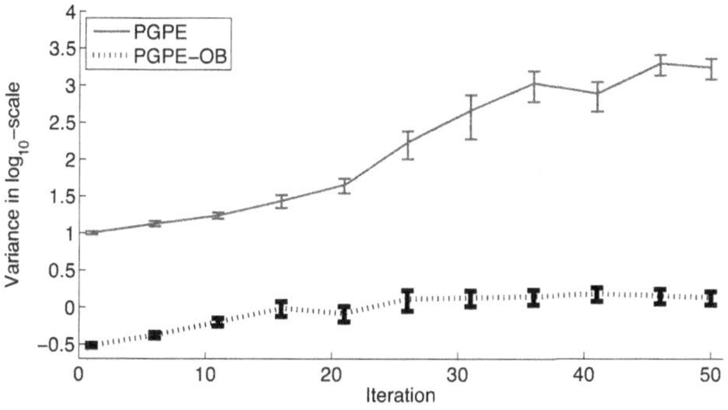

(b) PGPE and PGPE-OB

FIGURE 9.2: Mean and standard error of the variance of gradient estimators with respect to the mean parameter through policy-update iterations.

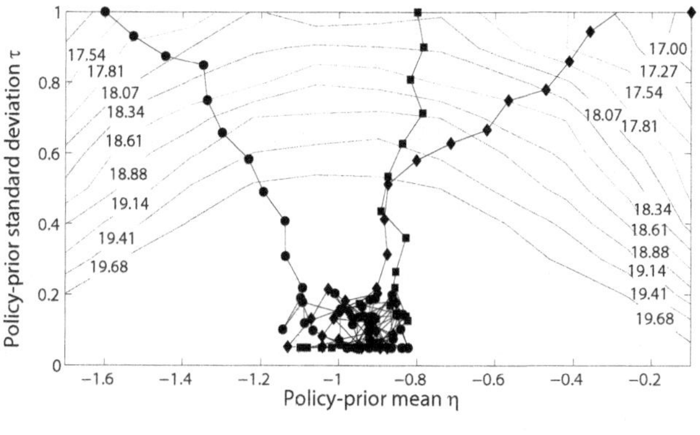

FIGURE 9.3: Trajectories of policy-prior parameter updates by PGPE.

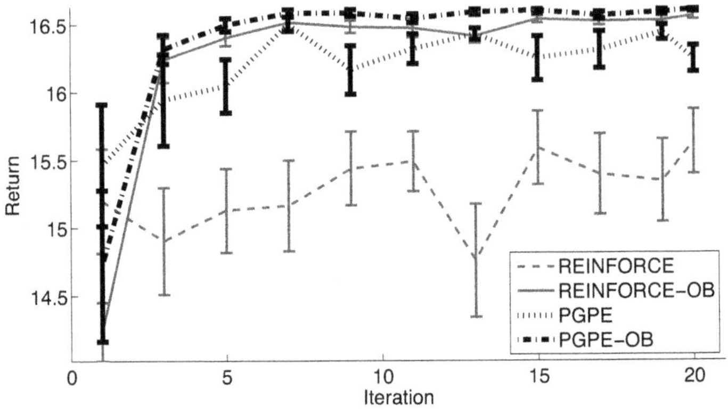

(a) Good initial policy

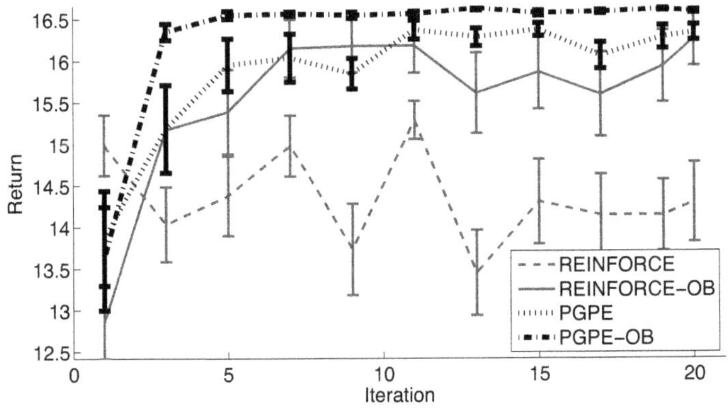

(b) Poor initial policy

FIGURE 9.4: Average and standard error of returns over 20 runs as functions of the number of episodic samples N.

plain PGPE also works reasonably well, although it is slightly unstable due to larger variance. The plain REINFORCE is highly unstable, which is caused by the huge variance of gradient estimators (see Figure 9.2 again). Figure 9.4(b) describes the results when initial mean parameter μ is chosen randomly from $[-3.0, -0.1]$, which tends to result in poorer performance. In this setup, the difference among the compared methods is more significant than the case with good initial policies, meaning that REINFORCE is sensitive to the choice of initial policies. Overall, the PGPE methods tend to outperform the REINFORCE methods, and among the PGPE methods, PGPE-OB works very well and converges quickly.

9.3 Sample Reuse in Policy-Prior Search

Although PGPE was shown to outperform REINFORCE, its behavior is still rather unstable if the number of data samples used for estimating the gradient is small. In this section, the sample-reuse idea is applied to PGPE. Technically, the original PGPE is categorized as an *on-policy* algorithm where data drawn from the current target policy is used to estimate policy-prior gradients. On the other hand, *off-policy* algorithms are more flexible in the sense that a data-collecting policy and the current target policy can be different. Here, PGPE is extended to the off-policy scenario using the importance-weighting technique.

9.3.1 Importance Weighting

Let us consider an off-policy scenario where a data-collecting policy and the current target policy are different in general. In the context of PGPE, two hyper-parameters are considered: $\boldsymbol{\rho}$ as the target policy to learn and $\boldsymbol{\rho}'$ as a policy for data collection. Let us denote the data samples collected with hyper-parameter $\boldsymbol{\rho}'$ by $\mathcal{H}'$:

$$\mathcal{H}' = \{(\boldsymbol{\theta}'_n, h'_n)\}_{n=1}^{N'} \overset{\text{i.i.d.}}{\sim} p(h|\boldsymbol{\theta})p(\boldsymbol{\theta}|\boldsymbol{\rho}').$$

If data $\mathcal{H}'$ is naively used to estimate policy-prior gradients by Eq. (9.1), we suffer an inconsistency problem:

$$\frac{1}{N'}\sum_{n=1}^{N'} \nabla_{\boldsymbol{\rho}} \log p(\boldsymbol{\theta}'_n|\boldsymbol{\rho})R(h'_n) \overset{N'\to\infty}{\nrightarrow} \nabla_{\boldsymbol{\rho}} J(\boldsymbol{\rho}),$$

where

$$\nabla_{\boldsymbol{\rho}} J(\boldsymbol{\rho}) = \iint p(h|\boldsymbol{\theta})p(\boldsymbol{\theta}|\boldsymbol{\rho})\nabla_{\boldsymbol{\rho}} \log p(\boldsymbol{\theta}|\boldsymbol{\rho})R(h)\mathrm{d}h\mathrm{d}\boldsymbol{\theta}$$

is the gradient of the expected return,

$$J(\boldsymbol{\rho}) = \iint p(h|\boldsymbol{\theta})p(\boldsymbol{\theta}|\boldsymbol{\rho})R(h)\mathrm{d}h\mathrm{d}\boldsymbol{\theta},$$

with respect to the policy hyper-parameter $\boldsymbol{\rho}$. Below, this naive method is referred to as *non-importance-weighted PGPE* (NIW-PGPE).

This inconsistency problem can be systematically resolved by *importance weighting*:

$$\nabla_{\boldsymbol{\rho}} \widehat{J}_{\mathrm{IW}}(\boldsymbol{\rho}) = \frac{1}{N'}\sum_{n=1}^{N'} w(\boldsymbol{\theta}'_n)\nabla_{\boldsymbol{\rho}} \log p(\boldsymbol{\theta}'_n|\boldsymbol{\rho})R(h'_n) \overset{N'\to\infty}{\longrightarrow} \nabla_{\boldsymbol{\rho}} J(\boldsymbol{\rho}),$$

where $w(\boldsymbol{\theta}) = p(\boldsymbol{\theta}|\boldsymbol{\rho})/p(\boldsymbol{\theta}|\boldsymbol{\rho}')$ is the importance weight. This extended method is called *importance-weighted PGPE* (IW-PGPE).

Below, the variance of gradient estimators in IW-PGPE is theoretically analyzed. See Zhao et al. (2013) for technical details. As described in Section 9.2.1, the deterministic linear policy model is used here:

$$\pi(a|\boldsymbol{s}, \boldsymbol{\theta}) = \delta(a = \boldsymbol{\theta}^\top \boldsymbol{\phi}(\boldsymbol{s})), \tag{9.3}$$

where $\delta(\cdot)$ is the *Dirac delta function* and $\boldsymbol{\phi}(\boldsymbol{s})$ is the B-dimensional basis function. Policy parameter $\boldsymbol{\theta} = (\theta_1, \ldots, \theta_B)^\top$ is drawn from the independent Gaussian prior, where policy hyper-parameter $\boldsymbol{\rho}$ consists of prior means $\boldsymbol{\eta} = (\eta_1, \ldots, \eta_B)^\top$ and prior standard deviations $\boldsymbol{\tau} = (\tau_1, \ldots, \tau_B)^\top$:

$$p(\boldsymbol{\theta}|\boldsymbol{\eta}, \boldsymbol{\tau}) = \prod_{b=1}^{B} \frac{1}{\tau_b\sqrt{2\pi}} \exp\left(-\frac{(\theta_b - \eta_b)^2}{2\tau_b^2}\right). \tag{9.4}$$

Let

$$G = \sum_{b=1}^{B} \tau_b^{-2},$$

and let $\mathbf{Var}_{p(h'|\boldsymbol{\theta}')p(\boldsymbol{\theta}'|\boldsymbol{\rho}')}$ denote the trace of the covariance matrix:

$$\begin{aligned}
&\mathbf{Var}_{p(h'|\boldsymbol{\theta}')p(\boldsymbol{\theta}'|\boldsymbol{\rho}')}[\boldsymbol{\zeta}] \\
&= \mathrm{tr}\Big(\mathbb{E}_{p(h'|\boldsymbol{\theta}')p(\boldsymbol{\theta}'|\boldsymbol{\rho}')}\big[(\boldsymbol{\zeta} - \mathbb{E}_{p(h'|\boldsymbol{\theta}')p(\boldsymbol{\theta}'|\boldsymbol{\rho}')}[\boldsymbol{\zeta}])(\boldsymbol{\zeta} - \mathbb{E}_{p(h'|\boldsymbol{\theta}')p(\boldsymbol{\theta}'|\boldsymbol{\rho}')}[\boldsymbol{\zeta}])^\top\big]\Big) \\
&= \mathbb{E}_{p(h'|\boldsymbol{\theta}')p(\boldsymbol{\theta}'|\boldsymbol{\rho}')}\left[\|\boldsymbol{\zeta} - \mathbb{E}_{p(h'|\boldsymbol{\theta}')p(\boldsymbol{\theta}'|\boldsymbol{\rho}')}[\boldsymbol{\zeta}]\|^2\right],
\end{aligned}$$

where $\mathbb{E}_{p(h'|\boldsymbol{\theta}')p(\boldsymbol{\theta}'|\boldsymbol{\rho}')}$ denotes the expectation over trajectory h' and policy parameter $\boldsymbol{\theta}'$ drawn from $p(h'|\boldsymbol{\theta}')p(\boldsymbol{\theta}'|\boldsymbol{\rho}')$. Then the following theorem holds:

Theorem 9.5 *Assume that for all* $\boldsymbol{s}$, a, *and* $\boldsymbol{s}'$, *there exists* $\beta > 0$ *such that* $r(\boldsymbol{s}, a, \boldsymbol{s}') \in [-\beta, \beta]$, *and, for all* $\boldsymbol{\theta}$, *there exists* $0 < w_{\max} < \infty$ *such that* $0 < w(\boldsymbol{\theta}) \leq w_{\max}$. *Then, the following upper bounds hold:*

$$\mathbf{Var}_{p(h'|\boldsymbol{\theta}')p(\boldsymbol{\theta}'|\boldsymbol{\rho}')}\left[\nabla_{\boldsymbol{\eta}} \widehat{J}_{\mathrm{IW}}(\boldsymbol{\eta}, \boldsymbol{\tau})\right] \leq \frac{\beta^2(1-\gamma^T)^2 G}{N'(1-\gamma)^2} w_{\max},$$

$$\mathbf{Var}_{p(h'|\boldsymbol{\theta}')p(\boldsymbol{\theta}'|\boldsymbol{\rho}')}\left[\nabla_{\boldsymbol{\tau}} \widehat{J}_{\mathrm{IW}}(\boldsymbol{\eta}, \boldsymbol{\tau})\right] \leq \frac{2\beta^2(1-\gamma^T)^2 G}{N'(1-\gamma)^2} w_{\max}.$$

It is interesting to note that the upper bounds are the same as the ones for the plain PGPE (Theorem 9.1 in Section 9.2.3) except for factor $w_{\max}$. When $w_{\max} = 1$, the bounds are reduced to those of the plain PGPE method. However, if the sampling distribution is significantly different from the target distribution, $w_{\max}$ can take a large value and thus IW-PGPE can produce a gradient estimator with large variance. Therefore, IW-PGPE may not be a reliable approach as it is.

Below, a variance reduction technique for IW-PGPE is introduced which leads to a practically useful algorithm.

9.3.2 Variance Reduction by Baseline Subtraction

Here, a baseline is introduced for IW-PGPE to reduce the variance of gradient estimators, in the same way as the plain PGPE explained in Section 9.2.2.

A policy-prior gradient estimator with a baseline $\xi \in \mathbb{R}$ is defined as

$$\nabla_{\boldsymbol{\rho}} \widehat{J}^{\xi}_{\mathrm{IW}}(\boldsymbol{\rho}) = \frac{1}{N'} \sum_{n=1}^{N'} (R(h'_n) - \xi) w(\boldsymbol{\theta}'_n) \nabla_{\boldsymbol{\rho}} \log p(\boldsymbol{\theta}'_n | \boldsymbol{\rho}).$$

Here, the baseline ξ is determined so that the variance is minimized. Let ξ^* be the optimal baseline for IW-PGPE that minimizes the variance:

$$\xi^* = \underset{\xi}{\operatorname{argmin}}\, \mathbf{Var}_{p(h'|\boldsymbol{\theta}')p(\boldsymbol{\theta}'|\boldsymbol{\rho}')}[\nabla_{\boldsymbol{\rho}} \widehat{J}^{\xi}_{\mathrm{IW}}(\boldsymbol{\rho})].$$

Then the optimal baseline for IW-PGPE is given as follows (Zhao et al., 2013):

$$\xi^* = \frac{\mathbb{E}_{p(h'|\boldsymbol{\theta}')p(\boldsymbol{\theta}'|\boldsymbol{\rho}')}[R(h') w^2(\boldsymbol{\theta}') \|\nabla_{\boldsymbol{\rho}} \log p(\boldsymbol{\theta}'|\boldsymbol{\rho})\|^2]}{\mathbb{E}_{p(\boldsymbol{\theta}'|\boldsymbol{\rho}')}[w^2(\boldsymbol{\theta}') \|\nabla_{\boldsymbol{\rho}} \log p(\boldsymbol{\theta}'|\boldsymbol{\rho})\|^2]},$$

where $\mathbb{E}_{p(\boldsymbol{\theta}'|\boldsymbol{\rho}')}$ denotes the expectation over policy parameter $\boldsymbol{\theta}'$ drawn from $p(\boldsymbol{\theta}'|\boldsymbol{\rho}')$. In practice, the expectations are approximated by the sample averages. The excess variance for a baseline ξ is given as

$$\begin{aligned}&\mathbf{Var}_{p(h'|\boldsymbol{\theta}')p(\boldsymbol{\theta}'|\boldsymbol{\rho}')}[\nabla_{\boldsymbol{\rho}} \widehat{J}^{\xi}_{\mathrm{IW}}(\boldsymbol{\rho})] - \mathbf{Var}_{p(h'|\boldsymbol{\theta}')p(\boldsymbol{\theta}'|\boldsymbol{\rho}')}[\nabla_{\boldsymbol{\rho}} \widehat{J}^{\xi^*}_{\mathrm{IW}}(\boldsymbol{\rho})]\\ &= \frac{(\xi - \xi^*)^2}{N'} \mathbb{E}_{p(\boldsymbol{\theta}'|\boldsymbol{\rho}')}[w^2(\boldsymbol{\theta}') \|\nabla_{\boldsymbol{\rho}} \log p(\boldsymbol{\theta}'|\boldsymbol{\rho})\|^2].\end{aligned}$$

Next, contributions of the optimal baseline to variance reduction in IW-PGPE are analyzed for the deterministic linear policy model (9.3) and the independent Gaussian prior (9.4). See Zhao et al. (2013) for technical details.

Theorem 9.6 *Assume that for all* $\boldsymbol{s}$, a, *and* $\boldsymbol{s}'$, *there exists* $\alpha > 0$ *such that* $r(\boldsymbol{s}, a, \boldsymbol{s}') \geq \alpha$, *and, for all* $\boldsymbol{\theta}$, *there exists* $w_{\min} > 0$ *such that* $w(\boldsymbol{\theta}) \geq w_{\min}$. *Then, the following lower bounds hold:*

$$\begin{aligned}&\mathbf{Var}_{p(h'|\boldsymbol{\theta}')p(\boldsymbol{\theta}'|\boldsymbol{\rho}')}\left[\nabla_{\boldsymbol{\eta}} \widehat{J}_{\mathrm{IW}}(\boldsymbol{\eta}, \boldsymbol{\tau})\right] - \mathbf{Var}_{p(h'|\boldsymbol{\theta}')p(\boldsymbol{\theta}'|\boldsymbol{\rho}')}\left[\nabla_{\boldsymbol{\eta}} \widehat{J}^{\xi^*}_{\mathrm{IW}}(\boldsymbol{\eta}, \boldsymbol{\tau})\right]\\ &\geq \frac{\alpha^2 (1 - \gamma^T)^2 G}{N'(1 - \gamma)^2} w_{\min},\\ &\mathbf{Var}_{p(h'|\boldsymbol{\theta}')p(\boldsymbol{\theta}'|\boldsymbol{\rho}')}\left[\nabla_{\boldsymbol{\tau}} \widehat{J}_{\mathrm{IW}}(\boldsymbol{\eta}, \boldsymbol{\tau})\right] - \mathbf{Var}_{p(h'|\boldsymbol{\theta}')p(\boldsymbol{\theta}'|\boldsymbol{\rho}')}\left[\nabla_{\boldsymbol{\tau}} \widehat{J}^{\xi^*}_{\mathrm{IW}}(\boldsymbol{\eta}, \boldsymbol{\tau})\right]\\ &\geq \frac{2\alpha^2 (1 - \gamma^T)^2 G}{N'(1 - \gamma)^2} w_{\min}.\end{aligned}$$

Assume that for all $\boldsymbol{s}$, a, *and* $\boldsymbol{s}'$, *there exists* $\beta > 0$ *such that* $r(\boldsymbol{s}, a, \boldsymbol{s}') \in$

$[-\beta, \beta]$, *and, for all* $\boldsymbol{\theta}$, *there exists* $0 < w_{\max} < \infty$ *such that* $0 < w(\boldsymbol{\theta}) \leq w_{\max}$. *Then, the following upper bounds hold:*

$$\mathbf{Var}_{p(h'|\boldsymbol{\theta}')p(\boldsymbol{\theta}'|\boldsymbol{\rho}')}\left[\nabla_{\boldsymbol{\eta}}\widehat{J}_{\mathrm{IW}}(\boldsymbol{\eta},\boldsymbol{\tau})\right] - \mathbf{Var}_{p(h'|\boldsymbol{\theta}')p(\boldsymbol{\theta}'|\boldsymbol{\rho}')}\left[\nabla_{\boldsymbol{\eta}}\widehat{J}^{\xi^*}_{\mathrm{IW}}(\boldsymbol{\eta},\boldsymbol{\tau})\right] \leq \frac{\beta^2(1-\gamma^T)^2 G}{N'(1-\gamma)^2} w_{\max},$$

$$\mathbf{Var}_{p(h'|\boldsymbol{\theta}')p(\boldsymbol{\theta}'|\boldsymbol{\rho}')}\left[\nabla_{\boldsymbol{\tau}}\widehat{J}_{\mathrm{IW}}(\boldsymbol{\eta},\boldsymbol{\tau})\right] - \mathbf{Var}_{p(h'|\boldsymbol{\theta}')p(\boldsymbol{\theta}'|\boldsymbol{\rho}')}\left[\nabla_{\boldsymbol{\tau}}\widehat{J}^{\xi^*}_{\mathrm{IW}}(\boldsymbol{\eta},\boldsymbol{\tau})\right] \leq \frac{2\beta^2(1-\gamma^T)^2 G}{N'(1-\gamma)^2} w_{\max}.$$

This theorem shows that the bounds of the variance reduction in IW-PGPE brought by the optimal baseline depend on the bounds of the importance weight, $w_{\min}$ and $w_{\max}$ — the larger the upper bound $w_{\max}$ is, the more optimal baseline subtraction can reduce the variance.

From Theorem 9.5 and Theorem 9.6, the following corollary can be immediately obtained:

Corollary 9.7 *Assume that for all* $\boldsymbol{s}$, a, *and* $\boldsymbol{s}'$, *there exists* $0 < \alpha < \beta$ *such that* $r(\boldsymbol{s}, a, \boldsymbol{s}') \in [\alpha, \beta]$, *and, for all* $\boldsymbol{\theta}$, *there exists* $0 < w_{\min} < w_{\max} < \infty$ *such that* $w_{\min} \leq w(\boldsymbol{\theta}) \leq w_{\max}$. *Then, the following upper bounds hold:*

$$\mathbf{Var}_{p(h'|\boldsymbol{\theta}')p(\boldsymbol{\theta}'|\boldsymbol{\rho}')}\left[\nabla_{\boldsymbol{\eta}}\widehat{J}^{\xi^*}_{\mathrm{IW}}(\boldsymbol{\eta},\boldsymbol{\tau})\right] \leq \frac{(1-\gamma^T)^2 G}{N'(1-\gamma)^2}(\beta^2 w_{\max} - \alpha^2 w_{\min}),$$

$$\mathbf{Var}_{p(h'|\boldsymbol{\theta}')p(\boldsymbol{\theta}'|\boldsymbol{\rho}')}\left[\nabla_{\boldsymbol{\tau}}\widehat{J}^{\xi^*}_{\mathrm{IW}}(\boldsymbol{\eta},\boldsymbol{\tau})\right] \leq \frac{2(1-\gamma^T)^2 G}{N'(1-\gamma)^2}(\beta^2 w_{\max} - \alpha^2 w_{\min}).$$

From Theorem 9.5 and this corollary, we can confirm that the upper bounds for the baseline-subtracted IW-PGPE are smaller than those for the plain IW-PGPE without baseline subtraction, because $\alpha^2 w_{\min} > 0$. In particular, if $w_{\min}$ is large, the upper bounds for the baseline-subtracted IW-PGPE can be much smaller than those for the plain IW-PGPE without baseline subtraction.

9.3.3 Numerical Examples

Here, we consider the controlling task of the humanoid robot *CB-i* (Cheng et al., 2007) shown in Figure 9.5(a). The goal is to lead the end effector of the right arm (right hand) to a target object. First, its simulated upper-body model, illustrated in Figure 9.5(b), is used to investigate the performance of the IW-PGPE-OB method. Then the IW-PGPE-OB method is applied to the real robot.

9.3.3.1 Setup

The performance of the following 4 methods is compared:

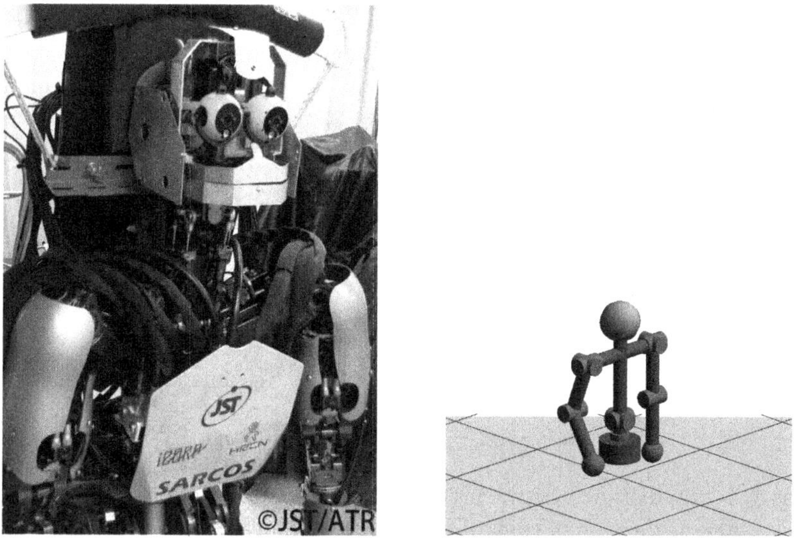

(a) CB-i (b) Simulated upper-body model

FIGURE 9.5: Humanoid robot CB-i and its upper-body model. The humanoid robot CB-i was developed by the JST-ICORP Computational Brain Project and ATR Computational Neuroscience Labs (Cheng et al., 2007).

- **IW-REINFORCE-OB:** Importance-weighted REINFORCE with the optimal baseline.
- **NIW-PGPE-OB:** Data-reuse PGPE-OB without importance weighting.
- **PGPE-OB:** Plain PGPE-OB without data reuse.
- **IW-PGPE-OB:** Importance-weighted PGPE with the optimal baseline.

The upper body of CB-i has 9 degrees of freedom: the shoulder pitch, shoulder roll, elbow pitch of the right arm; shoulder pitch, shoulder roll, elbow pitch of the left arm; waist yaw; torso roll; and torso pitch (Figure 9.5(b)). At each time step, the controller receives states from the system and sends out actions. The state space is 18-dimensional, which corresponds to the current angle and angular velocity of each joint. The action space is 9-dimensional, which corresponds to the target angle of each joint. Both states and actions are continuous.

Given the state and action in each time step, the physical control system calculates the torques at each joint by using a proportional-derivative (PD) controller as

$$\tau_i = K_{p_i}(a_i - s_i) - K_{d_i}\dot{s}_i,$$

where s_i, $\dot{s}_i$, and a_i denote the current angle, the current angular velocity, and the target angle of the i-th joint, respectively. K_{p_i} and K_{d_i} denote the position and velocity gains for the i-th joint, respectively. These parameters are set at

$$K_{p_i} = 200 \quad \text{and} \quad K_{d_i} = 10$$

for the elbow pitch joints, and

$$K_{p_i} = 2000 \quad \text{and} \quad K_{d_i} = 100$$

for other joints.

The initial position of the robot is fixed at the standing-up-straight pose with the arms down. The immediate reward r_t at the time step t is defined as

$$r_t = \exp(-10d_t) - 0.0005 \min(c_t, 10{,}000),$$

where d_t is the distance between the right hand of the robot and the target object, and c_t is the sum of control costs for each joint. The linear deterministic policy is used for the PGPE methods, and the Gaussian policy is used for IW-REINFORCE-OB. In both cases, the linear basis function $\phi(\boldsymbol{s}) = \boldsymbol{s}$ is used. For PGPE, the initial prior mean η is randomly chosen from the standard normal distribution, and the initial prior standard deviation τ is set at 1.

To evaluate the usefulness of data reuse methods with a small number of samples, the agent collects only $N = 3$ on-policy samples with trajectory length $T = 100$ at each iteration. All previous data samples are reused to estimate the gradients in the data reuse methods, while only on-policy samples are used to estimate the gradients in the plain PGPE-OB method. The discount factor is set at $\gamma = 0.9$.

9.3.3.2 Simulation with 2 Degrees of Freedom

First, the performance on the reaching task with only 2 degrees of freedom is investigated. The body of the robot is fixed and only the right shoulder pitch and right elbow pitch are used. Figure 9.6 depicts the averaged expected return over 10 trials as a function of the number of iterations. The expected return at each trial is computed from 50 newly drawn test episodic data that are not used for policy learning. The graph shows that IW-PGPE-OB nicely improves the performance over iterations with only a small number of on-policy samples. The plain PGPE-OB method can also improve the performance over iterations, but slowly. NIW-PGPE-OB is not as good as IW-PGPE-OB, especially at the later iterations, because of the inconsistency of the NIW estimator.

The distance from the right hand to the object and the control costs along the trajectory are also investigated for three policies: the initial policy, the policy obtained at the 20th iteration by IW-PGPE-OB, and the policy obtained at the 50th iteration by IW-PGPE-OB. Figure 9.7(a) plots the distance to the target object as a function of the time step. This shows that the policy obtained at the 50th iteration decreases the distance rapidly compared with

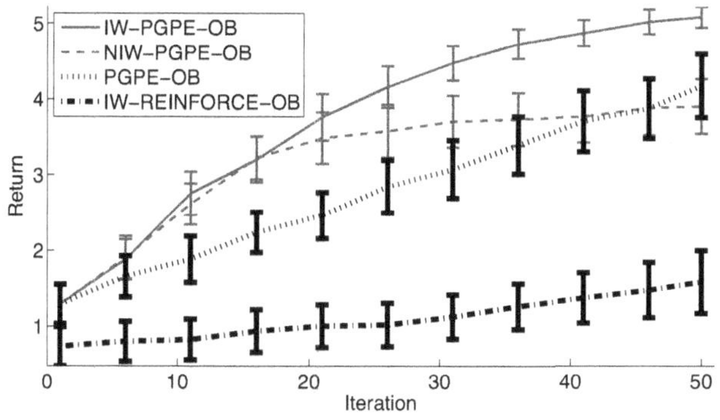

FIGURE 9.6: Average and standard error of returns over 10 runs as functions of the number of iterations for the reaching task with 2 degrees of freedom (right shoulder pitch and right elbow pitch).

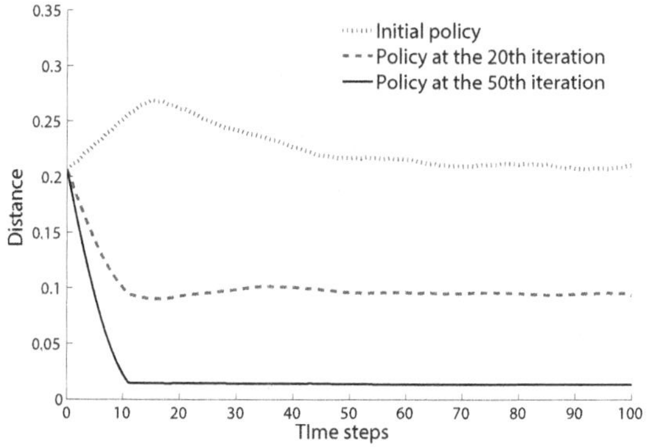

(a) Distance

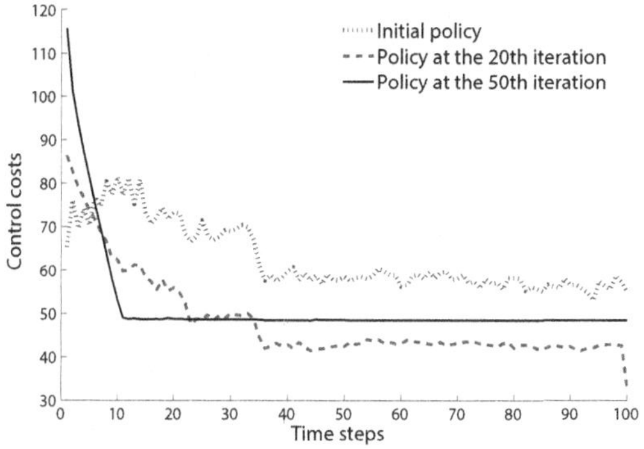

(b) Control costs

FIGURE 9.7: Distance and control costs of arm reaching with 2 degrees of freedom using the policy learned by IW-PGPE-OB.

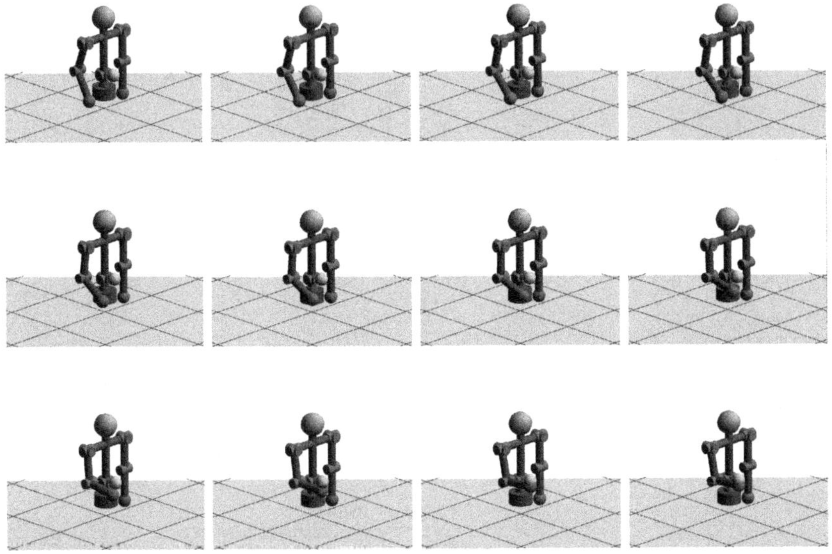

FIGURE 9.8: Typical example of arm reaching with 2 degrees of freedom using the policy obtained by IW-PGPE-OB at the 50th iteration (from left to right and top to bottom).

the initial policy and the policy obtained at the 20th iteration, which means that the robot can reach the object quickly by using the learned policy.

Figure 9.7(b) plots the control cost as a function of the time step. This shows that the policy obtained at the 50th iteration decreases the control cost steadily until the reaching task is completed. This is because the robot mainly adjusts the shoulder pitch in the beginning, which consumes a larger amount of energy than the energy required for controlling the elbow pitch. Then, once the right hand gets closer to the target object, the robot starts adjusting the elbow pitch to reach the target object. The policy obtained at the 20th iteration actually consumes less control costs, but it cannot lead the arm to the target object.

Figure 9.8 illustrates a typical solution of the reaching task with 2 degrees of freedom by the policy obtained by IW-PGPE-OB at the 50th iteration. The images show that the right hand is successfully led to the target object within only 10 time steps.

9.3.3.3 Simulation with All 9 Degrees of Freedom

Finally, the same experiment is carried out using all 9 degrees of freedom. The position of the target object is more distant from the robot so that it cannot be reached by only using the right arm.

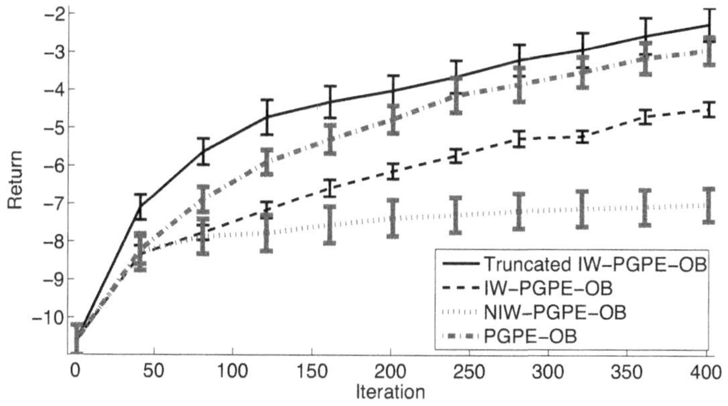

FIGURE 9.9: Average and standard error of returns over 10 runs as functions of the number of iterations for the reaching task with all 9 degrees of freedom.

Because all 9 joints are used, the dimensionality of the state space is much increased and this grows the values of importance weights exponentially. In order to mitigate the large values of importance weights, we decided not to reuse all previously collected samples, but only samples collected in the last 5 iterations. This allows us to keep the difference between the sampling distribution and the target distribution reasonably small, and thus the values of importance weights can be suppressed to some extent. Furthermore, following Wawrzynski (2009), we consider a version of IW-PGPE-OB, denoted as "truncated IW-PGPE-OB" below, where the importance weight is truncated as $w = \min(w, 2)$.

The results plotted in Figure 9.9 show that the performance of the truncated IW-PGPE-OB is the best. This implies that the truncation of importance weights is helpful when applying IW-PGPE-OB to high-dimensional problems.

Figure 9.10 illustrates a typical solution of the reaching task with all 9 degrees of freedom by the policy obtained by the truncated IW-PGPE-OB at the 400th iteration. The images show that the policy learned by our proposed method successfully leads the right hand to the target object, and the irrelevant parts are kept at the initial position for reducing the control costs.

9.3.3.4 Real Robot Control

Finally, the IW-PGPE-OB method is applied to the real CB-i robot shown in Figure 9.11 (Sugimoto et al., 2014).

The experimental setting is essentially the same as the above simulation studies with 9 joints, but policies are updated only every 5 trials and samples taken from the last 10 trials are reused for stabilization purposes. Figure 9.12

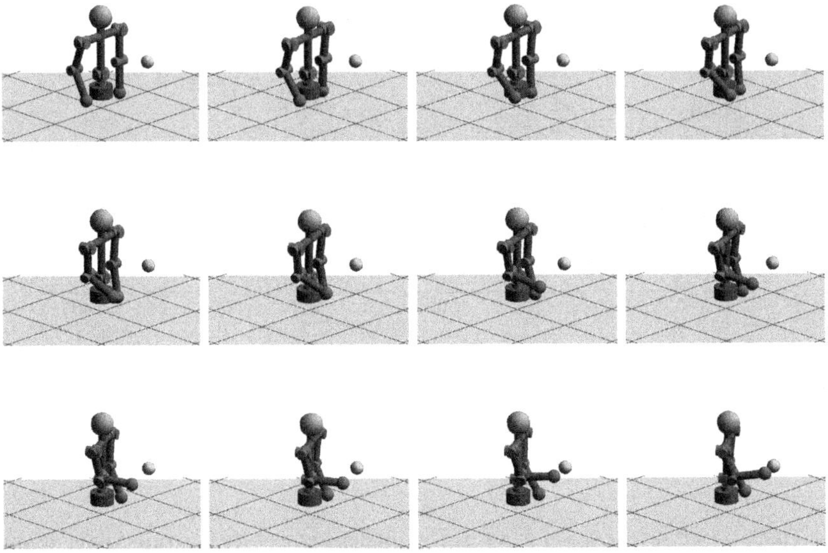

FIGURE 9.10: Typical example of arm reaching with all 9 degrees of freedom using the policy obtained by the truncated IW-PGPE-OB at the 400th iteration (from left to right and top to bottom).

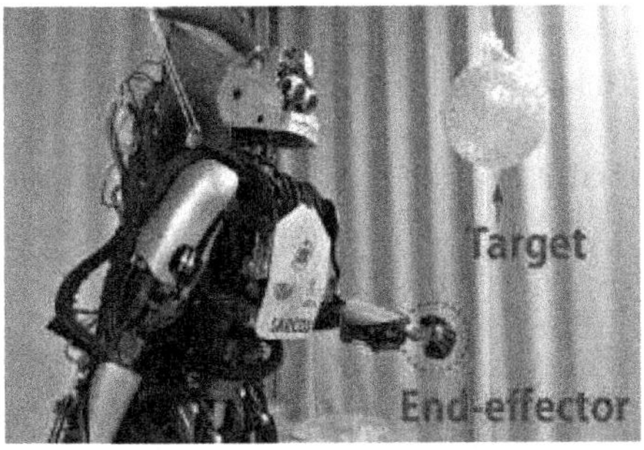

FIGURE 9.11: Reaching task by the real CB-i robot (Sugimoto et al., 2014).

plots the obtained rewards cumulated over policy update iterations, showing that rewards are steadily increased over iteration. Figure 9.13 exhibits the acquired reaching motion based on the policy obtained at the 120th iteration, showing that the end effector of the robot can successfully reach the target object.

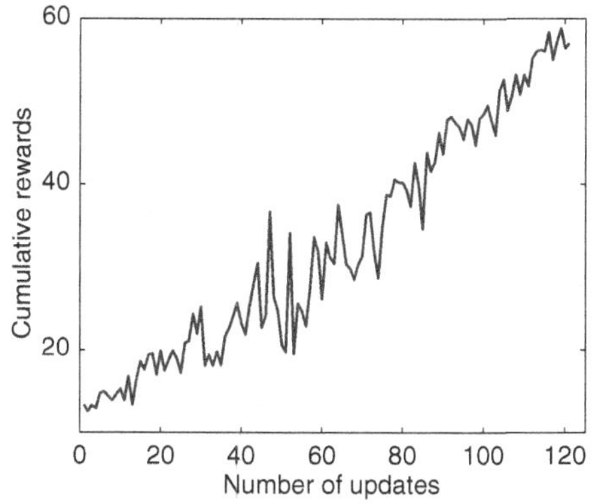

FIGURE 9.12: Obtained reward cumulated over policy updated iterations.

9.4 Remarks

When the trajectory length is large, direct policy search tends to produce gradient estimators with large variance, due to the randomness of stochastic policies. Policy-prior search can avoid this problem by using deterministic policies and introducing stochasticity by considering a prior distribution over policy parameters. Both theoretically and experimentally, advantages of policy-prior search over direct policy search were shown.

A sample reuse framework for policy-prior search was also introduced which is highly useful in real-world reinforcement learning problems with high sampling costs. Following the same line as the sample reuse methods for policy iteration described in Chapter 4 and direct policy search introduced in Chapter 8, *importance weighting* plays an essential role in sample-reuse policy-prior search. When the dimensionality of the state-action space is high, however, importance weights tend to take extremely large values, which causes instability of the importance weighting methods. To mitigate this problem, truncation of the importance weights is useful in practice.

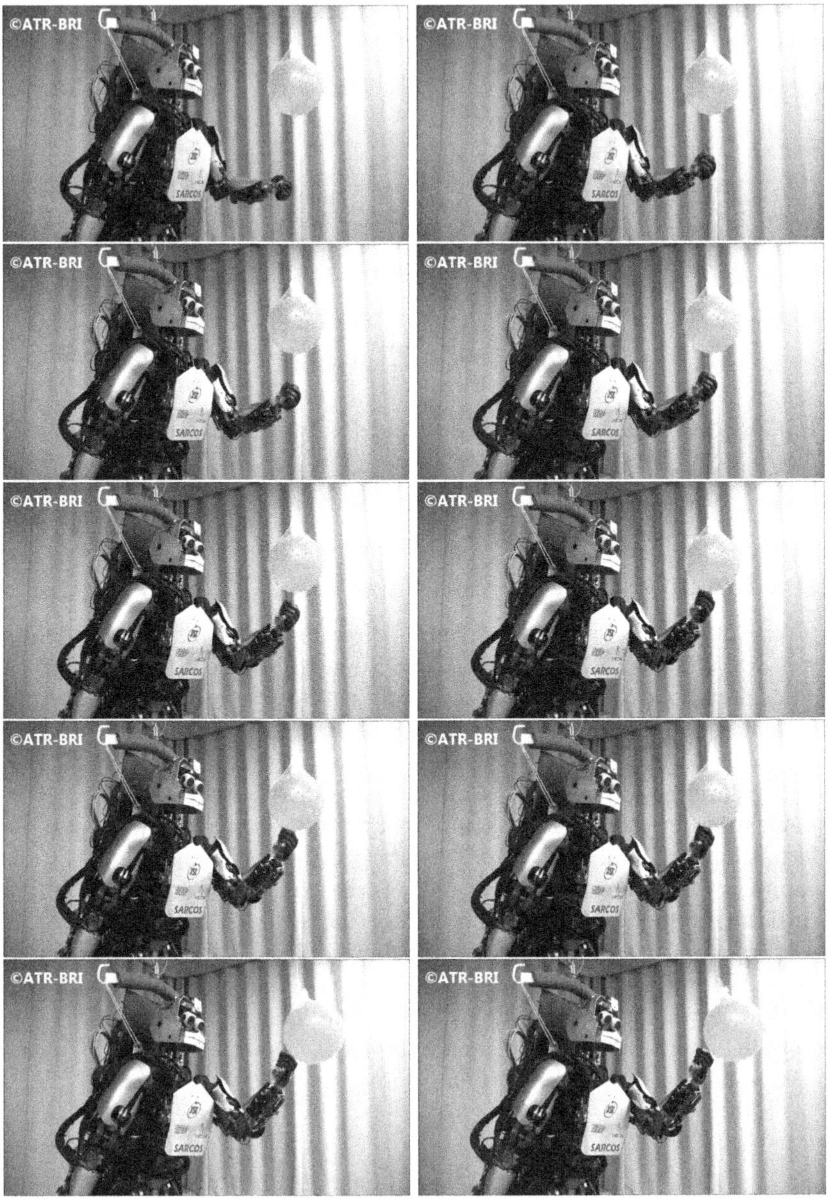

FIGURE 9.13: Typical example of arm reaching using the policy obtained by the IW-PGPE-OB method (from left to right and top to bottom).

Part IV

Model-Based Reinforcement Learning

The reinforcement learning methods explained in Part II and Part III are categorized into the *model-free* approach, meaning that policies are learned without explicitly modeling the unknown environment (i.e., the transition probability of the agent). On the other hand, in Part IV, we introduce an alternative approach called the *model-based* approach, which explicitly models the environment in advance and uses the learned environment model for policy learning.

In the model-based approach, no additional sampling cost is necessary to generate artificial samples from the learned environment model. Thus, the model-based approach is useful when data collection is expensive (e.g., robot control). However, accurately estimating the transition model from a limited amount of trajectory data in multi-dimensional continuous state and action spaces is highly challenging.

In Chapter 10, we introduce a non-parametric model estimator that possesses the optimal convergence rate with high computational efficiency, and demonstrate its usefulness through experiments. Then, in Chapter 11, we combine *dimensionality reduction* with model estimation to cope with high dimensionality of state and action spaces.

Chapter 10

Transition Model Estimation

In this chapter, we introduce transition probability estimation methods for *model-based reinforcement learning* (Wang & Dietterich, 2003; Deisenroth & Rasmussen, 2011). Among the methods described in Section 10.1, a non-parametric transition model estimator called *least-squares conditional density estimation* (LSCDE) (Sugiyama et al., 2010) is shown to be the most promising approach (Tangkaratt et al., 2014a). Then in Section 10.2, we describe how the transition model estimator can be utilized in model-based reinforcement learning. In Section 10.3, experimental performance of a model-based policy-prior search method is evaluated. Finally, in Section 10.4, this chapter is concluded.

10.1 Conditional Density Estimation

In this section, the problem of approximating the transition probability $p(\boldsymbol{s}'|\boldsymbol{s}, a)$ from independent transition samples $\{(\boldsymbol{s}_m, a_m, \boldsymbol{s}'_m)\}_{m=1}^{M}$ is addressed.

10.1.1 Regression-Based Approach

In the *regression*-based approach, the problem of transition probability estimation is formulated as a function approximation problem of predicting output $\boldsymbol{s}'$ given input $\boldsymbol{s}$ and a under Gaussian noise:

$$\boldsymbol{s}' = \boldsymbol{f}(\boldsymbol{s}, a) + \boldsymbol{\epsilon},$$

where $\boldsymbol{f}$ is an unknown regression function to be learned, $\boldsymbol{\epsilon}$ is an independent Gaussian noise vector with mean zero and covariance matrix $\sigma^2\boldsymbol{I}$, and $\boldsymbol{I}$ denotes the identity matrix.

Let us approximate $\boldsymbol{f}$ by the following linear-in-parameter model:

$$\boldsymbol{f}(\boldsymbol{s}, a, \boldsymbol{\Gamma}) = \boldsymbol{\Gamma}^\top \boldsymbol{\phi}(\boldsymbol{s}, a),$$

where $\boldsymbol{\Gamma}$ is the $B \times \dim(\boldsymbol{s})$ parameter matrix and $\boldsymbol{\phi}(\boldsymbol{s}, a)$ is the B-dimensional basis vector. A typical choice of the basis vector is the *Gaussian kernel*, which is defined for $B = M$ as

$$\phi_b(\boldsymbol{s}, a) = \exp\left(-\frac{\|\boldsymbol{s} - \boldsymbol{s}_b\|^2 + (a - a_b)^2}{2\kappa^2}\right),$$

and $\kappa > 0$ denotes the Gaussian kernel width. If B is too large, the number of basis functions may be reduced by only using a subset of samples as Gaussian centers. Different Gaussian widths for $\boldsymbol{s}$ and a may be used if necessary.

The parameter matrix $\boldsymbol{\Gamma}$ is learned so that the regularized squared error is minimized:

$$\widehat{\boldsymbol{\Gamma}} = \underset{\boldsymbol{\Gamma}}{\mathrm{argmin}}\left[\sum_{m=1}^{M}\left(\boldsymbol{f}(\boldsymbol{s}_m, a_m, \boldsymbol{\Gamma}) - \boldsymbol{f}(\boldsymbol{s}_m, a_m)\right)^2 + \mathrm{tr}\left(\boldsymbol{\Gamma}^\top \boldsymbol{R}\boldsymbol{\Gamma}\right)\right],$$

where $\boldsymbol{R}$ is the $B \times B$ positive semi-definite matrix called the regularization matrix. The solution $\widehat{\boldsymbol{\Gamma}}$ is given analytically as

$$\widehat{\boldsymbol{\Gamma}} = (\boldsymbol{\Phi}^\top\boldsymbol{\Phi} + \boldsymbol{R})^{-1}\boldsymbol{\Phi}^\top(\boldsymbol{s}'_1, \ldots, \boldsymbol{s}'_M)^\top,$$

where $\boldsymbol{\Phi}$ is the $M \times B$ *design matrix* defined as

$$\Phi_{m,b} = \phi_b(\boldsymbol{s}_m, a_m).$$

We can confirm that predicted output vector $\widehat{\boldsymbol{s}}' = \boldsymbol{f}(\boldsymbol{s}, a, \widehat{\boldsymbol{\Gamma}})$ actually follows the Gaussian distribution with mean

$$(\boldsymbol{s}'_1, \ldots, \boldsymbol{s}'_M)\boldsymbol{\Phi}(\boldsymbol{\Phi}^\top\boldsymbol{\Phi} + \boldsymbol{R})^{-1}\boldsymbol{\phi}(\boldsymbol{s}, a)$$

and covariance matrix $\widehat{\delta}^2\boldsymbol{I}$, where

$$\widehat{\delta}^2 = \sigma^2\mathrm{tr}\left((\boldsymbol{\Phi}^\top\boldsymbol{\Phi} + \boldsymbol{R})^{-2}\boldsymbol{\Phi}^\top\boldsymbol{\Phi}\right).$$

The tuning parameters such as the Gaussian kernel width κ and the regularization matrix $\boldsymbol{R}$ can be determined either by *cross-validation* or *evidence maximization* if the above method is regarded as *Gaussian process regression* in the Bayesian framework (Rasmussen & Williams, 2006).

This is the regression-based estimator of the transition probability density $p(\boldsymbol{s}'|\boldsymbol{s}, a)$ for an arbitrary test input $\boldsymbol{s}$ and a. Thus, by the use of kernel regression models, the regression function $\boldsymbol{f}$ (which is the conditional mean of outputs) is approximated in a non-parametric way. However, the conditional distribution of outputs itself is restricted to be Gaussian, which is highly restrictive in real-world reinforcement learning.

10.1.2 ϵ-Neighbor Kernel Density Estimation

When the conditioning variables $(\boldsymbol{s}, a)$ are discrete, the conditional density $p(\boldsymbol{s}'|\boldsymbol{s}, a)$ can be easily estimated by standard density estimators such as *kernel density estimation* (KDE) by only using samples $\{s'_i\}_i$ such that (s_i, a_i) agrees with the target values (s, a). ϵ-neighbor KDE (ϵKDE) extends this idea to the continuous case such that (s_i, a_i) are close to the target values (s, a).

More specifically, ϵKDE with the Gaussian kernel is given by

$$\widehat{p}(s'|s, a) = \frac{1}{|\mathcal{I}_{(s,a),\epsilon}|} \sum_{i \in \mathcal{I}_{(s,a),\epsilon}} \mathcal{N}(s'; s'_i, \sigma^2 I),$$

where $\mathcal{I}_{(s,a),\epsilon}$ is the set of sample indices such that $\|(s, a) - (s_i, a_i)\| \leq \epsilon$ and $\mathcal{N}(s'; s'_i, \sigma^2 I)$ denotes the Gaussian density with mean s'_i and covariance matrix $\sigma^2 I$. The Gaussian width σ and the distance threshold ϵ may be chosen by cross-validation.

ϵKDE is a useful non-parametric density estimator that is easy to implement. However, it is unreliable in high-dimensional problems due to the distance-based construction.

10.1.3 Least-Squares Conditional Density Estimation

A non-parametric conditional density estimator called *least-squares conditional density estimation* (LSCDE) (Sugiyama et al., 2010) possesses various useful properties:

- It can directly handle multi-dimensional multi-modal inputs and outputs.
- It was proved to achieve the optimal convergence rate (Kanamori et al., 2012).
- It has high numerical stability (Kanamori et al., 2013).
- It is robust against outliers (Sugiyama et al., 2010).
- Its solution can be analytically and efficiently computed just by solving a system of linear equations (Kanamori et al., 2009).
- Generating samples from the learned transition model is straightforward.

Let us model the transition probability $p(s'|s, a)$ by the following linear-in-parameter model:

$$\alpha^\top \phi(s, a, s'), \tag{10.1}$$

where α is the B-dimensional parameter vector and $\phi(s, a, s')$ is the B-dimensional basis function vector. A typical choice of the basis function is the *Gaussian kernel*, which is defined for $B = M$ as

$$\phi_b(s, a, s') = \exp\left(-\frac{\|s - s_b\|^2 + (a - a_b)^2 + \|s' - s'_b\|^2}{2\kappa^2}\right).$$

$\kappa > 0$ denotes the Gaussian kernel width. If B is too large, the number of basis functions may be reduced by only using a subset of samples as Gaussian centers. Different Gaussian widths for $\boldsymbol{s}$, a, and $\boldsymbol{s}'$ may be used if necessary.

The parameter $\boldsymbol{\alpha}$ is learned so that the following squared error is minimized:

$$\begin{aligned}
J_0(\boldsymbol{\alpha}) &= \frac{1}{2}\iiint \left(\boldsymbol{\alpha}^\top \boldsymbol{\phi}(\boldsymbol{s},a,\boldsymbol{s}') - p(\boldsymbol{s}'|\boldsymbol{s},a)\right)^2 p(\boldsymbol{s},a)\mathrm{d}\boldsymbol{s}\mathrm{d}a\mathrm{d}\boldsymbol{s}' \\
&= \frac{1}{2}\iiint \left(\boldsymbol{\alpha}^\top \boldsymbol{\phi}(\boldsymbol{s},a,\boldsymbol{s}')\right)^2 p(\boldsymbol{s},a)\mathrm{d}\boldsymbol{s}\mathrm{d}a\mathrm{d}\boldsymbol{s}' \\
&\quad - \iiint \boldsymbol{\alpha}^\top \boldsymbol{\phi}(\boldsymbol{s},a,\boldsymbol{s}')p(\boldsymbol{s},a,\boldsymbol{s}')\mathrm{d}\boldsymbol{s}\mathrm{d}a\mathrm{d}\boldsymbol{s}' + C,
\end{aligned}$$

where the identity $p(\boldsymbol{s}'|\boldsymbol{s},a) = p(\boldsymbol{s},a,\boldsymbol{s}')/p(\boldsymbol{s},a)$ is used in the second term and

$$C = \frac{1}{2}\iiint p(\boldsymbol{s}'|\boldsymbol{s},a)p(\boldsymbol{s},a,\boldsymbol{s}')\mathrm{d}\boldsymbol{s}\mathrm{d}a\mathrm{d}\boldsymbol{s}'.$$

Because C is constant independent of $\boldsymbol{\alpha}$, only the first two terms will be considered from here on:

$$J(\boldsymbol{\alpha}) = J_0(\boldsymbol{\alpha}) - C = \frac{1}{2}\boldsymbol{\alpha}^\top \boldsymbol{U}\boldsymbol{\alpha} - \boldsymbol{\alpha}^\top \boldsymbol{v},$$

where $\boldsymbol{U}$ is the $B \times B$ and $\boldsymbol{v}$ is the B-dimensional vector defined as

$$\begin{aligned}
\boldsymbol{U} &= \iint \overline{\boldsymbol{\Phi}}(\boldsymbol{s},a)p(\boldsymbol{s},a)\mathrm{d}\boldsymbol{s}\mathrm{d}a, \\
\boldsymbol{v} &= \iiint \boldsymbol{\phi}(\boldsymbol{s},a,\boldsymbol{s}')p(\boldsymbol{s},a,\boldsymbol{s}')\mathrm{d}\boldsymbol{s}\mathrm{d}a\mathrm{d}\boldsymbol{s}', \\
\overline{\boldsymbol{\Phi}}(\boldsymbol{s},a) &= \int \boldsymbol{\phi}(\boldsymbol{s},a,\boldsymbol{s}')\boldsymbol{\phi}(\boldsymbol{s},a,\boldsymbol{s}')^\top \mathrm{d}\boldsymbol{s}'.
\end{aligned}$$

Note that, for the Gaussian model (10.1), the (b,b')-th element of matrix $\overline{\boldsymbol{\Phi}}(\boldsymbol{s},a)$ can be computed analytically as

$$\begin{aligned}
\overline{\Phi}_{b,b'}(\boldsymbol{s},a) &= (\sqrt{\pi}\kappa)^{\dim(\boldsymbol{s}')} \exp\left(-\frac{\|\boldsymbol{s}'_b - \boldsymbol{s}'_{b'}\|^2}{4\kappa^2}\right) \\
&\quad \times \exp\left(-\frac{\|\boldsymbol{s}-\boldsymbol{s}_b\|^2 + \|\boldsymbol{s}-\boldsymbol{s}_{b'}\|^2 + (a-a_b)^2 + (a-a_{b'})^2}{2\kappa^2}\right).
\end{aligned}$$

Because $\boldsymbol{U}$ and $\boldsymbol{v}$ included in $J(\boldsymbol{\alpha})$ contain the expectations over unknown densities $p(\boldsymbol{s},a)$ and $p(\boldsymbol{s},a,\boldsymbol{s}')$, they are approximated by sample averages. Then we have

$$\widehat{J}(\boldsymbol{\alpha}) = \frac{1}{2}\boldsymbol{\alpha}^\top \widehat{\boldsymbol{U}}\boldsymbol{\alpha} - \widehat{\boldsymbol{v}}^\top \boldsymbol{\alpha},$$

where

$$\widehat{U} = \frac{1}{M}\sum_{m=1}^{M} \overline{\boldsymbol{\Phi}}(\boldsymbol{s}_m, a_m) \quad \text{and} \quad \widehat{\boldsymbol{v}} = \frac{1}{M}\sum_{m=1}^{M} \boldsymbol{\phi}(\boldsymbol{s}_m, a_m, \boldsymbol{s}'_m).$$

By adding an ℓ_2-regularizer to $\widehat{J}(\boldsymbol{\alpha})$ to avoid overfitting, the LSCDE optimization criterion is given as

$$\widetilde{\boldsymbol{\alpha}} = \underset{\boldsymbol{\alpha}\in\mathbb{R}^M}{\operatorname{argmin}} \left[\widehat{J}(\boldsymbol{\alpha}) + \frac{\lambda}{2}\|\boldsymbol{\alpha}\|^2\right],$$

where $\lambda \geq 0$ is the regularization parameter. The solution $\widetilde{\boldsymbol{\alpha}}$ is given analytically as

$$\widetilde{\boldsymbol{\alpha}} = (\widehat{\boldsymbol{U}} + \lambda \boldsymbol{I})^{-1}\widehat{\boldsymbol{v}},$$

where $\boldsymbol{I}$ denotes the identity matrix. Because conditional probability densities are non-negative by definition, the solution $\widetilde{\boldsymbol{\alpha}}$ is modified as

$$\widehat{\alpha}_b = \max(0, \widetilde{\alpha}_b).$$

Finally, the solution is normalized in the test phase. More specifically, given a test input point $(\boldsymbol{s}, a)$, the final LSCDE solution is given as

$$\widehat{p}(\boldsymbol{s}'|\boldsymbol{s}, a) = \frac{\widehat{\boldsymbol{\alpha}}^\top \boldsymbol{\phi}(\boldsymbol{s}, a, \boldsymbol{s}')}{\int \widehat{\boldsymbol{\alpha}}^\top \boldsymbol{\phi}(\boldsymbol{s}, a, \boldsymbol{s}'')\mathrm{d}\boldsymbol{s}''},$$

where, for the Gaussian model (10.1), the denominator can be analytically computed as

$$\int \widehat{\boldsymbol{\alpha}}^\top \boldsymbol{\phi}(\boldsymbol{s}, a, \boldsymbol{s}'')\mathrm{d}\boldsymbol{s}'' = (\sqrt{2\pi}\kappa)^{\dim(\boldsymbol{s}')} \sum_{b=1}^{B} \alpha_b \exp\left(-\frac{\|\boldsymbol{s} - \boldsymbol{s}_b\|^2 + (a - a_b)^2}{2\kappa^2}\right).$$

Model selection of the Gaussian width κ and the regularization parameter λ is possible by *cross-validation* (Sugiyama et al., 2010).

10.2 Model-Based Reinforcement Learning

Model-based reinforcement learning is simply carried out as follows.

1. Collect transition samples $\{(\boldsymbol{s}_m, a_m, \boldsymbol{s}'_m)\}_{m=1}^M$.
2. Obtain a transition model estimate $\widehat{p}(\boldsymbol{s}'|\boldsymbol{s}, a)$ from $\{(\boldsymbol{s}_m, a_m, \boldsymbol{s}'_m)\}_{m=1}^M$.

3. Run a model-free reinforcement learning method using trajectory samples $\{\widetilde{h}_t\}_{t=1}^{\widetilde{T}}$ artificially generated from estimated transition model $\widehat{p}(\boldsymbol{s}'|\boldsymbol{s}, a)$ and current policy $\pi(a|\boldsymbol{s}, \boldsymbol{\theta})$.

Model-based reinforcement learning is particularly advantageous when the sampling cost is limited. More specifically, in model-free methods, we need to fix the *sampling schedule* in advance — for example, whether many samples are gathered in the beginning or only a small batch of samples is collected for a longer period. However, optimizing the sampling schedule in advance is not possible without strong prior knowledge. Thus, we need to just blindly design the sampling schedule in practice, which can cause significant performance degradation. On the other hand, model-based methods do not suffer from this problem, because we can draw as many trajectory samples as we want from the learned transition model without additional sampling costs.

10.3 Numerical Examples

In this section, the experimental performance of the model-free and model-based versions of PGPE (*policy gradients with parameter-based exploration*) are evaluated:

M-PGPE(LSCDE): The model-based PGPE method with transition model estimated by LSCDE.

M-PGPE(GP): The model-based PGPE method with transition model estimated by Gaussian process (GP) regression.

IW-PGPE: The model-free PGPE method with sample reuse by importance weighting (the method introduced in Chapter 9).

10.3.1 Continuous Chain Walk

Let us first consider a simple continuous chain walk task, described in Figure 10.1.

10.3.1.1 Setup

Let

$$s \in \mathcal{S} = [0, 10], \quad a \in \mathcal{A} = [-5, 5], \quad \text{and} \quad r(s, a, s') = \begin{cases} 1 & (4 < s' < 6), \\ 0 & (\text{otherwise}). \end{cases}$$

That is, the agent receives positive reward $+1$ at the center of the state space. The trajectory length is set at $T = 10$ and the discount factor is set at

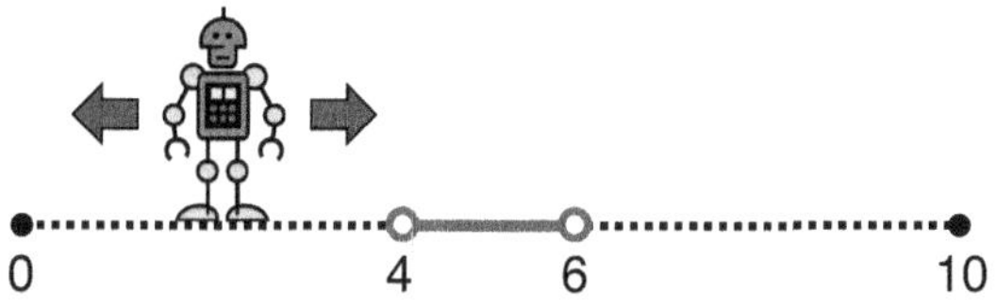

FIGURE 10.1: Illustration of continuous chain walk.

$\gamma = 0.99$. The following linear-in-parameter policy model is used in both the M-PGPE and IW-PGPE methods:

$$a = \sum_{i=1}^{6} \theta_i \exp\left(-\frac{(s - c_i)^2}{2}\right),$$

where $(c_1, \ldots, c_6) = (0, 2, 4, 6, 8, 10)$. If an action determined by the above policy is out of the action space, it is pulled back to be confined in the domain.

As transition dynamics, the following two scenarios are considered:

Gaussian: The true transition dynamics is given by

$$s_{t+1} = s_t + a_t + \varepsilon_t,$$

where ε_t is the Gaussian noise with mean 0 and standard deviation 0.3.

Bimodal: The true transition dynamics is given by

$$s_{t+1} = s_t \pm a_t + \varepsilon_t,$$

where ε_t is the Gaussian noise with mean 0 and standard deviation 0.3, and the sign of a_t is randomly chosen with probability 1/2.

If the next state is out of the state space, it is projected back to the domain. Below, the budget for data collection is assumed to be limited to $N = 20$ trajectory samples.

10.3.1.2 Comparison of Model Estimators

When the transition model is learned in the M-PGPE methods, all $N = 20$ trajectory samples are gathered randomly in the beginning at once. More specifically, the initial state s_1 and the action a_1 are chosen from the uniform distributions over $\mathcal{S}$ and $\mathcal{A}$, respectively. Then the next state s_2 and the immediate reward r_1 are obtained. After that, the action a_2 is chosen from the uniform distribution over $\mathcal{A}$, and the next state s_3 and the immediate reward r_2 are obtained. This process is repeated until r_T is obtained, by which a trajectory sample is obtained. This data generation process is repeated N times to obtain N trajectory samples.

Figure 10.2 and Figure 10.3 illustrate the true transition dynamics and

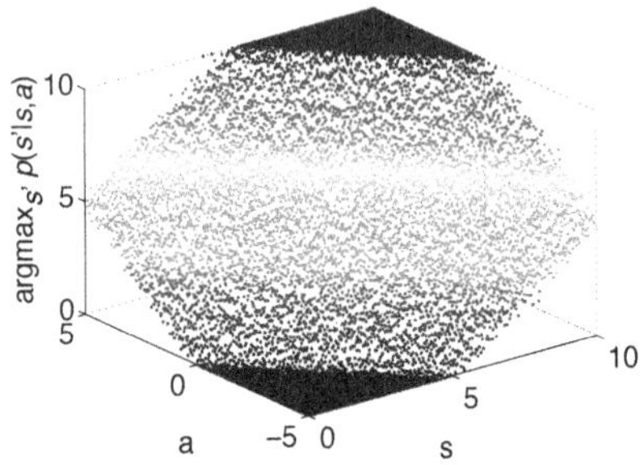

(a) True transition

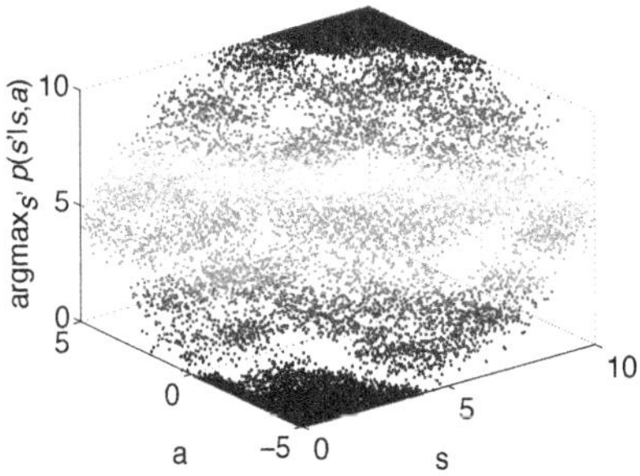

(b) Transition estimated by LSCDE

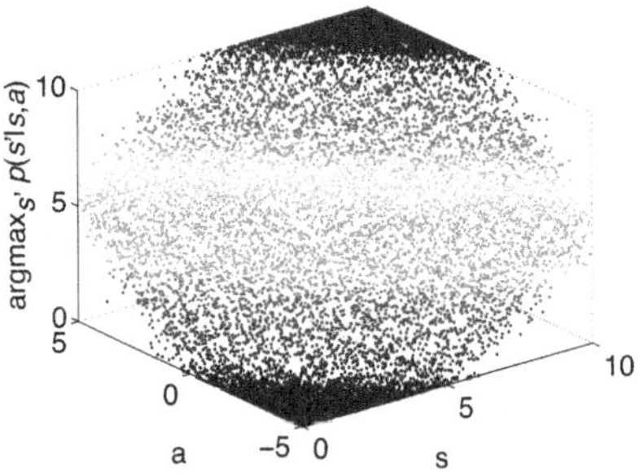

(c) Transition estimated by GP

FIGURE 10.2: Gaussian transition dynamics and its estimates by LSCDE and GP.

their estimates obtained by LSCDE and GP in the Gaussian and bimodal cases, respectively. Figure 10.2 shows that both LSCDE and GP can learn the entire profile of the true transition dynamics well in the Gaussian case. On the other hand, Figure 10.3 shows that LSCDE can still successfully capture the entire profile of the true transition dynamics well even in the bimodal case, but GP fails to capture the bimodal structure.

Based on the estimated transition models, policies are learned by the M-PGPE method. More specifically, from the learned transition model, 1000 artificial trajectory samples are generated for gradient estimation and another 1000 artificial trajectory samples are used for baseline estimation. Then policies are updated based on these artificial trajectory samples. This policy update step is repeated 100 times. For evaluating the return of a learned policy, 100 additional test trajectory samples are used which are not employed for policy learning. Figure 10.4 and Figure 10.5 depict the averages and standard errors of returns over 100 runs for the Gaussian and bimodal cases, respectively. The results show that, in the Gaussian case, the GP-based method performs very well and LSCDE also exhibits reasonable performance. In the bimodal case, on the other hand, GP performs poorly and LSCDE gives much better results than GP. This illustrates the high flexibility of LSCDE.

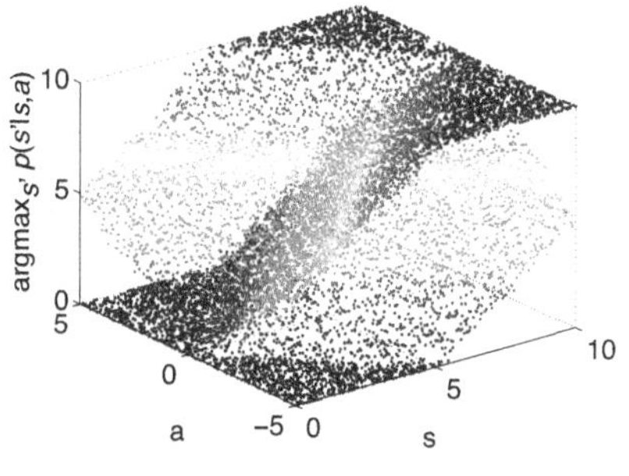

(a) True transition

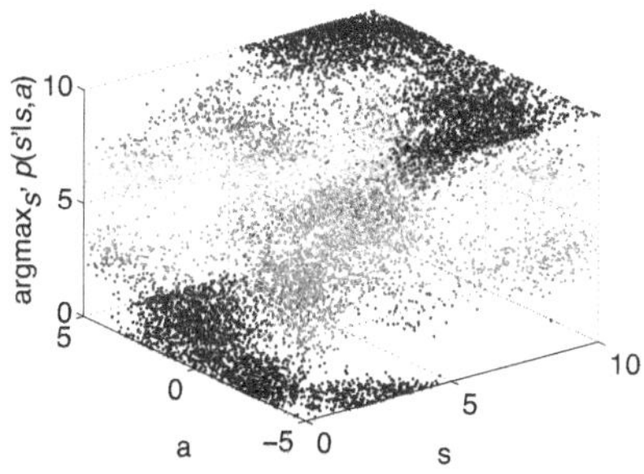

(b) Transition estimated by LSCDE

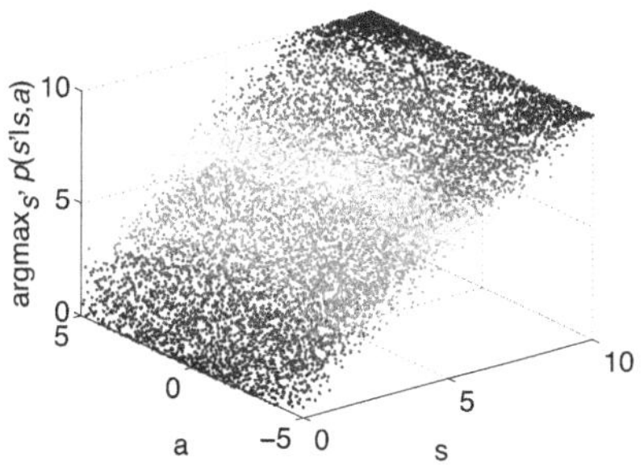

(c) Transition estimated by GP

FIGURE 10.3: Bimodal transition dynamics and its estimates by LSCDE and GP.

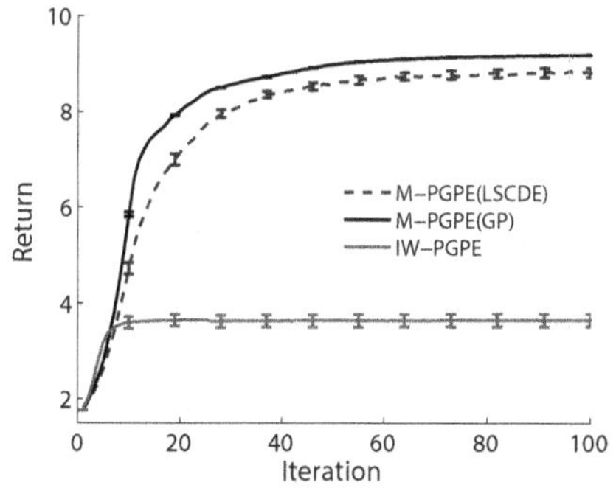

FIGURE 10.4: Averages and standard errors of returns of the policies over 100 runs obtained by M-PGPE with LSCDE, M-PGPE with GP, and IW-PGPE for Gaussian transition.

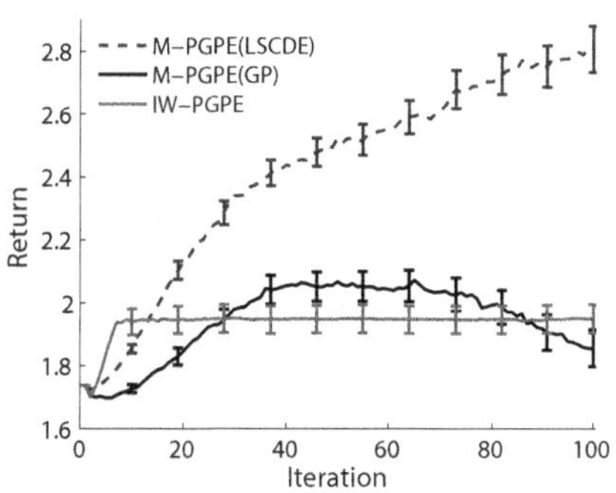

FIGURE 10.5: Averages and standard errors of returns of the policies over 100 runs obtained by M-PGPE with LSCDE, M-PGPE with GP, and IW-PGPE for bimodal transition.

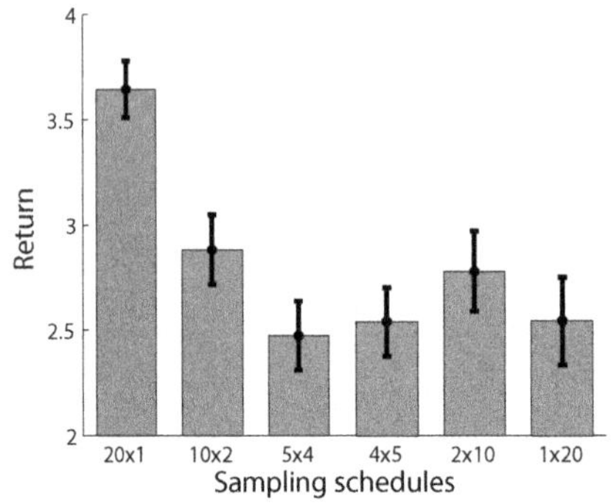

FIGURE 10.6: Averages and standard errors of returns obtained by IW-PGPE over 100 runs for Gaussian transition with different sampling schedules (e.g., 5×4 means gathering $k = 5$ trajectory samples 4 times).

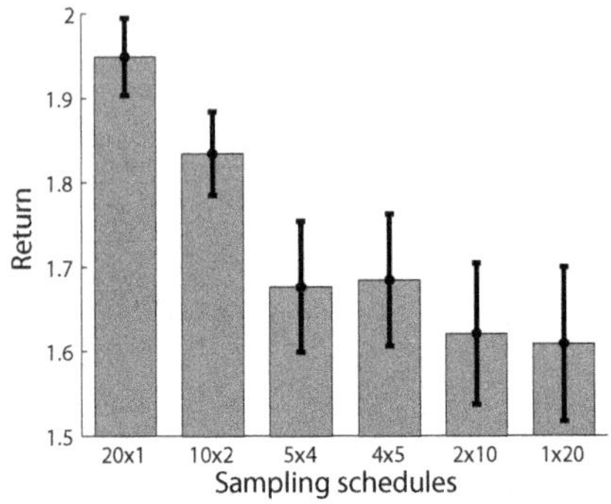

FIGURE 10.7: Averages and standard errors of returns obtained by IW-PGPE over 100 runs for bimodal transition with different sampling schedules (e.g., 5×4 means gathering $k = 5$ trajectory samples 4 times).

10.3.1.3 Comparison of Model-Based and Model-Free Methods

Next, the performance of the model-based and model-free PGPE methods are compared.

Under the fixed budget scenario, the schedule of collecting 20 trajectory samples needs to be determined for the IW-PGPE method. First, the influence of the choice of sampling schedules is illustrated. Figure 10.6 and Figure 10.7 show expected returns averaged over 100 runs under the sampling schedule that a batch of k trajectory samples are gathered $20/k$ times for different values of k. Here, policy update is performed 100 times after observing each batch of k trajectory samples, because this performed better than the usual scheme of updating the policy only once. Figure 10.6 shows that the performance of IW-PGPE depends heavily on the sampling schedule, and gathering $k = 20$ trajectory samples at once is shown to be the best choice in the Gaussian case. Figure 10.7 shows that gathering $k = 20$ trajectory samples at once is also the best choice in the bimodal case.

Although the best sampling schedule is not accessible in practice, the optimal sampling schedule is used for evaluating the performance of IW-PGPE. Figure 10.4 and Figure 10.5 show the averages and standard errors of returns obtained by IW-PGPE over 100 runs as functions of the sampling steps. These graphs show that IW-PGPE can improve the policies only in the beginning, because all trajectory samples are gathered at once in the beginning. The performance of IW-PGPE may be further improved if it is possible to gather more trajectory samples. However, this is prohibited under the fixed budget scenario. On the other hand, returns of M-PGPE keep increasing over iterations, because artificial trajectory samples can be kept generated without additional sampling costs. This illustrates a potential advantage of model-based reinforcement learning (RL) methods.

10.3.2 Humanoid Robot Control

Finally, the performance of M-PGPE is evaluated on a practical control problem of a simulated upper-body model of the humanoid robot *CB-i* (Cheng et al., 2007), which was also used in Section 9.3.3; see Figure 9.5 for the illustrations of CB-i and its simulator.

10.3.2.1 Setup

The simulator is based on the upper body of the CB-i humanoid robot, which has 9 joints for shoulder pitch, shoulder roll, elbow pitch of the right arm, and shoulder pitch, shoulder roll, elbow pitch of the left arm, waist yaw, torso roll, and torso pitch. The state vector is 18-dimensional and real-valued, which corresponds to the current angle in degree and the current angular velocity for each joint. The action vector is 9-dimensional and real-valued, which corresponds to the target angle of each joint in degree. The goal of the control problem is to lead the end effector of the right arm (right hand) to the target object. A noisy control system is simulated by perturbing action vectors with independent bimodal Gaussian noise. More specifically, for each element of the action vector, Gaussian noise with mean 0 and standard deviation 3 is added with probability 0.6, and Gaussian noise with mean -5 and standard deviation 3 is added with probability 0.4.

The initial posture of the robot is fixed to be standing up straight with arms down. The target object is located in front of and above the right hand, which is reachable by using the controllable joints. The reward function at each time step is defined as

$$r_t = \exp(-10d_t) - 0.000005 \min\{c_t, 1,000,000\},$$

where d_t is the distance between the right hand and target object at time step t, and c_t is the sum of control costs for each joint. The deterministic policy model used in M-PGPE and IW-PGPE is defined as $a = \boldsymbol{\theta}^\top \boldsymbol{\phi}(\boldsymbol{s})$ with the basis function $\boldsymbol{\phi}(\boldsymbol{s}) = \boldsymbol{s}$. The trajectory length is set at $T = 100$ and the discount factor is set at $\gamma = 0.9$.

10.3.2.2 Experiment with 2 Joints

First, we consider using only 2 joints among the 9 joints, i.e., only the right shoulder pitch and right elbow pitch are allowed to be controlled, while the other joints remain still at each time step (no control signal is sent to these joints). Therefore, the dimensionalities of state vector $\boldsymbol{s}$ and action vector $\boldsymbol{a}$ are 4 and 2, respectively.

We suppose that the budget for data collection is limited to $N = 50$ trajectory samples. For the M-PGPE methods, all trajectory samples are collected at first using the uniformly random initial states and policy. More specifically, the initial state is chosen from the uniform distribution over $\mathcal{S}$. At each time step, the action a_i of the i-th joint is first drawn from the uniform distribution on $[s_i - 5, s_i + 5]$, where s_i denotes the state for the i-th joint. In total, 5000 transition samples are collected for model estimation. Then, from the learned transition model, 1000 artificial trajectory samples are generated for gradient estimation and another 1000 artificial trajectory samples are generated for baseline estimation in each iteration. The sampling schedule of the IW-PGPE method is chosen to collect $k = 5$ trajectory samples $50/k$ times, which performs well, as shown in Figure 10.8. The average and standard error of the return obtained by each method over 10 runs are plotted in Figure 10.9, showing that M-PGPE(LSCDE) tends to outperform both M-PGPE(GP) and IW-PGPE.

Figure 10.10 illustrates an example of the reaching motion with 2 joints obtained by M-PGPE(LSCDE) at the 60th iteration. This shows that the learned policy successfully leads the right hand to the target object within only 13 steps in this noisy control system.

10.3.2.3 Experiment with 9 Joints

Finally, the performance of M-PGPE(LSCDE) and IW-PGPE is evaluated on the reaching task with all 9 joints.

The experimental setup is essentially the same as the 2-joint case, but the budget for gathering $N = 1000$ trajectory samples is given to this complex and high-dimensional task. The position of the target object is moved to far left, which is not reachable by using only 2 joints. Thus, the robot is required to move other joints to reach the object with the right hand. Five thousand randomly chosen transition samples are used as Gaussian centers for M-PGPE(LSCDE). The sampling schedule for IW-PGPE is set at gathering 1000 trajectory samples at once, which is the best sampling schedule according to Figure 10.11. The averages and standard errors of returns obtained by M-PGPE(LSCDE) and IW-PGPE over 30 runs are plotted in Figure 10.12, showing that M-PGPE(LSCDE) tends to outperform IW-PGPE.

Figure 10.13 exhibits a typical reaching motion with 9 joints obtained by M-PGPE(LSCDE) at the 1000th iteration. This shows that the right hand is led to the distant object successfully within 14 steps.

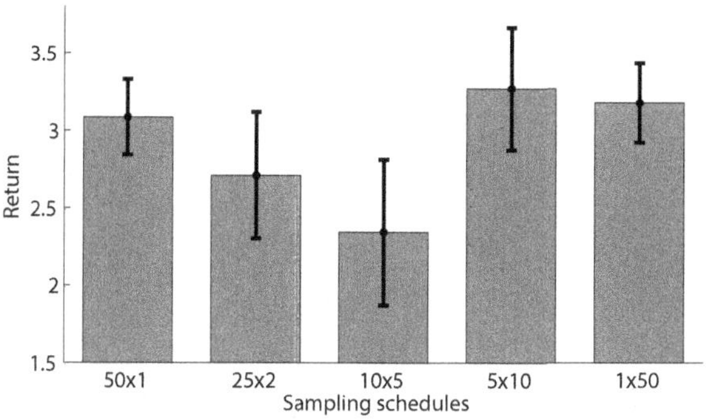

FIGURE 10.8: Averages and standard errors of returns obtained by IW-PGPE over 10 runs for the 2-joint humanoid robot simulator for different sampling schedules (e.g., 5×10 means gathering $k = 5$ trajectory samples 10 times).

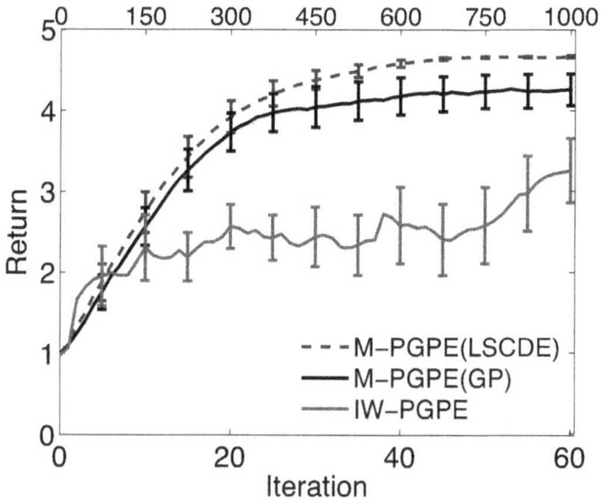

FIGURE 10.9: Averages and standard errors of obtained returns over 10 runs for the 2-joint humanoid robot simulator. All methods use 50 trajectory samples for policy learning. In M-PGPE(LSCDE) and M-PGPE(GP), all 50 trajectory samples are gathered in the beginning and the environment model is learned; then 2000 artificial trajectory samples are generated in each update iteration. In IW-PGPE, a batch of 5 trajectory samples is gathered for 10 iterations, which was shown to be the best sampling scheduling (see Figure 10.8). Note that policy update is performed 100 times after observing each batch of trajectory samples, which we confirmed to perform well. The bottom horizontal axis is for the M-PGPE methods, while the top horizontal axis is for the IW-PGPE method.

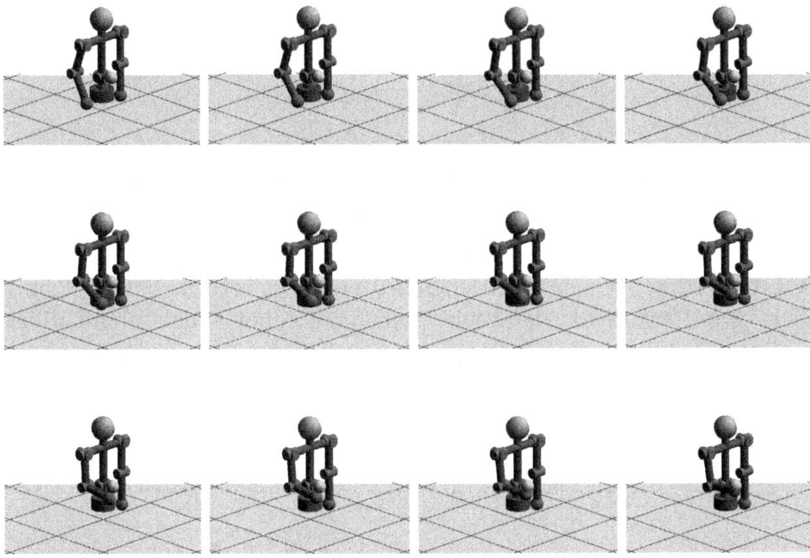

FIGURE 10.10: Example of arm reaching with 2 joints using a policy obtained by M-PGPE(LSCDE) at the 60th iteration (from left to right and top to bottom).

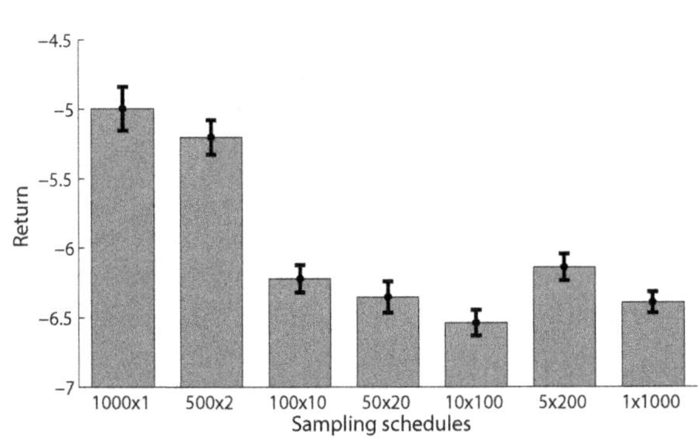

FIGURE 10.11: Averages and standard errors of returns obtained by IW-PGPE over 30 runs for the 9-joint humanoid robot simulator for different sampling schedules (e.g., 100×10 means gathering $k = 100$ trajectory samples 10 times).

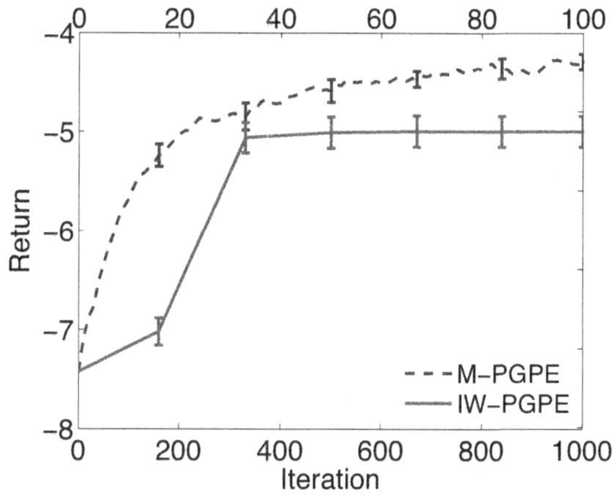

FIGURE 10.12: Averages and standard errors of obtained returns over 30 runs for the humanoid robot simulator with 9 joints. Both methods use 1000 trajectory samples for policy learning. In M-PGPE(LSCDE), all 1000 trajectory samples are gathered in the beginning and the environment model is learned; then 2000 artificial trajectory samples are generated in each update iteration. In IW-PGPE, a batch of 1000 trajectory samples is gathered at once, which was shown to be the best scheduling (see Figure 10.11). Note that policy update is performed 100 times after observing each batch of trajectory samples. The bottom horizontal axis is for the M-PGPE method, while the top horizontal axis is for the IW-PGPE method.

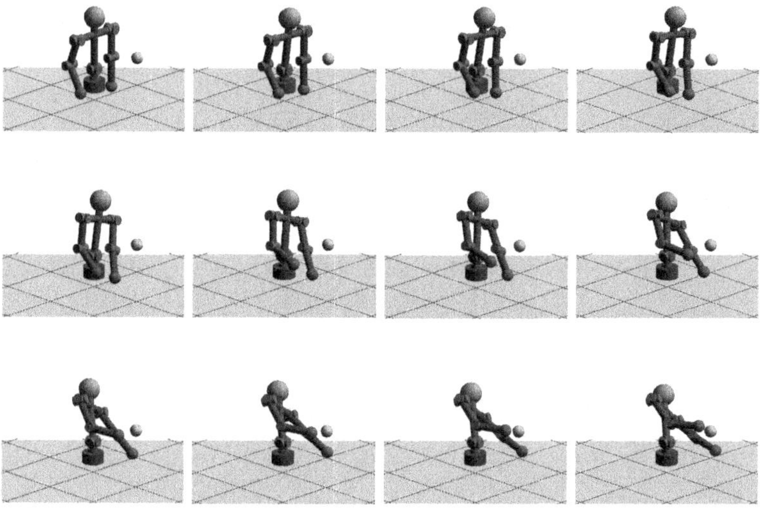

FIGURE 10.13: Example of arm reaching with 9 joints using a policy obtained by M-PGPE(LSCDE) at the 1000th iteration (from left to right and top to bottom).

10.4 Remarks

Model-based reinforcement learning is a promising approach, given that the transition model can be estimated accurately. However, estimating the high-dimensional conditional density is challenging. In this chapter, a non-parametric conditional density estimator called *least-squares conditional density estimation* (LSCDE) was introduced, and model-based PGPE with LSCDE was shown to work excellently in experiments.

Under the fixed sampling budget, the model-free approach requires us to design the sampling schedule appropriately in advance. However, this is practically very hard unless strong prior knowledge is available. On the other hand, model-based methods do not suffer from this problem, which is an excellent practical advantage over the model-free approach.

In robotics, the model-free approach seems to be preferred because accurately learning the transition dynamics of complex robots is challenging (Deisenroth et al., 2013). Furthermore, model-free methods can utilize the prior knowledge in the form of policy demonstration (Kober & Peters, 2011). On the other hand, the model-based approach is advantageous in that no interaction with the real robot is required once the transition model has been learned and the learned transition model can be utilized for further simulation.

Actually, the choice of model-free or model-based methods is not only an ongoing research topic in machine learning, but also a big debatable issue in neuroscience. Therefore, further discussion would be necessary to more deeply understand the pros and cons of the model-based and model-free approaches. Combining or switching the model-free and model-based approaches would also be an interesting direction to be further investigated.

Chapter 11

Dimensionality Reduction for Transition Model Estimation

Least-squares conditional density estimation (LSCDE), introduced in Chapter 10, is a practical transition model estimator. However, transition model estimation is still challenging when the dimensionality of state and action spaces is high. In this chapter, a *dimensionality reduction* method is introduced to LSCDE which finds a low-dimensional expression of the original state and action vector that is relevant to predicting the next state. After mathematically formulating the problem of dimensionality reduction in Section 11.1, a detailed description of the dimensionality reduction algorithm based on *squared-loss conditional entropy* is provided in Section 11.2. Then numerical examples are given in Section 11.3, and this chapter is concluded in Section 11.4.

11.1 Sufficient Dimensionality Reduction

Sufficient dimensionality reduction (Li, 1991; Cook & Ni, 2005) is a framework of dimensionality reduction in a supervised learning setting of analyzing an input-output relation — in our case, input is the state-action pair $(\boldsymbol{s}, a)$ and output is the next state $\boldsymbol{s}'$. Sufficient dimensionality reduction is aimed at finding a low-dimensional expression $\boldsymbol{z}$ of input $(\boldsymbol{s}, a)$ that contains "sufficient" information about output $\boldsymbol{s}'$.

Let $\boldsymbol{z}$ be a linear projection of input $(\boldsymbol{s}, a)$. More specifically, using matrix $\boldsymbol{W}$ such that $\boldsymbol{W}\boldsymbol{W}^\top = \boldsymbol{I}$ where $\boldsymbol{I}$ denotes the identity matrix, $\boldsymbol{z}$ is given by

$$\boldsymbol{z} = \boldsymbol{W} \begin{pmatrix} \boldsymbol{s} \\ a \end{pmatrix}.$$

The goal of sufficient dimensionality reduction is, from independent transition samples $\{(\boldsymbol{s}_m, a_m, \boldsymbol{s}'_m)\}_{m=1}^M$, to find $\boldsymbol{W}$ such that $\boldsymbol{s}'$ and $(\boldsymbol{s}, a)$ are *conditionally independent* given $\boldsymbol{z}$. This conditional independence means that $\boldsymbol{z}$ contains all information about $\boldsymbol{s}'$ and is equivalently expressed as

$$p(\boldsymbol{s}'|\boldsymbol{s}, a) = p(\boldsymbol{s}'|\boldsymbol{z}). \tag{11.1}$$

11.2 Squared-Loss Conditional Entropy

In this section, the dimensionality reduction method based on the *squared-loss conditional entropy* (SCE) is introduced.

11.2.1 Conditional Independence

SCE is defined and expressed as

$$\begin{aligned}\mathrm{SCE}(\boldsymbol{s}'|\boldsymbol{z}) &= -\frac{1}{2}\iint p(\boldsymbol{s}'|\boldsymbol{z})p(\boldsymbol{s}',\boldsymbol{z})\mathrm{d}\boldsymbol{z}\mathrm{d}\boldsymbol{s}' \\ &= -\frac{1}{2}\iint \left(p(\boldsymbol{s}'|\boldsymbol{z})-1\right)^2 p(\boldsymbol{z})\mathrm{d}\boldsymbol{z}\mathrm{d}\boldsymbol{s}' - 1 + \frac{1}{2}\int \mathrm{d}\boldsymbol{s}'.\end{aligned}$$

It was shown in Tangkaratt et al. (2015) that

$$\mathrm{SCE}(\boldsymbol{s}'|\boldsymbol{z}) \geq \mathrm{SCE}(\boldsymbol{s}'|\boldsymbol{s},a),$$

and the equality holds if and only if Eq. (11.1) holds. Thus, sufficient dimensionality reduction can be performed by minimizing $\mathrm{SCE}(\boldsymbol{s}'|\boldsymbol{z})$ with respect to $\boldsymbol{W}$:

$$\boldsymbol{W}^* = \underset{\boldsymbol{W}\in\mathbb{G}}{\mathrm{argmin}}\ \mathrm{SCE}(\boldsymbol{s}'|\boldsymbol{z}).$$

Here, $\mathbb{G}$ denotes the *Grassmann manifold*, which is the set of matrices $\boldsymbol{W}$ such that $\boldsymbol{W}\boldsymbol{W}^\top = \boldsymbol{I}$ without redundancy in terms of the span.

Since SCE contains unknown densities $p(\boldsymbol{s}'|\boldsymbol{z})$ and $p(\boldsymbol{s}',\boldsymbol{z})$, it cannot be directly computed. Here, let us employ the LSCDE method introduced in Chapter 10 to obtain an estimator $\widehat{p}(\boldsymbol{s}'|\boldsymbol{z})$ of conditional density $p(\boldsymbol{s}'|\boldsymbol{z})$. Then, by replacing the expectation over $p(\boldsymbol{s}',\boldsymbol{z})$ with the sample average, SCE can be approximated as

$$\widehat{\mathrm{SCE}}(\boldsymbol{s}'|\boldsymbol{z}) = -\frac{1}{2M}\sum_{m=1}^{M}\widehat{p}(\boldsymbol{s}'_m|\boldsymbol{z}_m) = -\frac{1}{2}\widetilde{\boldsymbol{\alpha}}^\top\widehat{\boldsymbol{v}},$$

where

$$\boldsymbol{z}_m = \boldsymbol{W}\begin{pmatrix}\boldsymbol{s}_m\\ a_m\end{pmatrix} \quad \text{and} \quad \widehat{\boldsymbol{v}} = \frac{1}{M}\sum_{m=1}^{M}\boldsymbol{\phi}(\boldsymbol{z}_m,\boldsymbol{s}'_m).$$

$\boldsymbol{\phi}(\boldsymbol{z},\boldsymbol{s}')$ is the basis function vector used in LSCDE given by

$$\phi_b(\boldsymbol{z},\boldsymbol{s}') = \exp\left(-\frac{\|\boldsymbol{z}-\boldsymbol{z}_b\|^2 + \|\boldsymbol{s}'-\boldsymbol{s}'_b\|^2}{2\kappa^2}\right),$$

where $\kappa > 0$ denotes the Gaussian kernel width. $\widetilde{\boldsymbol{\alpha}}$ is the LSCDE solution given by

$$\widetilde{\boldsymbol{\alpha}} = (\widehat{\boldsymbol{U}} + \lambda \boldsymbol{I})^{-1}\widehat{\boldsymbol{v}},$$

where $\lambda \geq 0$ is the regularization parameter and

$$\widehat{U}_{b,b'} = \frac{(\sqrt{\pi}\kappa)^{\dim(\boldsymbol{s}')}}{M} \exp\left(-\frac{\|\boldsymbol{s}'_b - \boldsymbol{s}'_{b'}\|^2}{4\kappa^2}\right) \times \sum_{m=1}^{M} \exp\left(-\frac{\|\boldsymbol{z}_m - \boldsymbol{z}_b\|^2 + \|\boldsymbol{z}_m - \boldsymbol{z}_{b'}\|^2}{2\kappa^2}\right).$$

11.2.2 Dimensionality Reduction with SCE

With the above SCE estimator, a practical formulation for sufficient dimensionality reduction is given by

$$\widehat{\boldsymbol{W}} = \underset{\boldsymbol{W} \in \mathbb{G}}{\operatorname{argmax}}\ S(\boldsymbol{W}), \quad \text{where } S(\boldsymbol{W}) = \widetilde{\boldsymbol{\alpha}}^\top \widehat{\boldsymbol{v}}.$$

The gradient of $S(\boldsymbol{W})$ with respect to $W_{\ell,\ell'}$ is given by

$$\frac{\partial S}{\partial W_{\ell,\ell'}} = -\widetilde{\boldsymbol{\alpha}}^\top \frac{\partial \widehat{\boldsymbol{U}}}{\partial W_{\ell,\ell'}} \widetilde{\boldsymbol{\alpha}} + 2 \frac{\partial \widehat{\boldsymbol{v}}^\top}{\partial W_{\ell,\ell'}} \widetilde{\boldsymbol{\alpha}}.$$

In the Euclidean space, the above gradient gives the steepest direction (see also Section 7.3.1). However, on the Grassmann manifold, the *natural gradient* (Amari, 1998) gives the steepest direction. The natural gradient at $\boldsymbol{W}$ is the projection of the ordinary gradient to the tangent space of the Grassmann manifold. If the tangent space is equipped with the canonical metric $\langle \boldsymbol{W}, \boldsymbol{W}' \rangle = \frac{1}{2}\mathrm{tr}(\boldsymbol{W}^\top \boldsymbol{W}')$, the natural gradient at $\boldsymbol{W}$ is given as follows (Edelman et al., 1998):

$$\frac{\partial S}{\partial \boldsymbol{W}} \boldsymbol{W}_\perp^\top \boldsymbol{W}_\perp,$$

where $\boldsymbol{W}_\perp$ is the matrix such that $[\boldsymbol{W}^\top, \boldsymbol{W}_\perp^\top]$ is an orthogonal matrix.

The *geodesic* from $\boldsymbol{W}$ to the direction of the natural gradient over the Grassmann manifold can be expressed using $t \in \mathbb{R}$ as

$$\boldsymbol{W}_t = \begin{bmatrix} \boldsymbol{I} & \boldsymbol{O} \end{bmatrix} \exp\left(-t \begin{bmatrix} \boldsymbol{O} & \frac{\partial S}{\partial \boldsymbol{W}} \boldsymbol{W}_\perp^\top \\ -\boldsymbol{W}_\perp \frac{\partial S}{\partial \boldsymbol{W}}^\top & \boldsymbol{O} \end{bmatrix}\right) \begin{bmatrix} \boldsymbol{W} \\ \boldsymbol{W}_\perp \end{bmatrix},$$

where "exp" for a matrix denotes the *matrix exponential* and $\boldsymbol{O}$ denotes the zero matrix. Then line search along the geodesic in the natural gradient direction is performed by finding the maximizer from $\{\boldsymbol{W}_t \mid t \geq 0\}$ (Edelman et al., 1998).

Once $\boldsymbol{W}$ is updated by the natural gradient method, SCE is re-estimated for new $\boldsymbol{W}$ and natural gradient ascent is performed again. This entire procedure is repeated until $\boldsymbol{W}$ converges, and the final solution is given by

$$\widehat{p}(\boldsymbol{s}'|\boldsymbol{z}) = \frac{\widehat{\boldsymbol{\alpha}}^\top \boldsymbol{\phi}(\boldsymbol{z}, \boldsymbol{s}')}{\int \widehat{\boldsymbol{\alpha}}^\top \boldsymbol{\phi}(\boldsymbol{z}, \boldsymbol{s}'')\mathrm{d}\boldsymbol{s}''},$$

where $\widehat{\alpha}_b = \max(0, \widetilde{\alpha}_b)$, and the denominator can be analytically computed as

$$\int \widehat{\boldsymbol{\alpha}}^\top \boldsymbol{\phi}(\boldsymbol{z}, \boldsymbol{s}'')\mathrm{d}\boldsymbol{s}'' = (\sqrt{2\pi}\kappa)^{\dim(\boldsymbol{s}')} \sum_{b=1}^{B} \alpha_b \exp\left(-\frac{\|\boldsymbol{z} - \boldsymbol{z}_b\|^2}{2\kappa^2}\right).$$

When SCE is re-estimated, performing cross-validation for LSCDE in every step is computationally expensive. In practice, cross-validation may be performed only once every several gradient updates. Furthermore, to find a better local optimal solution, this gradient ascent procedure may be executed multiple times with randomly chosen initial solutions, and the one achieving the largest objective value is chosen.

11.2.3 Relation to Squared-Loss Mutual Information

The above dimensionality reduction method minimizes SCE:

$$\mathrm{SCE}(\boldsymbol{s}'|\boldsymbol{z}) = -\frac{1}{2}\iint \frac{p(\boldsymbol{z}, \boldsymbol{s}')^2}{p(\boldsymbol{z})}\mathrm{d}\boldsymbol{z}\mathrm{d}\boldsymbol{s}'.$$

On the other hand, the dimensionality reduction method proposed in Suzuki and Sugiyama (2013) maximizes *squared-loss mutual information* (SMI):

$$\mathrm{SMI}(\boldsymbol{z}, \boldsymbol{s}') = \frac{1}{2}\iint \frac{p(\boldsymbol{z}, \boldsymbol{s}')^2}{p(\boldsymbol{z})p(\boldsymbol{s}')}\mathrm{d}\boldsymbol{z}\mathrm{d}\boldsymbol{s}'.$$

Note that SMI can be approximated almost in the same way as SCE by the least-squares method (Suzuki & Sugiyama, 2013). The above equations show that the essential difference between SCE and SMI is whether $p(\boldsymbol{s}')$ is included in the denominator of the density ratio, and SCE is reduced to the negative SMI if $p(\boldsymbol{s}')$ is uniform. However, if $p(\boldsymbol{s}')$ is not uniform, the density ratio function $\frac{p(\boldsymbol{z},\boldsymbol{s}')}{p(\boldsymbol{z})p(\boldsymbol{s}')}$ included in SMI may be more fluctuated than $\frac{p(\boldsymbol{z},\boldsymbol{s}')}{p(\boldsymbol{z})}$ included in SCE. Since a smoother function can be more accurately estimated from a small number of samples in general (Vapnik, 1998), SCE-based dimensionality reduction is expected to work better than SMI-based dimensionality reduction.

11.3 Numerical Examples

In this section, experimental behavior of the SCE-based dimensionality reduction method is illustrated.

11.3.1 Artificial and Benchmark Datasets

The following dimensionality reduction schemes are compared:

- **None:** No dimensionality reduction is performed.
- **SCE (Section 11.2):** Dimensionality reduction is performed by minimizing the least-squares SCE approximator using natural gradients over the Grassmann manifold (Tangkaratt et al., 2015).
- **SMI (Section 11.2.3):** Dimensionality reduction is performed by maximizing the least-squares SMI approximator using natural gradients over the Grassmann manifold (Suzuki & Sugiyama, 2013).
- **True:** The "true" subspace is used (only for artificial datasets).

After dimensionality reduction, the following conditional density estimators are run:

- **LSCDE (Section 10.1.3):** Least-squares conditional density estimation (Sugiyama et al., 2010).
- **ϵKDE (Section 10.1.2):** ϵ-neighbor kernel density estimation, where ϵ is chosen by least-squares cross-validation.

First, the behavior of SCE-LSCDE is compared with the plain LSCDE with no dimensionality reduction. The datasets have 5-dimensional input $\boldsymbol{x} = (x^{(1)}, \ldots, x^{(5)})^\top$ and 1-dimensional output y. Among the 5 dimensions of $\boldsymbol{x}$, only the first dimension $x^{(1)}$ is relevant to predicting the output y and the other 4 dimensions $x^{(2)}, \ldots, x^{(5)}$ are just standard Gaussian noise. Figure 11.1 plots the first dimension of input and output of the samples in the datasets and conditional density estimation results. The graphs show that the plain LSCDE does not perform well due to the irrelevant noise dimensions in input, while SCE-LSCDE gives much better estimates.

Next, artificial datasets with 5-dimensional input $\boldsymbol{x} = (x^{(1)}, \ldots, x^{(5)})^\top$ and 1-dimensional output y are used. Each element of $\boldsymbol{x}$ follows the standard Gaussian distribution and y is given by

(a) $y = x^{(1)} + (x^{(1)})^2 + (x^{(1)})^3 + \varepsilon$,

(b) $y = (x^{(1)})^2 + (x^{(2)})^2 + \varepsilon$,

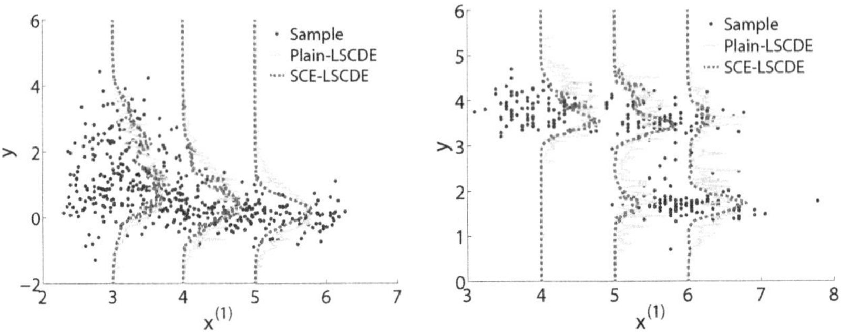

(a) Bone mineral density (b) Old Faithful geyser

FIGURE 11.1: Examples of conditional density estimation by plain LSCDE and SCE-LSCDE.

where ε is the Gaussian noise with mean zero and standard deviation $1/4$.

The top row of Figure 11.2 shows the dimensionality reduction error between true $\boldsymbol{W}^*$ and its estimate $\widehat{\boldsymbol{W}}$ for different sample size n, measured by

$$\mathrm{Error}_{\mathrm{DR}} = \|\widehat{\boldsymbol{W}}^\top \widehat{\boldsymbol{W}} - \boldsymbol{W}^{*\top} \boldsymbol{W}^*\|_{\mathrm{Frobenius}},$$

where $\|\cdot\|_{\mathrm{Frobenius}}$ denotes the Frobenius norm. The SMI-based and SCE-based dimensionality reduction methods both perform similarly for the dataset (a), while the SCE-based method clearly outperforms the SMI-based method for the dataset (b). The histograms of $\{y\}_{i=1}^{400}$ plotted in the 2nd row of Figure 11.2 show that the profile of the histogram (which is a sample approximation of $p(y)$) in the dataset (b) is much sharper than that in the dataset (a). As explained in Section 11.2.3, the density ratio function used in SMI contains $p(y)$ in the denominator. Therefore, it would be highly non-smooth and thus is hard to approximate. On the other hand, the density ratio function used in SCE does not contain $p(y)$. Therefore, it would be smoother than the one used in SMI and thus is easier to approximate.

The 3rd and 4th rows of Figure 11.2 plot the conditional density estimation error between true $p(y|\boldsymbol{x})$ and its estimate $\widehat{p}(y|\boldsymbol{x})$, evaluated by the squared loss (without a constant):

$$\mathrm{Error}_{\mathrm{CDE}} = \frac{1}{2n'} \sum_{i=1}^{n'} \int \widehat{p}(y|\widetilde{\boldsymbol{x}}_i)^2 \mathrm{d}y - \frac{1}{n'} \sum_{i=1}^{n'} \widehat{p}(\widetilde{y}_i|\widetilde{\boldsymbol{x}}_i),$$

where $\{(\widetilde{\boldsymbol{x}}_i, \widetilde{y}_i)\}_{i=1}^{n'}$ is a set of test samples that have not been used for conditional density estimation. We set $n' = 1000$. The graphs show that LSCDE overall outperforms ϵKDE for both datasets. For the dataset (a), SMI-LSCDE and SCE-LSCDE perform equally well, and are much better than

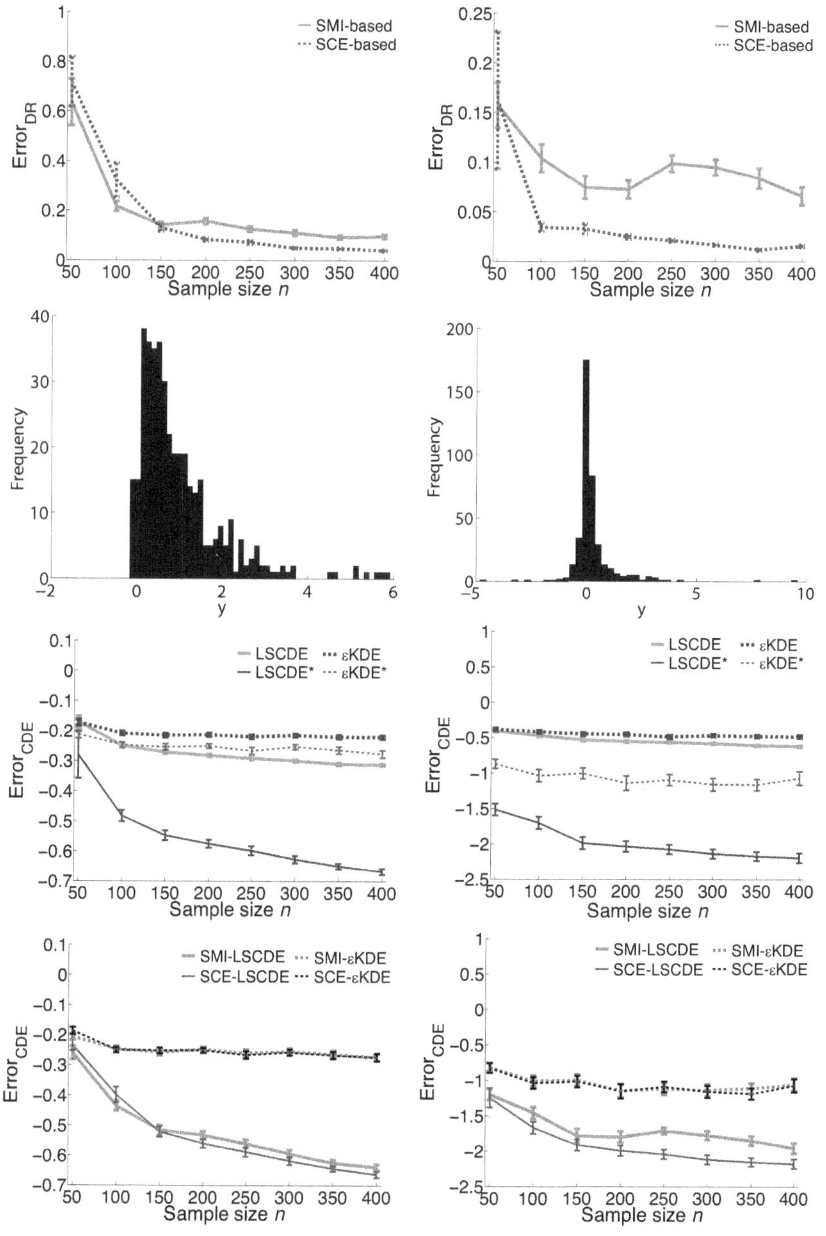

FIGURE 11.2: Top row: The mean and standard error of the dimensionality reduction error over 20 runs on the artificial datasets. 2nd row: Histograms of output $\{y_i\}_{i=1}^{400}$. 3rd and 4th rows: The mean and standard error of the conditional density estimation error over 20 runs.

plain LSCDE with no dimensionality reduction (LSCDE) and comparable to LSCDE with the true subspace (LSCDE*). For the dataset (b), SCE-LSCDE outperforms SMI-LSCDE and LSCDE and is comparable to LSCDE*.

Next, the UCI benchmark datasets (Bache & Lichman, 2013) are used for performance evaluation. n samples are selected randomly from each dataset for conditional density estimation, and the rest of the samples are used to measure the conditional density estimation error. Since the dimensionality of $\boldsymbol{z}$ is unknown for the benchmark datasets, it was determined by cross-validation. The results are summarized in Table 11.1, showing that SCE-LSCDE works well overall. Table 11.2 describes the dimensionalities selected by cross-validation, showing that both the SCE-based and SMI-based methods reduce the dimensionality significantly.

11.3.2 Humanoid Robot

Finally, SCE-LSCDE is applied to transition estimation of a humanoid robot. We use a simulator of the upper-body part of the humanoid robot *CB-i* (Cheng et al., 2007) (see Figure 9.5).

The robot has 9 controllable joints: shoulder pitch, shoulder roll, elbow pitch of the right arm, and shoulder pitch, shoulder roll, elbow pitch of the left arm, waist yaw, torso roll, and torso pitch joints. Posture of the robot is described by 18-dimensional real-valued state vector $\boldsymbol{s}$, which corresponds to the angle and angular velocity of each joint in radian and radian-per-second, respectively. The robot is controlled by sending an action command $\boldsymbol{a}$ to the system. The action command $\boldsymbol{a}$ is a 9-dimensional real-valued vector, which corresponds to the target angle of each joint. When the robot is currently at state $\boldsymbol{s}$ and receives action $\boldsymbol{a}$, the physical control system of the simulator calculates the amount of torque to be applied to each joint (see Section 9.3.3 for details).

In the experiment, the action vector $\boldsymbol{a}$ is randomly chosen and a noisy control system is simulated by adding a bimodal Gaussian noise vector. More specifically, the action a_i of the i-th joint is first drawn from the uniform distribution on $[s_i - 0.087, s_i + 0.087]$, where s_i denotes the state for the i-th joint. The drawn action is then contaminated by Gaussian noise with mean 0 and standard deviation 0.034 with probability 0.6 and Gaussian noise with mean -0.087 and standard deviation 0.034 with probability 0.4. By repeatedly controlling the robot M times, transition samples $\{(\boldsymbol{s}_m, \boldsymbol{a}_m, \boldsymbol{s}'_m)\}_{m=1}^{M}$ are obtained. Our goal is to learn the system dynamics as a state transition probability $p(\boldsymbol{s}'|\boldsymbol{s}, \boldsymbol{a})$ from these samples.

The following three scenarios are considered: using only 2 joints (right shoulder pitch and right elbow pitch), only 4 joints (in addition, right shoulder roll and waist yaw), and all 9 joints. These setups correspond to 6-dimensional input and 4-dimensional output in the 2-joint case, 12-dimensional input and 8-dimensional output in the 4-joint case, and 27-dimensional input and 18-dimensional output in the 9-joint case. Five hundred, 1000, and 1500 transition

TABLE 11.1: Mean and standard error of the conditional density estimation error over 10 runs for various datasets (smaller is better). The best method in terms of the mean error and comparable methods according to the two-sample paired t-test at the significance level 5% are specified by bold face.

Dataset	$(d_{\mathbf{x}}, d_{\mathbf{y}})$	n	SCE-based		SMI-based		No reduction		Scale
			LSCDE	ϵKDE	LSCDE	ϵKDE	LSCDE	ϵKDE	
Housing	(13, 1)	100	**−1.73(.09)**	−1.57(.11)	**−1.91(.05)**	−1.62(.08)	−1.41(.05)	−1.13(.01)	×1
Auto MPG	(7, 1)	100	**−1.80(.04)**	**−1.74(.06)**	**−1.85(.04)**	**−1.77(.05)**	**−1.75(.04)**	−1.46(.04)	×1
Servo	(4, 1)	50	**−2.92(.18)**	**−3.03(.14)**	**−2.69(.18)**	**−2.95(.11)**	−2.62(.09)	−2.72(.06)	×1
Yacht	(6, 1)	80	**−6.46(.02)**	**−6.23(.14)**	−5.63(.26)	−5.47(.29)	−1.72(.04)	−2.95(.02)	×1
Physicochem	(9, 1)	500	**−1.19(.01)**	−0.99(.02)	**−1.20(.01)**	−0.97(.02)	**−1.19(.01)**	−0.91(.01)	×1
White Wine	(11, 1)	400	−2.31(.01)	**−2.47(.15)**	**−2.35(.02)**	**−2.60(.12)**	−2.06(.01)	−1.89(.01)	×1
Red Wine	(11, 1)	300	**−2.85(.02)**	−1.95(.17)	**−2.82(.03)**	−1.93(.17)	−2.03(.02)	−1.13(.04)	×1
Forest Fires	(12, 1)	100	**−7.18(.02)**	−6.93(.03)	−6.93(.04)	−6.93(.02)	−3.40(.07)	−6.96(.02)	×1
Concrete	(8, 1)	300	**−1.36(.03)**	−1.20(.06)	**−1.30(.03)**	−1.18(.04)	−1.11(.02)	−0.80(.03)	×1
Energy	(8, 2)	200	**−7.13(.04)**	−4.18(.22)	−6.04(.47)	−3.41(.49)	−2.12(.06)	−1.95(.14)	×10
Stock	(7, 2)	100	−8.37(.53)	**−9.75(.37)**	**−9.42(.50)**	**−10.27(.33)**	−7.35(.13)	−9.25(.14)	×1
2 Joints	(6, 4)	100	**−10.49(.86)**	−7.50(.54)	**−8.00(.84)**	−7.44(.60)	−3.95(.13)	−3.65(.14)	×1
4 Joints	(12, 8)	200	**−2.81(.21)**	−1.73(.14)	−2.06(.25)	−1.38(.16)	−0.83(.03)	−0.75(.01)	×10
9 Joints	(27, 18)	500	**−8.37(.83)**	−2.44(.17)	**−9.74(.63)**	−2.37(.51)	−1.60(.36)	−0.89(.02)	×100

TABLE 11.2: Mean and standard error of the chosen subspace dimensionality over 10 runs for benchmark and robot transition datasets.

Dataset	$(d_{\mathbf{x}}, d_{\mathbf{y}})$	SCE-based		SMI-based	
		LSCDE	ϵKDE	LSCDE	ϵKDE
Housing	$(13, 1)$	3.9(0.74)	2.0(0.79)	2.0(0.39)	1.3(0.15)
Auto MPG	$(7, 1)$	3.2(0.66)	1.3(0.15)	2.1(0.67)	1.1(0.10)
Servo	$(4, 1)$	1.9(0.35)	2.4(0.40)	2.2(0.33)	1.6(0.31)
Yacht	$(6, 1)$	1.0(0.00)	1.0(0.00)	1.0(0.00)	1.0(0.00)
Physicochem	$(9, 1)$	6.5(0.58)	1.9(0.28)	6.6(0.58)	2.6(0.86)
White Wine	$(11, 1)$	1.2(0.13)	1.0(0.00)	1.4(0.31)	1.0(0.00)
Red Wine	$(11, 1)$	1.0(0.00)	1.3(0.15)	1.2(0.20)	1.0(0.00)
Forest Fires	$(12, 1)$	1.2(0.20)	4.9(0.99)	1.4(0.22)	6.8(1.23)
Concrete	$(8, 1)$	1.0(0.00)	1.0(0.00)	1.2(0.13)	1.0(0.00)
Energy	$(8, 2)$	5.9(0.10)	3.9(0.80)	2.1(0.10)	2.0(0.30)
Stock	$(7, 2)$	3.2(0.83)	2.1(0.59)	2.1(0.60)	2.7(0.67)
2 Joints	$(6, 4)$	2.9(0.31)	2.7(0.21)	2.5(0.31)	2.0(0.00)
4 Joints	$(12, 8)$	5.2(0.68)	6.2(0.63)	5.4(0.67)	4.6(0.43)
9 Joints	$(27, 18)$	13.8(1.28)	15.3(0.94)	11.4(0.75)	13.2(1.02)

samples are generated for the 2-joint, 4-joint, and 9-joint cases, respectively. Then randomly chosen $n = 100$, 200, and 500 samples are used for conditional density estimation, and the rest is used for evaluating the test error. The results are summarized in Table 11.1, showing that SCE-LSCDE performs well for the all three cases. Table 11.2 describes the dimensionalities selected by cross-validation. This shows that the dimensionalities are much reduced, implying that transition of the humanoid robot is highly redundant.

11.4 Remarks

Coping with high dimensionality of the state and action spaces is one of the most important challenges in model-based reinforcement learning. In this chapter, a dimensionality reduction method for conditional density estimation was introduced. The key idea was to use the squared-loss conditional entropy (SCE) for dimensionality reduction, which can be estimated by least-squares conditional density estimation. This allowed us to perform dimensionality reduction and conditional density estimation simultaneously in an integrated manner. In contrast, dimensionality reduction based on squared-loss mutual information (SMI) yields a two-step procedure of first reducing the dimensionality and then the conditional density is estimated. SCE-based dimensionality reduction was shown to outperform the SMI-based method, particularly when output follows a skewed distribution.

References

Abbeel, P., & Ng, A. Y. (2004). Apprenticeship learning via inverse reinforcement learning. *Proceedings of International Conference on Machine Learning* (pp. 1–8).

Abe, N., Melville, P., Pendus, C., Reddy, C. K., Jensen, D. L., Thomas, V. P., Bennett, J. J., Anderson, G. F., Cooley, B. R., Kowalczyk, M., Domick, M., & Gardinier, T. (2010). Optimizing debt collections using constrained reinforcement learning. *Proceedings of ACM SIGKDD International Conference on Knowledge Discovery and Data Mining* (pp. 75–84).

Amari, S. (1967). Theory of adaptive pattern classifiers. *IEEE Transactions on Electronic Computers*, *EC-16*, 299–307.

Amari, S. (1998). Natural gradient works efficiently in learning. *Neural Computation*, *10*, 251–276.

Amari, S., & Nagaoka, H. (2000). *Methods of information geometry*. Providence, RI, USA: Oxford University Press.

Bache, K., & Lichman, M. (2013). UCI machine learning repository. `http://archive.ics.uci.edu/ml/`

Baxter, J., Bartlett, P., & Weaver, L. (2001). Experiments with infinite-horizon, policy-gradient estimation. *Journal of Artificial Intelligence Research*, *15*, 351–381.

Bishop, C. M. (2006). *Pattern recognition and machine learning*. New York, NY, USA: Springer.

Boyd, S., & Vandenberghe, L. (2004). *Convex optimization*. Cambridge, UK: Cambridge University Press.

Bradtke, S. J., & Barto, A. G. (1996). Linear least-squares algorithms for temporal difference learning. *Machine Learning*, *22*, 33–57.

Chapelle, O., Schölkopf, B., & Zien, A. (Eds.). (2006). *Semi-supervised learning*. Cambridge, MA, USA: MIT Press.

Cheng, G., Hyon, S., Morimoto, J., Ude, A., Joshua, G. H., Colvin, G., Scroggin, W., & Stephen, C. J. (2007). CB: A humanoid research platform for exploring neuroscience. *Advanced Robotics*, *21*, 1097–1114.

Chung, F. R. K. (1997). *Spectral graph theory.* Providence, RI, USA: American Mathematical Society.

Coifman, R., & Maggioni, M. (2006). Diffusion wavelets. *Applied and Computational Harmonic Analysis, 21*, 53–94.

Cook, R. D., & Ni, L. (2005). Sufficient dimension reduction via inverse regression. *Journal of the American Statistical Association, 100*, 410–428.

Dayan, P., & Hinton, G. E. (1997). Using expectation-maximization for reinforcement learning. *Neural Computation, 9*, 271–278.

Deisenroth, M. P., Neumann, G., & Peters, J. (2013). A survey on policy search for robotics. *Foundations and Trends in Robotics, 2*, 1–142.

Deisenroth, M. P., & Rasmussen, C. E. (2011). PILCO: A model-based and data-efficient approach to policy search. *Proceedings of International Conference on Machine Learning* (pp. 465–473).

Demiriz, A., Bennett, K. P., & Shawe-Taylor, J. (2002). Linear programming boosting via column generation. *Machine Learning, 46*, 225–254.

Dempster, A. P., Laird, N. M., & Rubin, D. B. (1977). Maximum likelihood from incomplete data via the EM algorithm. *Journal of the Royal Statistical Society, series B, 39*, 1–38.

Dijkstra, E. W. (1959). A note on two problems in connexion [sic] with graphs. *Numerische Mathematik, 1*, 269–271.

Edelman, A., Arias, T. A., & Smith, S. T. (1998). The geometry of algorithms with orthogonality constraints. *SIAM Journal on Matrix Analysis and Applications, 20*, 303–353.

Efron, B., Hastie, T., Johnstone, I., & Tibshirani, R. (2004). Least angle regression. *Annals of Statistics, 32*, 407–499.

Engel, Y., Mannor, S., & Meir, R. (2005). Reinforcement learning with Gaussian processes. *Proceedings of International Conference on Machine Learning* (pp. 201–208).

Fishman, G. S. (1996). *Monte Carlo: Concepts, algorithms, and applications.* Berlin, Germany: Springer-Verlag.

Fredman, M. L., & Tarjan, R. E. (1987). Fibonacci heaps and their uses in improved network optimization algorithms. *Journal of the ACM, 34*, 569–615.

Goldberg, A. V., & Harrelson, C. (2005). Computing the shortest path: A* search meets graph theory. *Proceedings of Annual ACM-SIAM Symposium on Discrete Algorithms* (pp. 156–165).

Gooch, B., & Gooch, A. (2001). *Non-photorealistic rendering.* Natick, MA, USA: A.K. Peters Ltd.

Greensmith, E., Bartlett, P. L., & Baxter, J. (2004). Variance reduction techniques for gradient estimates in reinforcement learning. *Journal of Machine Learning Research, 5*, 1471–1530.

Guo, Q., & Kunii, T. L. (2003). "Nijimi" rendering algorithm for creating quality black ink paintings. *Proceedings of Computer Graphics International* (pp. 152–159).

Henkel, R. E. (1976). *Tests of significance.* Beverly Hills, CA, USA.: SAGE Publication.

Hertzmann, A. (1998). Painterly rendering with curved brush strokes of multiple sizes. *Proceedings of Annual Conference on Computer Graphics and Interactive Techniques* (pp. 453–460).

Hertzmann, A. (2003). A survey of stroke based rendering. *IEEE Computer Graphics and Applications, 23*, 70–81.

Hoerl, A. E., & Kennard, R. W. (1970). Ridge regression: Biased estimation for nonorthogonal problems. *Technometrics, 12*, 55–67.

Huber, P. J. (1981). *Robust statistics.* New York, NY, USA: Wiley.

Kakade, S. (2002). A natural policy gradient. *Advances in Neural Information Processing Systems 14* (pp. 1531–1538).

Kanamori, T., Hido, S., & Sugiyama, M. (2009). A least-squares approach to direct importance estimation. *Journal of Machine Learning Research, 10*, 1391–1445.

Kanamori, T., Suzuki, T., & Sugiyama, M. (2012). Statistical analysis of kernel-based least-squares density-ratio estimation. *Machine Learning, 86*, 335–367.

Kanamori, T., Suzuki, T., & Sugiyama, M. (2013). Computational complexity of kernel-based density-ratio estimation: A condition number analysis. *Machine Learning, 90*, 431–460.

Kober, J., & Peters, J. (2011). Policy search for motor primitives in robotics. *Machine Learning, 84*, 171–203.

Koenker, R. (2005). *Quantile regression.* Cambridge, MA, USA: Cambridge University Press.

Kohonen, T. (1995). *Self-organizing maps.* Berlin, Germany: Springer.

Kullback, S., & Leibler, R. A. (1951). On information and sufficiency. *Annals of Mathematical Statistics, 22*, 79–86.

Lagoudakis, M. G., & Parr, R. (2003). Least-squares policy iteration. *Journal of Machine Learning Research, 4*, 1107–1149.

Li, K. (1991). Sliced inverse regression for dimension reduction. *Journal of the American Statistical Association, 86*, 316–342.

Mahadevan, S. (2005). Proto-value functions: Developmental reinforcement learning. *Proceedings of International Conference on Machine Learning* (pp. 553–560).

Mangasarian, O. L., & Musicant, D. R. (2000). Robust linear and support vector regression. *IEEE Transactions on Pattern Analysis and Machine Intelligence, 22*, 950–955.

Morimura, T., Sugiyama, M., Kashima, H., Hachiya, H., & Tanaka, T. (2010a). Nonparametric return distribution approximation for reinforcement learning. *Proceedings of International Conference on Machine Learning* (pp. 799–806).

Morimura, T., Sugiyama, M., Kashima, H., Hachiya, H., & Tanaka, T. (2010b). Parametric return density estimation for reinforcement learning. *Conference on Uncertainty in Artificial Intelligence* (pp. 368–375).

Peters, J., & Schaal, S. (2006). Policy gradient methods for robotics. *Processing of the IEEE/RSJ International Conference on Intelligent Robots and Systems* (pp. 2219–2225).

Peters, J., & Schaal, S. (2007). Reinforcement learning by reward-weighted regression for operational space control. *Proceedings of International Conference on Machine Learning* (pp. 745–750). Corvallis, Oregon, USA.

Precup, D., Sutton, R. S., & Singh, S. (2000). Eligibility traces for off-policy policy evaluation. *Proceedings of International Conference on Machine Learning* (pp. 759–766).

Rasmussen, C. E., & Williams, C. K. I. (2006). *Gaussian processes for machine learning.* Cambridge, MA, USA: MIT Press.

Rockafellar, R. T., & Uryasev, S. (2002). Conditional value-at-risk for general loss distributions. *Journal of Banking & Finance, 26*, 1443–1471.

Rousseeuw, P. J., & Leroy, A. M. (1987). *Robust regression and outlier detection.* New York, NY, USA: Wiley.

Schaal, S. (2009). *The SL simulation and real-time control software package* (Technical Report). Computer Science and Neuroscience, University of Southern California.

Sehnke, F., Osendorfer, C., Rückstiess, T., Graves, A., Peters, J., & Schmidhuber, J. (2010). Parameter-exploring policy gradients. *Neural Networks, 23*, 551–559.

Shimodaira, H. (2000). Improving predictive inference under covariate shift by weighting the log-likelihood function. *Journal of Statistical Planning and Inference, 90*, 227–244.

Siciliano, B., & Khatib, O. (Eds.). (2008). *Springer handbook of robotics.* Berlin, Germany: Springer-Verlag.

Sugimoto, N., Tangkaratt, V., Wensveen, T., Zhao, T., Sugiyama, M., & Morimoto, J. (2014). Efficient reuse of previous experiences in humanoid motor learning. *Proceedings of IEEE-RAS International Conference on Humanoid Robots* (pp. 554–559).

Sugiyama, M. (2006). Active learning in approximately linear regression based on conditional expectation of generalization error. *Journal of Machine Learning Research, 7*, 141–166.

Sugiyama, M., Hachiya, H., Towell, C., & Vijayakumar, S. (2008). Geodesic Gaussian kernels for value function approximation. *Autonomous Robots, 25*, 287–304.

Sugiyama, M., & Kawanabe, M. (2012). *Machine learning in non-stationary environments: Introduction to covariate shift adaptation.* Cambridge, MA, USA: MIT Press.

Sugiyama, M., Krauledat, M., & Müller, K.-R. (2007). Covariate shift adaptation by importance weighted cross validation. *Journal of Machine Learning Research, 8*, 985–1005.

Sugiyama, M., Suzuki, T., & Kanamori, T. (2012). Density ratio matching under the Bregman divergence: A unified framework of density ratio estimation. *Annals of the Institute of Statistical Mathematics, 64*, 1009–1044.

Sugiyama, M., Takeuchi, I., Suzuki, T., Kanamori, T., Hachiya, H., & Okanohara, D. (2010). Least-squares conditional density estimation. *IEICE Transactions on Information and Systems, E93-D*, 583–594.

Sutton, R. S., & Barto, G. A. (1998). *Reinforcement learning: An introduction.* Cambridge, MA, USA: MIT Press.

Suzuki, T., & Sugiyama, M. (2013). Sufficient dimension reduction via squared-loss mutual information estimation. *Neural Computation, 25*, 725–758.

Takeda, A. (2007). *Support vector machine based on conditional value-at-risk minimization* (Technical Report B-439). Department of Mathematical and Computing Sciences, Tokyo Institute of Technology.

Tangkaratt, V., Mori, S., Zhao, T., Morimoto, J., & Sugiyama, M. (2014). Model-based policy gradients with parameter-based exploration by least-squares conditional density estimation. *Neural Networks, 57*, 128–140.

Tangkaratt, V., Xie, N., & Sugiyama, M. (2015). Conditional density estimation with dimensionality reduction via squared-loss conditional entropy minimization. *Neural Computation, 27*, 228–254.

Tesauro, G. (1994). TD-gammon, a self-teaching backgammon program, achieves master-level play. *Neural Computation, 6*, 215–219.

Tibshirani, R. (1996). Regression shrinkage and subset selection with the lasso. *Journal of the Royal Statistical Society, Series B, 58*, 267–288.

Tomioka, R., Suzuki, T., & Sugiyama, M. (2011). Super-linear convergence of dual augmented Lagrangian algorithm for sparsity regularized estimation. *Journal of Machine Learning Research, 12*, 1537–1586.

Vapnik, V. N. (1998). *Statistical learning theory.* New York, NY, USA: Wiley.

Vesanto, J., Himberg, J., Alhoniemi, E., & Parhankangas, J. (2000). *SOM toolbox for Matlab 5* (Technical Report A57). Helsinki University of Technology.

Wahba, G. (1990). *Spline models for observational data.* Philadelphia, PA, USA: Society for Industrial and Applied Mathematics.

Wang, X., & Dietterich, T. G. (2003). Model-based policy gradient reinforcement learning. *Proceedings of International Conference on Machine Learning* (pp. 776–783).

Wawrzynski, P. (2009). Real-time reinforcement learning by sequential actor-critics and experience replay. *Neural Networks, 22*, 1484–1497.

Weaver, L., & Baxter, J. (1999). *Reinforcement learning from state and temporal differences* (Technical Report). Department of Computer Science, Australian National University.

Weaver, L., & Tao, N. (2001). The optimal reward baseline for gradient-based reinforcement learning. *Proceedings of Conference on Uncertainty in Artificial Intelligence* (pp. 538–545).

Williams, J. D., & Young, S. J. (2007). Partially observable Markov decision processes for spoken dialog systems. *Computer Speech and Language, 21*, 393–422.

Williams, R. J. (1992). Simple statistical gradient-following algorithms for connectionist reinforcement learning. *Machine Learning, 8*, 229–256.

Xie, N., Hachiya, H., & Sugiyama, M. (2013). Artist agent: A reinforcement learning approach to automatic stroke generation in oriental ink painting. *IEICE Transactions on Information and Systems, E95-D*, 1134–1144.

Xie, N., Laga, H., Saito, S., & Nakajima, M. (2011). Contour-driven Sumi-e rendering of real photos. *Computers & Graphics, 35*, 122–134.

Zhao, T., Hachiya, H., Niu, G., & Sugiyama, M. (2012). Analysis and improvement of policy gradient estimation. *Neural Networks*, *26*, 118–129.

Zhao, T., Hachiya, H., Tangkaratt, V., Morimoto, J., & Sugiyama, M. (2013). Efficient sample reuse in policy gradients with parameter-based exploration. *Neural Computation*, *25*, 1512–1547.

Index

Printed in the United States
by Baker & Taylor Publisher Services